Who or What is God?

Who or What is God?

And Other Investigations

John Hick

Seabury Books

Unless otherwise noted, the Scripture quotations contained herein are from the New Revised Standard Version Bible, copyright © 1989 by the Division of Christian Education of the National Council of Churches of Christ in the U.S.A. Used by permission. All rights reserved.

Cover design by Brenda Klinger
Typeset by Regent Typesetting, London

Library of Congress Cataloging-in-Publication Data

A catalog record of this book is available from the Library of Congress

ISBN: 978-1-59627-116-6

First published in the United Kingdom in 2008 by SCM Press
13–17 Long Lane,
London EC1A 9PN
www.scm-canterburypress.co.uk
SCM Press is a division of SCM-Canterbury Press Ltd

First published in North America in 2009 by
Seabury Books
445 Fifth Avenue
New York, New York 10016

www.seaburybooks.com

An imprint of Church Publishing Incorporated

5 4 3 2 1

Contents

Acknowledgements   vii

Introduction   ix

1   Who or What is God?   1

2   Mystical Experience as Cognition   14

3   The Religious Meaning of Life   31

4   On Being Mortal   47

5   Reincarnation   53

6   Believable Christianity   65

7   Literal and Metaphorical Incarnation   75

8   The Resurrection of Jesus   88

9   Is the Doctrine of Atonement a Mistake?   96

10   Christianity and Islam   118

11   Apartheid Observed (1980)   130

12   Is there a Global Ethic?   149

13   Mahatma Gandhi's Significance for Today   161

14   The Second Form of the Ontological Argument   179

Index   195

Acknowledgements

'Mystical Experience as Cognition' first appeared in *Mystics and Scholars*, edited by Harold Coward and Terence Penelhum in 1976, published by the Wilfred Laurier University Press, Canada, and now reprinted with permission. 'The Religious Meaning of Life' was first published in *The Meaning of Life in the World Religions*, edited by Joseph Runzo and Nancy Martin, and is now reprinted with the permission of the publisher, One World, Oxford. 'On Being Mortal' first appeared in *Sermons from Great St Mary's*, edited by Hugh Montefiore in 1968. 'Believable Christianity' is a lecture given at Carrs Lane United Reformed Church, Birmingham, UK, in their annual series of Lectures on Radical Christian Faith. 'Literal and Metaphorical Incarnation' was first published in *Jesus Then and Now*, edited by Marvin Meyer and Charles Hughes, and is now reprinted with the permission of the publisher, Trinity Press International. 'The Resurrection of Jesus' is a lecture given to a church group in Birmingham. 'Is the Doctrine of Atonement a Mistake?' was first published in *Philosophy and Theological Discourse*, edited by Stephen T. Davis (1997), and is reprinted with permission. 'Christianity and Islam' is a lecture given to the Institute for Interreligious Dialogue in Tehran in 2005. 'Apartheid Observed' is a report published as a pamphlet by AFFOR (All Faiths For One Race) in Birmingham in 1980, ten years before the end of apartheid in South Africa. 'Is there a Global Ethic?' is a lecture given to the Global Ethics seminar at the University of Birmingham, UK. 'Mahatma Gandhi's Significance for Today' is a public lecture given under the auspices of the Institute for Advanced Research in Arts and Social Sciences at the University of Birmingham, UK. And 'The Second Form of the Ontological Argument' first appeared in John Hick and Arthur McGill, eds, *The Many-Faced Argument*, 1968, Macmillan & Co. Ltd, and is reproduced with permission of Palgrave Macmillan.

Introduction

The chapters of this book are a collection of previously published articles, reports and lectures on a wide range of issues centred on two themes, the search for truth, and the search for justice and peace. The search for truth concerns the ultimate reality to which the world's great religions point, involving discussion of religious experience, religious language, the relations between religions, life and death, and Christian belief. The search for justice and peace is pursued in the quest for a global ethic and in the life and thought of Mahatma Gandhi and again in South Africa during the apartheid era.

'Who or What is God?' begins with the ordinary concept of God found today in most churches and in common discourse – the God whom such writers as Richard Dawkins in *The God Delusion* and Christopher Hitchins in *God Is Not Great* reject. I also reject this concept, but not the experience of transcendent reality that it so inadequately expresses. This leads to a distinction, drawn in different ways within each of the world faiths, between God or the Ultimate in itself and that reality as humanly known in terms of human concepts and in historically and regionally different forms. As Thomas Aquinas wrote, 'Things known are in the knower according to the mode of the knower',[1] and in religion the mode of the knower varies between the different human cultures. The implications of this for interfaith relations are explored.

The heart of true religion is not the religious institutions but religious experience. In 1976 the University of Calgary, Canada, held a conference of practising mystics in dialogue with scholars of various disciplines. The mystics were from different traditions – Brother David Steindl-Rast, a Dominican monk; Roshi Shimano, a Zen master; Swami Prabuddhananda, a monk of the Ramakrishna order; Rabbi Zalman Schachter; and Rufus Goodstriker of the Blood Indians of Alberta. I was one of the scholars in discussion with them, together with John Heintz, Ninian Smart, Terence Penelhum, and Joseph Eppes Brown, and my own paper was on 'Mystical Experience as Cognition'.

Religious experience, of which mystical experience is the peak, leads directly to questions of the meaning of life and of death. 'The Religious Meaning of Life' explores this in the different world faiths, and the sermon 'On Being Mortal', preached at Great St Mary's Church in Cambridge, looks at death as an inevitably approaching reality, but not one to fear. In 'Reincarnation' I look at what seems to me, from a religious as opposed to a naturalistic point of view, to be the most likely form of life after death.

Reincarnation has never been an orthodox Christian belief, but it is consistent with (although not required by) other unorthodox views that I have come over the years to hold. These, and the reasons for them, are explained in 'Believable Christianity', which is a lecture delivered in 2006 at Carrs Lane United Reformed Church in Birmingham, UK, as part of their annual series on Radical Christian Faith. One aspect of it is amplified in 'Literal and Metaphorical Incarnation' and others in 'The Resurrection of Jesus' and 'Is the Doctrine of Atonement a Mistake?' There are in reality today two Christianities, one conservative, predominantly evangelical and including a large and powerful fundamentalist element, and the other liberal or progressive. The practical dividing line however is not so much theological as in moral outlook, focused in particular today on the issue of homosexuality. Can the churches accept actively gay members, ministers, priests, bishops? This is the question that is today splitting the worldwide Anglican Communion. To those outside the churches, and also to many of us within them, it seems astonishing and deplorable that this should be seen as the crucial issue in the relations between Christians.

It is the more progressive individuals within Christianity who are able to engage in fruitful dialogue with people of other religions. 'Christianity and Islam' is a lecture that I gave in Tehran in February 2005. The relationship and interactions between Islam and Christianity in the world today are of immense importance to us all; and in my opinion it is essential, despite our differences and the often disastrous historical conflicts of the past and today, to develop the basis for a mutual acceptance of each faith by the other as an authentic awareness of and response to God. With this in mind it may be of interest to recount this visit to Iran, which has not been visited by most British theologians and philosophers of religion. Iran is a Shia Muslim country. Several of my books and a number of articles had been translated into Persian, that is, Farsi, and this is no doubt the reason why I was invited. The then President, Mohammed Khatami, was a reformer, but had been blocked again and again in his reforms by the Supreme Leader, Ayatollah Ali

Khameini. It was later, in the summer of that year, that Mahmoud Ahmajinidad became President.

I was invited by the Institute for Interreligious Dialogue in Tehran to give some lectures there and elsewhere in the city. At Tehran airport I was met by a young lady speaking excellent English, accompanied by a turbaned, bearded and robed cleric who was able to take me through the procedures at speed. My overwhelming impression from the moment of landing was of the generous hospitality that I received everywhere. I was put up in a modern hotel, my room on the 72nd floor, and a car and driver were available to take me everywhere. My time was crowded, going from event to event most of each day. The afternoon I arrived, after only a few minutes at the hotel, I was driven to give my first lecture at what is to me the unusual time of 3 p.m. The traffic in Tehran is horrific. Millions of cars, cheap petrol, people driving at speed a few inches apart and interweaving all the time! We arrived at 3 o'clock and I expected to go straight into the lecture hall. Instead I was taken upstairs and greeted by Mr Ali Rashad, the director of this particular institute, the Institute for Islamic Culture and Thought, with an embrace and a kiss on each cheek, and tea and fruit, before going down to the crowded lecture hall, with lights and TV cameras. The front row was occupied mainly by turbaned clerics with their names on cards in front of them. This was the only occasion when something unwelcome happened. Before the chairman was able to introduce me, Mr Rashad came up and took his place and read out a long speech in Persian. My friend Dr Amir Akrami, who had come to do all the translating, whispered to me an outline of what he was saying. After a fulsome welcome, he launched into a lengthy criticism of religious pluralism. Without having read the text in English I could not possibly give a considered reply, and said so (Amir translating into Persian), and felt, possibly wrongly, that I had to shorten my own paper, on 'Islam and Religious Pluralism', because of the time already taken by Mr Rashad. I later asked him to send me either his Persian text or a translation so that I could then respond to it, and he agreed to do so. (The most recent letter of apology and promise to send his text came more than a year after my visit, and I have still not received his text.) After that, the questions from the audience, beginning with the front row, were good, much the same as the questions raised by English philosophers, and I gave much the same answers. The whole discussion proceeded in a rational and reasoned way, with no slogans or dogmatic assertions.

Immediately after this I was whisked away by the Islamic Republic of Iran Broadcasting Corporation (IRIBC – their equivalent of the BBC) for an hour's interview in English by a well prepared interviewer. Then to a restaurant for dinner. There was a table piled high with good things. I assumed that this was the meal, and filled my plate. But it turned out to be only the hors d'oeuvre, followed by a substantial meal served at the table, with rather nice non-alcoholic beer. After that back to my hotel for a good night's sleep. I gave lectures or held discussions at the Institute for Interreligious Dialogue, the Iranian Institute for Philosophy, and Tarbiat Modarres University, all translated paragraph by paragraph by Amir. The discussions were well focused, many of the participants having read some of my books or articles, and wanting to raise questions about them. The questions and discussions were on a high level. Many of the scholars were familiar with Western thought. They knew their Kant and Heidegger and other major Western philosophers. They were not however so well aware of modern developments within Christian theology. It probably came as a surprise that my own (unorthodox) understanding of Jesus, as a great prophet and teacher, was similar to that of the Qur'an, in which he is spoken about in the most exalted terms short of deifying him. The only differences were that I believed that Jesus did indeed die on the cross, which is denied in the Qur'an, but did not believe in his virgin birth which *is* taught in the Qur'an. On this latter point Muslims are nearer than I to conservative Christian belief!

One afternoon I was driven on a tour of the city, or as much of it as there was time for. A modern centre, with many high rise buildings and streets of the kind of shops that indicate wealth, is surrounded by less affluent areas and then slums. In all the streets we went through I never saw women covering their heads with more than a scarf, sometimes gaily coloured. They were often wearing trousers under their robes and often Western trainers.

I had a splendid dinner on another day with Mr Rashad. He had just come from a meeting with the President, who sent me his good wishes. After dinner Rashad told me at length, through Amir, why Islam was the best, because the most comprehensive, religion. I don't believe that there is a 'best' religion, but there was no time to argue the matter. And on my last evening I had another splendid dinner, this time with my host, the Director of the Institute for Interreligious Dialogue and his wife and others in the restaurant on the top floor of my hotel, after which they presented me with a wonderful piece of Isfahan handcraft with birds and branches in silver against a black satin background, now on my dining room wall. Another present was a tray of silver teacups from the IRIBC, another a Persian rug, and another a book of photos of the ancient sites of Persia.

Many of the issues and difficulties about religious pluralism raised from a Muslim point of view were essentially the same as those raised in the West from a Christian point of view, though both faiths include within themselves a variety of emphases and outlooks. My own position, in brief, is similar to that of some of the great Sufi thinkers, such as al-Arabi and Rumi, and can be summarized in Rumi's words, 'The lamps are different, but the Light is the same; it comes from Beyond.'[2] This is not, of course, a view that is acceptable to either Muslim or Christian conservatives, but is nevertheless the subject of very wide discussion and gradually growing both acceptance and resistance in the West, particularly the USA and Britain, with new books and articles coming out every month, exploring various models of religious pluralism.

I was concerned in my own lectures in Tehran to make it clear that religious pluralism is not a form of relativism, since it involves criteria for distinguishing between good and bad religion; and is not a product of the Western Enlightenment of the eighteenth century, since it had already long been a familiar idea for many centuries in India, going back as far as the Buddhist emperor Ashoka in the second century BCE, and including such thinkers as Kabir, Nanak, and many more, as well as some of the great Sufis of Islam. Although in my own way of presenting it philosophically I make use of Kant's distinction between noumenal and phenomenal reality, it is not dependent upon Kant's philosophy and only makes use of one aspect of it – a use of which Kant himself would not have approved, for he had a quite different philosophy of religion. But I could equally well have developed my own without any reference to Kant, relying instead on the critical realism developed by American philosophers in the first half of the twentieth century, and supported by more recent work in social psychology and the sociology of knowledge.

But a bigger and more important long-term issue is that of the relation between Christianity and the other world faiths. It is possible to have a relatively orthodox theology but to adapt it to acknowledge the equal authenticity of those other faiths. But this is not possible for conservative Christians, including both evangelical/fundamentalist Protestant Christians and Catholics who accept the position laid down in such Vatican documents as *Dominus Iesus* in 2000. These all maintain the unique superiority of Christianity. On this issue there are two Christianities, although they remain at present, albeit with increasing strain, under the same organizational umbrellas. It will be clear from the arguments in this book that I advocate the second Christianity. But my own version of it is of course not the only version, and there is endless scope for constructive discussion among liberal thinkers.

This emerging second Christianity is a force for world peace. It has been well said (by Hans Küng) that there will never be peace between the nations until there is peace between the world religions. And I would add that there will never be real peace between the world religions until each is able to accept the equal validity of the others. This can only be done from within each faith community. I have tried here and elsewhere to point to the path along which Christianity can reach this goal. And so we next move in three papers on to the practical implications of a religious understanding of life. Nelson Mandela was in prison on Robben Island in 1980, and the end of apartheid was still ten years in the future, when I spent three months in South Africa, including an excursion to free Botswana, to see for myself the appalling brutality of apartheid and to write a report on it, which was promptly banned by the South African government as soon as copies arrived there.

Apartheid, as well as today's dictatorships in several countries, and indeed the general state of the world today with destructive violence in several regions, raises the question whether there can be a global ethic. 'Is there a Global Ethic?' is a paper delivered to the Global Ethics Seminar at Birmingham University in 2007.

Gandhi was a great exemplar of ethics at work. He was not only the leader of the non-violent campaign that led in 1947 to Indian independence but was also one of the world's great spiritual teachers. He lived what he taught. Few can say with him, 'My life is my message', but his life embodied the power of non-violence, of love for one's enemies, of forgiveness and reconciliation. His life has since influenced many others, including Vinoba Bhave in India, Martin Luther King in his leadership of the civil rights movement in the United States, Nelson Mandela in his spirit of forgiveness in South Africa, expressed in the Truth and Reconciliation Commission chaired by Archbishop Desmond Tutu; and many lesser-known figures in many countries.

Finally, there is a paper criticizing what has come to be known as the second form of the ontological argument for the existence of God. This is the most philosophically interesting of the 'theistic proofs'. Originated by Anselm in the twelfth century, the twentieth-century rediscovery of its more subtle second form was made independently by the American philosophers Charles Hartshorne and Norman Malcolm, and it is their formulations that I criticize in this paper. The ontological argument is perennially fascinating and will always be studied by students and practitioners of the philosophy of religion. An examination of it illustrates the way in which the critical stance of philosophy can make a contribution to theology.

Notes

1 *Summa Theologica*, II/II, Q. 1, art. 2.
2 Rumi: *Rumi, Poet and Mystic*, trans. R. A. Nicholson, London: Unwin Mandala Books, 1978, p. 166.

I

Who or What is God?

If you ask the educated man or woman in the street, or in a church, what they mean by 'God', they will probably say something like this: God is the infinite personal Being who has created the universe, whom religious people worship and to whom they pray, and who has the power, when he (or she) so decides, to intervene in human affairs in response to our prayerful requests. And so in church we pray for world peace, for the victims of flood, earthquake, famine, war and other disasters, that the rulers of the nations may have wisdom and, in a Church of England service, for the health and well-being of the Queen and the royal family; and we pray privately for ourselves and our own family and friends, especially those in any special need or danger. Thus God is seen as an active all-powerful force who is motivated by a limitless love, tempered by justice, and who has knowledge and wisdom infinitely surpassing our own. When our prayers are not answered, this is because he always knows better than we do, and indeed knows infallibly, what is the best thing to do or refrain from doing.

I think this is a fair depiction of the concept of God that operates today in Western society, and has operated for many centuries. It applies to Jews and Muslims as well as to Christians, and it applies to atheists as much as to theists. This is the 'God' whom people wholeheartedly or tentatively believe in, and equally whom people wholeheartedly or tentatively believe not to exist, and whom Nietzsche declared to be dead.

This concept of God can be described as anthropomorphic. That is to say, God is a being like ourselves in the fundamental respect that we are both – God and ourselves – persons. But whereas we are finite, created, dependent persons, God is an infinite, eternal, uncreated and omnipotent Person. Some theologians, uncomfortable with such an explicitly anthropomorphic characterization, say that God is not *a* person, but rather is personal. But this is a distinction without a difference. We cannot conceive of a personal being who is not a person. And we know what a person is only because we are ourselves persons. God, then, is like us – or rather we are like God – in this very basic respect.

I am not going to bring in here the doctrine of the Trinity, which distinguishes Christianity theologically from Judaism and Islam, because I don't think that it makes any practical difference within Christian worship. Trinitarian language is of course firmly embedded in our liturgies; but is not prayer itself in practice invariably addressed to God our heavenly Father? We add 'through' or 'in the name of' our Lord Jesus Christ – except of course in the prayer which he himself taught, the Lord's Prayer, in which we address God directly. But adding 'we ask this in the name of' does not alter the fact that we are consciously addressing the heavenly Father. So I am leaving aside for now the trinitarian complication.

The central aspect of this prevailing concept of God, on which I want to focus, is divine activity in the course of nature and of human life. God can and does perform miracles, in the sense of making things happen which would not otherwise have happened, and preventing things from happening which otherwise would have happened. These interventions are either manifest or – much more often – discernible only to the eyes of faith. But it is believed that God *does* sometimes intervene in answer to prayer. The Bible, and church history, and contemporary religious discourse are full of accounts of such occasions. And prayers of intercession in church and in private devotion presuppose that he at least sometimes operates on earth in these ways. Otherwise, what is the point of those prayers? And how often have we heard in the media someone telling of their miraculous escape when, for example, they survived unhurt in a car crash in which the two others were killed, or even more dramatically how a soldier in war was saved by wearing a medallion which stopped the bullet that would have killed him, or how when a family were at their wits' end in some terrible dilemma something unexpectedly happened to save the situation? Or there was recently the American who on winning $5 million in the US lottery said, 'I just praised God and Jesus.' Of course most of those who speak like this today in our pervasively secular age are not using the word 'miracle' in a religious sense but merely as an expression of wonder and relief. Likewise 'Thank God for that' is usually no more than an expression of heartfelt relief. But seriously devout believers who give God thanks for a lucky escape, or for recovery from a serious illness, or for the resolution of some problem, do often believe that they have experienced a divine intervention on their behalf, a miracle which confirms and strengthens their faith and evokes gratitude to God.

It is this serious and literal use of the idea of divine intervention that concerns us here. The problem that it raises has led many to atheism.

For example, in the car crash case, if God intervened to save only one of the people in the car, who then gave God thanks for a miraculous delivery, this implies not only that God decided to save *that* person, but equally that he decided *not* to save the other two. It presupposes that it is, so to speak, OK from God's point of view to intervene whenever he so chooses, and this inevitably poses the question why he intervenes so seldom, leaving unprotected the great majority of innocent victims of natural disasters and of human cruelty and neglect. Some years ago the then atheist (but now deist) philosopher Antony Flew wrote:

> Someone tells us that God loves us as a father loves his children. We are reassured. But then we see a child dying of inoperable cancer of the throat. His earthly father is driven frantic in his efforts to help, but his Heavenly Father reveals no sign of concern.[1]

And given the biblical and traditional assumption that God does intervene miraculously whenever he so decides, one can understand why this belief led Flew and many others to atheism. It is this implied picture of God as arbitrary, protecting some but not others, and thus as deliberately leaving so many in pain, hardship, misery and peril, that is so repugnant to so many people. If there is such a Being, why regard him or her as good and as worthy of worship, except by the chosen few who benefit from the special divine interventions?

The problem arises from the belief that it is, as I put it, OK from God's point of view to intervene on earth whenever he chooses. Suppose, however, that, regardless of whether or not it is within God's power to intervene, it is for some good reason *not* OK from the divine point of view to do so. Suppose this would be counter-productive from the point of view of a creative purpose which requires both human freedom (which is directly or indirectly the source of much the greater part of human suffering) and also elements of contingency and unpredictability in the evolution of the universe. The kind of theodicy sketched in this brief formula has been developed in a number of works, including my own *Evil and the God of Love*.[2] This does not require the idea of special divine interventions in the form of open or covert miracles. However, as we shall see presently, while I still think this is a viable position I now want to suggest going a good deal further.

A non-intervening anthropomorphic God, who does not act within human history and human life, who does not cause things to happen which would not otherwise have happened and does not prevent things from happening which would otherwise have happened, seems religiously unsatisfying to many practising Christians, a kind of deism which is little better than atheism.

So we have a dilemma. Can we find any way through it or beyond it? At this point I want to suggest enlarging our field of vision – since we are no longer living in the BC (Before Computers) age and have so greatly extended our database – by taking account of the other world religions as well as our own. After all, the large majority of religious people in the world are not Christians, and yet their religions involve forms of life and thought that claim to lead to a transforming relationship, of limitless value, with an eternal reality that both transcends, and in the case of the Eastern traditions is also immanent within, us. But Buddhism and Taoism and Confucianism and some strands of Hinduism do not see that eternal reality as an infinite Person. Suppose then, as an experiment, we now use the word 'God' as our Western term for the ultimate reality which some do and others do not believe to be an infinite person. We then broaden the question, Who or what is God? by not confining it at the outset to a particular concept of the religious ultimate. When we do this some prefer not to use the term 'God', finding it almost impossible to detach it in most people's minds from the notion of an infinite divine person, and use instead such terms as Ultimate Reality, or the Ultimate, or the Real. But let us for our present purpose stick with the familiar term 'God', reminding ourselves however from time to time that we are not now using it in a sense restricted to what are called the Western monotheisms – although in fact none of them originated in the West.

Where do we now go from here? I suggest that at this point it will be helpful to take account of an enormously important distinction drawn by some of the great Christian mystics, as well as by mystics of the other major traditions. Although the writer who has been given the derogatory sounding name of Pseudo-Dionysius is largely unknown outside the history of Christian mysticism, he has in fact probably been the most influential single individual in that history. He wrote in the name of Dionysius, the disciple of St Paul (Acts 17.34), thus assuming a near apostolic authority, and he was a major theological influence throughout the thousand years prior to the Reformation. Thomas Aquinas, for example, quotes him as an authority some 1,700 times. He is generally believed today to have been a Syrian monk writing around the year 500, and whether he would have exerted the same immense influence if this had been known before Erasmus and others became suspicious of his identity is one of history's fascinating unanswered questions. But he did exert this immense influence, and in my opinion it was a very creative influence. For it reinforced the existing emphasis on the ultimate ineffability of God. I am not fond of the word 'ineffable' and prefer 'transcategorial', meaning beyond the range of our human systems of concepts or mental categories. Theologians have nearly always taken the ultimate divine ineffability or transcategoriality for granted, though usually without taking its implications to their logical conclusion. Augustine, for example, about a century before Pseudo-Dionysius, said that 'God transcends even the mind',[3] but did not develop this further. But Dionysius – or Denys, to give him a more user-friendly name – makes the divine ineffability central and begins at least to struggle with its implications. In his central work, *The Mystical Theology*, he says in every way he can think of that God is utterly and totally transcategorial. God is 'indescribable', 'beyond all being and knowledge'. God, the ultimate One, is:

> not soul or mind, nor does it possess imagination, conviction, speech, or understanding . . . It cannot be spoken of and it cannot be grasped by understanding . . . It does not live nor is it life. It is not a substance, nor is it eternity or time. It cannot be grasped by the understanding . . . It is neither one nor oneness, divinity nor goodness . . . It is not sonship or fatherhood . . . There is no speaking of it, nor name nor knowledge of it . . . It is beyond assertion and denial.[4]

This last statement, that that to which the term 'God' refers is beyond assertion *and* denial, is crucial. For Denys is not simply doing negative theology, saying that God does not have this or that attribute but, much more radically, that our entire range of attribute-concepts do not apply to God at all, either positively or negatively. To apply them to God in God's ultimacy is, in modern philosophical terms, a category mistake. To say, for example, that molecules are not stupid, although true, is misleading because it assumes that molecules are the sort of thing of which it makes sense to say that they are either stupid or not stupid. And to say that God is not 'one nor oneness, divinity nor goodness', although true would likewise, by itself, be deeply misleading because it assumes that God is the kind of reality to which such qualities could be rightly or wrongly attributed. We have to take on board the much more radical idea of a reality which is what it is, but whose nature lies beyond the scope of our conceptual and linguistic systems. When we speak about such a reality we are not, then, speaking about it as it is in itself, totally beyond the range of our comprehension, but about its impact upon us, the difference that it makes within the realm of human experience, to which our concepts and hence our languages do apply.

It is worth stressing that the divine ineffability does not entail that the ultimate reality, which we are calling God, is an empty blank, but rather that God's inner nature is beyond the range of our human conceptual resources. This is also, incidentally, what Mahayana Buddhism intends when it speaks of the Ultimate Reality as *sunyata*, emptiness: it is empty of everything that the human mind inevitably projects in its acts of cognition. Going back to Denys, although he himself does not make this further qualification, modern philosophical discussions of ineffability have introduced a distinction between, on the one hand, what we can call substantial attributes, meaning attributes which tell us something positive about the divine nature, and on the other hand purely formal, linguistically generated attributes, which do not tell us anything about the divine nature. Thus that God is ineffable formally entails that God has the attribute of ineffability. And even to refer to God at all entails that God has the attribute of being able to be referred to. But such purely formal attributes give rise only to trivial truths, trivial in the sense that they do not in any way contradict or undermine the divine ineffability.

But given divine ineffability, problems immediately arise for Christian theology. Denys was, we presume, a devout worshipping Christian monk. And as well as teaching the total divine transcategoriality, he also took for granted the main body of Christian doctrine. Although Denys takes surprisingly little interest in the traditional dogmas, he does nevertheless take it for granted that God is a Trinity of Father, Son and Holy Spirit, and that the second person became incarnate as Jesus Christ. But how can one both hold that God is totally ineffable and also profess to know all these substantial truths about God? God cannot both have no humanly knowable attributes and also have such humanly knowable attributes as being a Trinity, and so forth. On the face of it this is a sheer contradiction. And Denys saw this quite clearly. He asks, in his book on *The Divine Names*:

> How then can we speak of the divine names [that is, attributes]? How can we do this if the Transcendent surpasses all discourse and knowledge, if it abides beyond the reach of mind and of being, if it encompasses and circumscribes, embraces and anticipates all things while itself eluding their grasp and escaping from any perception, imagination, opinion, name, discourse, apprehension, or understanding?[5]

And he makes at least a beginning in answering this question. He has said that God is self-revealed in the scriptures. But then he goes on to say that the scriptural language about God is metaphorical. He does not use the modern term 'metaphor', but a later Denys, Denys Turner of Yale, points out very clearly that when Dionysius speaks of symbols he means what today we call metaphors.[6] Denys – the early medieval one – says that 'the Word of God makes use of poetic imagery',[7] and he speaks of 'what scripture has revealed to us in symbolic and uplifting fashion' (121A), and of how the divine Light makes truth known to us 'by way of representative symbols' (121B). Further, he says that the function of the scriptural symbols and poetry is practical, to draw us forward on our pilgrim's progress: 'By itself [the ineffable One] generously reveals a firm, transcendent beam, granting enlightenments proportionate to each being, and thereby draws sacred minds upward to its permitted contemplation, to participation and to the state of becoming like it'.[8] Again, God 'uses scriptural passages in an uplifting fashion as a way . . . to uplift our mind in a manner suitable to our nature'.[9] When I translate this into my own terms I hear Denys saying that in the scriptures we speak about God in true myths, that is to say, descriptions which are not literally true but which nevertheless have the effect of evoking in us an appropriate dispositional response to the ultimate subject-matter of the myths. He does not however go beyond the scriptural ascriptions to apply the same principle to Christian doctrines. If he had he would have been in tune with the teaching of the Buddha, a thousand or so years earlier, that the function of religious doctrines, as 'skilful means', is to help us onward at particular stages of our spiritual journey and that when they have served their purpose they are to be left behind.

But while Denys makes a good start – indeed in the context of his time he was an extremely bold and original thinker – there is another aspect of the religious life which his writings do not cover, namely religious experience. I do not mean at this point the ultimate ineffable unity with the divine of which he does speak, but more ordinary religious experience – the worshipper's occasional sense of God's presence, or sense of being in God's presence, the occasional vivid I–Thou experience in prayer, the sense of divine presence through the liturgy or in some moments of daily life, the transformed consciousness sometimes found through meditation or, moving up a notch, the mystical visions and auditions reported in all ages. But without moving up that notch, religious experience, particularly the sense of being in God's presence, and the transformed consciousness reached in meditation, is central to the religious life. Without it, religion would consist simply in human, all-too-human institutions. Within these institutions there has usually also been space for the inner reality of religious experience and its transforming influence in human life. But if there were only the institutions, devoid of the experiential aspect of the religious life, the religions would be simply cultural frameworks and exercises of social control which have done at least as much harm as good in the course of human history.

So given the centrality of religious experience, who or what is it that is being experienced? If it is the experience of the loving presence of the heavenly Father of Jesus' teaching, this is clearly not the ineffable Ultimate Reality of which Denys has been speaking. What, then, is the relation between that ultimate reality and the available God of the Bible and of Christian worship? This is the question which Pseudo-Dionysius does not tackle.

Nor do subsequent medieval theologians. Aquinas, for example, declares that 'by its immensity, the divine substance surpasses every form that our intellect reaches',[10] and that 'The first cause surpasses human understanding and speech.'[11] He tries to bridge the gap between God's ineffability and our doctrines about God with his use of analogy. But this does not really help. For although we know, according to Aquinas, that God possesses the divine analogues of human goodness, wisdom, and so forth, we do not have the faintest idea what these divine analogues are. Although we know what it is for a human to be good and wise, we have no conception of what it is for God to be analogically good or analogically wise. Indeed, according to Aquinas, the divine nature is absolutely simple, not made up of a number of distinct attributes.[12] So such attributes as goodness, wisdom and love are constructs which arise at the human level as a result of the divine impact upon us, but are not reflections on the human scale of the same attributes in God. Because of the ultimate divine simplicity, which is only divided up into distinct attributes in the human mind, these so-called divine attributes refer to the impact of God's presence on us, expressed in our human categories of thought.

Now let us come down through the centuries from Pseudo-Dionysius to another original genius, the thirteenth- and fourteenth-century mystic Meister Eckhart. Eckhart was profoundly influenced by Denys, whom he quotes as speaking of 'the unknown God above all gods',[13] echoed in Paul Tillich's 'the God above the god of theism'.[14] Eckhart himself distinguishes between the utterly transcategorial Godhead (*Gottheit, deitas*) and the worshipped God (*Gott, deus*). 'God and the Godhead', he says, 'are as different from each other as heaven and earth' (Sermon 27). It is clear that by God, in distinction from the Godhead, he means the God of the Bible and of Christian devotion. He says, 'God acts. The Godhead does not' (Sermon 27). Further, he sees very clearly the implication that the known and describable God of Christian experience and worship exists only in relation to the experiencing and worshipping community. 'For before there were creatures,' he says, 'God was not god, but, rather, he was what he was. When creatures came to be . . . then God was no longer God as he is in himself, but god as he is with creatures' (Sermon 28), so that 'before there were creatures God was not "God"' (Sermon 52), that is, not the humanly known God. Eckhart does not of course mean that with the creation of humanity the Godhead ceased to exist, but that there then also came to be the humanly experienced God of Christian worship.

This distinction between the ultimate divine reality and its humanly thinkable and experienceable form (or forms) is also found within each of the other great traditions. To refer to these very briefly, Advaitic Hinduism distinguishes between *nirguna* Brahman, which is the totally 'formless' or transcategorial Ultimate Reality, and *saguna* Brahman, which is that same reality as manifested within human experience as the realm of the worshipped gods and goddesses. The *trikaya* doctrine of Mahayana Buddhism distinguishes between the utterly transcategorial *dharmakaya* and its manifestation in the realm of the heavenly Buddhas (the *nirmanakaya)*, one or other of whom becomes incarnate on earth from time to time. The Jewish mystics of the Zoharic and Lurianic Kabbala distinguished between *Eyn Sof*, the Infinite, and the God of the scriptures. The Sufi mystics of Islam distinguished between the ineffable ultimate reality, *Al-Haqq*, usually translated as the Real, and the revealed God of the Qur'an. Thus al-Arabi says in *The Bezels of Wisdom*:

> God is absolute or restricted as He pleases; and the God of religious beliefs is subject to limitations, for He is the God contained in the heart of His servants. But the absolute God is not contained in anything . . . Thus, He is not known [as Allah] until we are known.[15]

Now I want to suggest that this generic distinction within the mystical strand of religion worldwide between, on the one hand, the transcategorial – or if you prefer the older term, the ineffable – Godhead or the Real and, on the other hand, the form or forms in which that ultimate reality is manifested within our human conceptual frameworks and modes of experience, makes possible a religious interpretation of the data of the history of religions.

Suppose that, as is in fact the case, I participate in some small degree in the very wide and varied realm of religious experience. And suppose that, as is again the case, I hold the basic religious faith that this is not purely imaginative projection, but that while clearly employing my own conceptual and imaginative resources, it is at the same time also a response to the presence to me of a transcendent reality. I then notice that others within the same, in my case Christian, tradition also report moments of religious experience, though often taking different forms. And I then notice that people within the other religious traditions like-wise report a yet wider range of such experiences. Applying a kind of philosophical Golden Rule, it would be unreasonable not to grant to religious experience within other traditions what I affirm of it within my own tradition. And so I have to take account of the worldwide varieties of religious experience. I now have the two-level picture of the ultimate ineffable Real, or the Godhead, being responded to in this range of different forms of religious experience, the differences between them arising from our different culturally formed conceptual systems and imaginative repertoires, embodied in and reinforced by our different kinds of spiritual practice.

The basic principle that we are aware of anything, not as it is in itself unobserved, but always and necessarily as it appears to beings with our particular cognitive equipment, was brilliantly stated by Aquinas when he said that 'Things known are in the knower according to the mode of the knower.'[16] And in the case of religious awareness, the mode of the knower differs significantly from one religious tradition to another. And so my hypothesis is that the ultimate reality of which the religions speak, and which we refer to as God, is being differently conceived, and there-fore differently experienced, and therefore differently responded to in historical forms of life within the different religions.

What does this mean for the different, and often conflicting, belief-systems of the religions? It means that they are descriptions of *different* manifestations of the Ultimate; and as such they do not conflict with one another. They each arise from some immensely powerful moment or period of religious experience, notably the Buddha's experience of enlightenment under the Bo tree at Bodh Gaya, Jesus' sense of the pres-ence of the heavenly Father, Muhammad's experience of hearing the words that became the Qur'an, and also the experiences of Vedic sages, of Hebrew prophets, of Taoist sages. But these experiences are always formed in the terms available to that individual or community at that time and are then further elaborated within the resulting new religious movements. This process of elaboration is one of philosophical or theo-logical construction. Christian experience of the presence of God, for example, at least in the early days and again since the thirteenth- and fourteenth-century rediscovery of the centrality of the divine love, is the sense of a greater, much more momentously important, much more pro-foundly loving, personal presence than that of one's fellow humans. But that this higher presence is eternal, is omnipotent, is omniscient, is the creator of the universe, is infinite in goodness and love is not, because it cannot be, given in the experience itself. In sense perception we can see as far as our horizon but cannot see how much further the universe stretches beyond it, and so likewise we can experience a high degree of goodness or of love but cannot experience that it reaches beyond this to infinity. That God has these infinite qualities, and likewise that God is a divine Trinity, can only be an inference, or a theory, or a supposedly revealed truth, but not an experienced fact. And so Jesus himself will have understood the experienced loving and demanding presence to be the God of his Jewish tradition, and specifically of that aspect of the tradition that emphasized the divine goodness and love, as well as justice and power. But as his teaching about the heavenly Father was further elaborated, and indeed transformed, within the expanding gentile Church, it grew into the philosophical conception of God as an infinite co-equal trinity of Father, Son and Holy Spirit. And so what we inherit today is a complex totality in which religious experience and philosophical speculation embodied in theological doctrine have interacted over the centuries and have to a considerable degree fused. In the other great traditions the same process has taken place, in each case taking its own distinctive forms. For religious experience always has to take some specific form, and the forms developed within a given tradition 'work' for people within that tradition but not, in many cases, for people formed by a different tradition.

There also emerges here an answer to the question, Why should we think that there is an ultimate transcendent reality, the Real or the Godhead, in distinction from the experienced personal Gods and non-personal Absolutes of the different traditions? For surely if it is the case that not only our own Christian experience, but also the different forms of experience within the other great religious traditions, are indeed responsive and not purely projective, it is not surprising that within human awareness many different God-figures have formed. Phenomenologically – that is, as describable – the Holy Trinity is different from the Allah of Islam, which is different from the Adonai, the Lord, of rabbinic Judaism, which is different again from the Vishnu and the Shiva of theistic Hinduism, and even more different from the non-personal Tao, or Dharma, or Brahman. All these are, in Kantian language, divine phenomena in distinction from the divine noumenon of which they are its appearances to humanity. Thus we need – I am suggesting – a two-level model, with the experienced realities in relation to which the religious life is lived as manifestations of an ultimate reality beyond them.

Let me offer a couple of analogies to illustrate this. The sun's light is refracted by the earth's atmosphere into the spectrum of the different colours of the rainbow. Perhaps the ultimate light of the universal divine presence is refracted by our different human religious cultures into the spectrum of the different world faiths.

And concerning the different, and indeed often conflicting, belief systems of the religions: our earth is a three-dimensional globe. But when you map it on a two-dimensional surface you have to distort it. You cannot get three dimensions into two without distortion. And there are a variety of projections used by cartographers which are different systematic ways of distorting the earth's curvature to represent it on a flat surface. But if a map made in one projection is correct it does not follow that maps made in other projections are incorrect. If they are properly made they are all correct, and yet they all distort. Perhaps our different theologies, both within the same religion and between different religions, are human maps of the infinite divine reality made in different projections, which is to say, in different conceptual systems. These all necessarily distort, since that infinite reality as it is in itself cannot be represented in our finite human terms. But all may be equally useful in guiding our journey through life.

But finally, let us return to the point at which we started, namely prayer, particularly petitionary prayer, prayer for other people. In my opinion it is an observable fact that such prayer does sometimes 'work'. I do not however see this as a matter of our asking an omnipotent God to intervene miraculously on earth and his then graciously acting accordingly. I see it rather as depending upon a mental field or network, below the level of normal consciousness, within which we are all connected and through which our thoughts, and even more our emotions, are all the time affecting one another. These influences are usually largely filtered out by the mechanism that preserves our individual autonomy. But when in 'prayer', or what Buddhists call loving-kindness meditation, we concentrate upon some particular individual who is in a distressed state of anxiety, fear, anger, despair, and so on, concretely visualizing a better possibility for them, this can have a positive effect. Even in the case of bodily distress our thought may affect the patient's mind and sometimes through this his or her bodily state. And I would suggest – outrageously, from the point of view of the contemporary secular mindset – that quite possibly the thou of whom we are sometimes aware in prayer is a reality, but is what the Eastern religions call a *deva*, a god in distinction from God, or in Western terms an angel. This does not of course mean that what I have referred to elsewhere as the personae of the Real – Jahweh, Trinity, Allah – with their omni-attributes, are *devas* or angels.

So here is a large-scale hypothesis which constitutes a religious, as distinguished from a naturalistic, interpretation of religion. And like all such hypotheses, it presents itself for consideration and invites others who find it inadequate to offer a better hypothesis.

Notes

1 Antony Flew, 'Theology and Falsification', in Antony Flew and Alasdair Macintyre (eds), *New Essays in Philosophical Theology*, London: SCM Press, 1955, pp. 98–9.

2 John Hick, *Evil and the God of Love*, 3rd edn, Basingstoke: Palgrave Macmillan, 2007.

3 Augustine, *On True Religion*, 3.6.67.

4 Dionysius, *The Mystical Theology*, 1045DB1048B.

5 Dionysius, *The Divine Names*, 593ABB.

6 Denys Turner, *The Darkness of God*, Cambridge: Cambridge University Press, 1995, p. 35.

7 Dionysius, *The Celestial Hierarchy*, 137ABB.

8 Dionysius, *Divine Names*, 588CBD.

9 Dionysius, *Celestial Hierarchy*, 137B.

10 Aquinas, *Summa contra Gentiles*, 1:14.3.

11 Aquinas, *De Causis*, 6.

12 Aquinas, *Summa Theologica*, I/I, Q. 3, art. 7.

13 Meister Eckhart, Sermon 39.

14 Paul Tillich, *The Courage to Be*, New Haven: Yale University Press, 1952, p. 189.

15 Al-Arabi, *Bezels of Wisdom*, 92.

16 Aquinas, *ST*, II/II, Q. 1, art. 2.

2

Mystical Experience as Cognition

The Centrality of Religious and Mystical Experience

Our 'practising mystics' have spoken both of mystical experience and of the mystic's practices and disciplines. I should like to discuss the former, the religious experience and its significance, rather than the practices and techniques which serve it. Mystical experience, as our mystics (and others as well) describe it, does not seem to me to be anything other than first-hand religious experience as such. This is however, I believe, the essence of religion. Religion has often been understood, particularly within our modern science-oriented Western culture, as an attempt (though a primitive and unsuccessful attempt) to explain certain puzzling phenomena, from cosmic puzzles concerning the origin of the world and the source of its order, to local puzzles about why the rains are late this year or what last night's thunder signified. There is, certainly, an explanatory side to religion, although modern religious thought applies these explanatory resources to the existence or the meaning of the world as a whole rather than to the occurrence of particular events within it. How far this movement away from a theological explanation of the genesis of particular events can or should be taken is an important question which, however, I shall not be taking up here. The point I wish to make is rather that the explanatory function of religion is secondary and derivative. Religion consists primarily in experiencing our life in its relation to the Transcendent and living on the basis of that experience. And mysticism, I take it, is simply religion understood in this way. Or, rather, it is a name for one, but the most important, aspect of the total phenomenon of religion. In terms of Ninian Smart's six-dimensional analysis – distinguishing the ritual, mythological, doctrinal, ethical, social and experiential dimensions of religion – mysticism is a general name for religious experience together with part at least of the network of religious practices which support it.

I am encouraged to equate mysticism in this way with the experimental core of religion by the fact that two of our practising mystics have said something very like this, while nothing was said by the other three to suggest dissent. Brother David defined mysticism as 'experience of communion with the source of meaning'; and he stressed that all who worship, and indeed all who are conscious of the divine, are mystics. And Swami Prabuddhananda defined mysticism as the realization of a relationship between the individual soul and the infinite reality, and again, being consciously in relation to God or to Brahman. This would in turn mean that all who are conscious of existing in the presence of the divine are mystics. This would in turn mean, in both cases, that rather than religious people being divided into a small minority of mystics and a large majority of non-mystics, we should equate mysticism with religious experience or religious consciousness as such, but recognizing of course many degrees of consciousness of the Transcendent, as well as many forms which this consciousness takes.

Thus far it is not clear why we need the term 'mysticism' in addition to 'religious experience' and 'devotional practice'. Nevertheless, we do have the word, and its use in the title of this chapter is a sign of its continuing life. The word clearly meets a need; and that need is, I think, twofold. There is first the inevitable distinction between what can be variously called conventional, nominal, external or secondhand religion on the one hand, and real, true, or first-hand religion on the other. The former has always, in all large traditions, been the major part of the total phenomenon of religion. And it has seemed convenient, and perhaps reassuring, to the mass of ordinary adherents of a religious tradition, to whom their faith means conformity to the customary creed and ritual of their society, to bestow a special label upon the minority among them who live by a first-hand experience of the Transcendent, with the implied suggestion that the latter follow a special and peculiar way which is not for everyone. And second, there is the fact that mysticism, in the broad sense of what may be called first-hand religion as such, is continuous with rare forms of religious experience which are reported by a minority within the minority and which involve such phenomena as seeing visions or hearing voices, and in yet rarer experiences of a oneness with the Transcendent which language cannot begin to express.

Any philosophical understanding of mysticism, or of religious experience, must take account both of the kind of experiences reported by our practising mystics and also of the rarer experiences of visions and voices and of the unitive life to which the label 'mysticism' is sometimes restricted. However, I shall confine myself here to the level or stage of religious experience described by our three reporters, this constituting – as I presume – a stage on a spiritual journey which leads eventually to the unitive life in God; or to *fana*, the annihilation of the soul in God; or to *moksha*; or nirvana.

Implications of Mystical Experience

Let us reserve for later the question, which is of course ultimately all-important, whether it is reasonable for those who experience life religiously to base their beliefs upon this experience. For, as we are all well aware in this sceptical age, it is always in principle possible to dismiss religious experience as a fantasy or projection; and I shall in due course come to this crucial issue. But for the moment let us bracket off that question and assume that the several reports of the mystics, from within the wider traditions of belief out of which they come, are true. Let us assume that these are substantially accurate accounts of experiences on the interface between the human and the divine. What metaphysical hypothesis, or picture of the universe, is implied in this supposition? Any answer, within the confines of this paper, must of course be in very large and general terms.

First, the Transcendent of which the mystics speak is of the nature of mind rather than of matter; and accordingly a distinction between matter, on the one hand, and spirit, soul, mind or consciousness, on the other, is implicit in a great deal that they have said. The Transcendent, let us then say, is Infinite Spirit.

It follows, second, that the material universe is other than the Infinite Spirit, or at any rate other than the Infinite Spirit per se. Matter may (as the Semitic religions teach) be wholly other than, and created out of nothing by, the Infinite Spirit, or (as the religions of Indian origin teach) it may be a kind of illusion or dream experienced at some level of the infinite Consciousness, or again it may be related to that Consciousness somewhat as body to mind. But on any of these views, matter is not simply identical with the Infinite Spirit as such. And because the material universe is thus either really or illusorily other than the eternal Spirit its real existence, or its existence as a real illusion, is not self-explanatory. Indeed, so far from being self-explanatory, its existence constitutes for us, who are part of it, the ultimate mystery. There seems to be a metaphysical analogue of Gödel's theorem, to the effect that, from the point of view of a consciousness which is part of the universe, any systematic interpretation of the universe must generate at least one question which that system can never answer. And for the religious systems it is essentially the same question, though posed in different terms within the different traditions. For the theistic religions it is the question why a perfect and self-sufficient God has created something other than, and of necessity inferior to, himself. For the non-theistic system of Advaita Vedanta it is the question why the illusion of finite and material existence occurs at all – for an illusion is just as truly something whose occurrence demands an explanation as a non-illusion: the existence of the material world has not become any less problematic when it has been labelled an illusion. For non-theistic Buddhism, the unanswerable question is why the wheel of *samsara* turns. (One has to define the problem as its turning rather than its existing; for *samsara* is a process, consisting wholly in a series of events.) The immediate answer is that it turns by the power of *tanha* (craving, desire); but why is there this apparently otiose phenomenon of finite consciousness and its cravings? This is the Buddhist form of the unanswerable question which appears elsewhere as the questions why there is *maya* and why there is a created universe.

There is, then, the mysterious fact of material existence. And accepting it as a fact, we can see that, whether or not by design, it has the effect of allowing a plurality of finite individuals existing over against one another. We are distinct beings because consciousness is exercised in us through separate bodily organisms in virtue of which we are aware of the world from particular points within it. Further, we are conscious from the point of view of living organisms each programmed for its own survival. And whether we are parts or aspects of the Infinite Spirit, somehow separated from it (even though the separation be an illusion of our finite consciousness) or are real beings created *ex nihilo* by the Infinite Spirit, we have in either case a certain all-important affinity with that supreme Infinite Spirit. And such conscious relationship, which Schleiermacher called God-consciousness, and which more broadly we can call consciousness of the Transcendent, is, as it seems to me, the essential religious or mystical experience.

Experience as Interpretation

What is the nature of our human consciousness of the Transcendent?

In the mysticism of our reporters, it occurs within the context of this world, for they are men and women living on this earth. And the epistemological character of this experience enjoyed by the soul *in via* is not, I suggest, peculiar to religious consciousness. On the contrary, what is going on is not fundamentally different in character from what is going on in other forms of awareness which we take to be awareness of our environment. For in all our conscious experiencing there is an important element of cognitive choice, and this element in religious awareness is continuous with the element of subjective interpretation in our other awarenesses. I mean by this that when we are aware of a thing (such as this fountain pen) or aware of being in a particular kind of situation (such as our present situation of participating in a conference) we are interpreting what is before us, or around us, in terms of concepts. And by 'interpreting' here I do not mean the intellectual exercise of theory-construction, as when we speak of the prosecution's interpretation of the evidence in a court of law, or, on a grander scale, of a philosopher's interpretation of the universe. I am referring to interpretation in the sense in which this enters continuously into our ordinary sense experience. For it is a commonplace today that in our ordinary everyday perception of our physical environment as having the character that we perceive it to have, the mind is constantly active – comparing, remembering, selecting, grouping, presuming, recognizing – that is to say, being aware of our environment as having the particular character that we perceive (and of course often misperceive) it to have.

For example, I want to say that in seeing this fountain pen, I am seeing what is before me *as* a fountain pen – borrowing and extending the notion of 'seeing as' which Wittgenstein discussed in the *Philosophical Investigations*. Wittgenstein himself thought that the notion only applies to special cases, like puzzle pictures: for example, you can see Jastrow's duck/rabbit *as* a picture of a duck or *as* a picture of a rabbit. But I want to say that *all* conscious experiencing is experiencing-as. That is to say, it involves *recognizing* objects and situations by means of concepts; or in other words, perceiving them as having this or that particular character or significance. For consider this pen. Surely, you might say, it is impossible to see it as anything other than a pen; and therefore the idea of seeing-as, implying as it does some sort of ambiguity in what is seen, is not appropriate. But to be conscious of seeing a pen, to be identifying *this* as a fountain pen, is to be using a concept which has been created within a particular culture and which functions within certain cultures and not in others. We in North America and Europe see certain things as fountain pens; two centuries ago our ancestors did not. Of course those who lack this concept could soon acquire it, and would then be able to see this as a fountain pen. But the dispositional capacity to recognize it as such, to see it in this way, is not innate to the human mind but is a cultural product. Again, to experience what is now going on as a seminar discussion presupposes a certain cultural background: beings from the planet Mars might well suppose something quite different to be taking place.

This second example, of being aware of the nature of a situation, is more to the point than the previous example of recognizing an individual object. For we are all the time within situations of various kinds, indeed usually within a number of different situations at the same time – for example, the situation of being in this room (on which our attention might become focused if someone were to shout out that there is a bomb concealed in it); the situation of participating in a discussion (on which our attention is I hope in fact focused); the situation of being a Canadian or American or British citizen; the situation of being a father, mother, son or daughter, brother or sister, or colleague; of being *a* human being within the mystery of existence; or – could it be? – the situation of being in the presence of God, or of being part of the *samsaric* process which leads to eventual oneness with the eternal reality. And these are not mutually exclusive situations; someone could be in all of them at once but with the spotlight of his attention moving back and forth among them.

Let us speak, then, of our experiencing situations as having this or that character, it being always the case that in order so to experience we have to have a certain conceptual and interpretative equipment, often a very complex equipment. And one feature of situational awareness to which I should like to draw attention is that it involves tendencies or dispositions to act in ways appropriate to the perceived character of the situation. For one important thing about a situation in which we find ourselves is that we are *in* it, part of it, and have therefore to conduct ourselves in terms of its character as we perceive it. The appropriate action may of course often be inaction, or just going on doing the same thing. Every form of situational awareness has its own practical dispositional aspect. Thus, to be conscious of being in a certain kind of situation is, among other things, to be in a dispositional state to act in this rather than that way or range of ways. And this is as true of religious as of secular cases. To be conscious of living in the presence of the Transcendent has all kinds of practical implications. For example, to be conscious of existing in the presence of God as Jesus depicted him is not to be anxious about the future, not to be afraid of other people but on the contrary full of love for them, and it is to believe that whatever happens to one, one is in the divine presence and within God's loving providence. Again, to be conscious of being a 'spark of divinity', wrapped in illusion but struggling towards the clear light of reality, is to be set upon overcoming one's own egoity and upon breaking the many threads of selfish desire which hold one back.

I have been suggesting, then, that religious experience exhibits a common structure, which it shares with all our other cognitive experience, and that this is the experiencing of situations in terms of certain concepts. And awareness of a situation as having a certain character includes an appropriate dispositional stance. We can call the experienced character of a situation, in virtue of which we are in a certain dispositional state in relation to it, its meaning – or, more precisely, the meaning that we have found in it. Meaning, then, is the experienced character of a situation such that to experience it as having that character is to be in a distinctive dispositional state in relation to it. And so we can speak of the different meanings of human life – of the global human situation – which different religious traditions enable people to be aware of and to live in terms of.

God and the Godhead

This diversity of religious meanings is brought out by comparing the reports of our practising mystics. If we assumed that they were all deluded, the differences between their delusions would not present any serious problem. But assuming, as I am, that they are not deluded, one has to consider whether the diversity of these experiences is compatible with their all being experiences of the same transcendent reality.

Clearly, the possibility to be explored is that the concepts which we have seen to be involved in all experience may account for the same transcendent reality being experienced in different ways.

Does Christian consciousness differ from Hindu, and Jewish from Buddhist, because in these different traditions different concepts of the Transcendent enter into the formation of one's religious experience? And if so, how is it that the Transcendent is capable of being conceptualized in such different ways?

In order to answer these questions we need, I think, a broadly Kantian epistemology. There are, of course, many difficult and disputed questions of Kantian interpretation. But the main outlines of his epistemology are clear enough. He distinguished between the noumenal world, which exists independently of human perception of it, and the phenomenal world, which is that world experienced in terms of the various forms and categories that constitute the structure of human consciousness. All that we know about the noumenal world is that it is the unknown reality whose impact upon us produces the phenomenal world of conscious experience. An analogous distinction has to be drawn, and has indeed often been drawn, in man's thought of the

Transcendent. Perhaps its most explicit form is the Hindu distinction between *nirguna* Brahman, Brahman without attributes, beyond the scope of human language, and *saguna* Brahman, Brahman with attributes, known within human religious experience as Ishvara, the personal creator and governor of the universe. In the West the Christian mystic Meister Eckhart distinguished between the Godhead (*deitas*) and God (*deus*);[1] and Rudolf Otto, in his comparative study of Eckhart and Shankara, says, 'Herein lies the most extraordinary analogy between Eckhart and Sankara: high above God and the personal Lord abides the "Godhead", having an almost identical relationship to God as that of Brahman to Ishvara'.[2] More recently, Paul Tillich has spoken of the 'God above the God of theism'.[3] Whitehead, and the process theologians who have followed him, distinguish between the primordial and the consequent natures of God, the former being God's nature in himself, and the latter being formed by his response to and inclusion of the world.[4] And Gordon Kaufman distinguishes between the 'real God' and the 'available God', the former being an 'utterly unknowable X', and the latter 'essentially a mental or imaginative construction'.[5] A traditional Christian form of the distinction is that between God in himself, in his infinite self-existent being, beyond the grasp of the human mind, and God in relation to mankind, revealed as creator and redeemer. In one form or another the distinction seems unavoidable for any view which is not willing to reduce God to a finite being who can, in principle, be wholly known by the human mind and defined within human concepts. If God is infinite, he must pass out into sheer mystery beyond the reach of our knowledge and comprehension, and in his limitless transcendence he is *nirguna*, the ultimate Godhead, the God above the God of theism.

But if we see such concepts as *nirguna* Brahman, the Godhead, and the God above the God of theism as pointing to the unknowable divine noumenon, we need not necessarily follow the advaitist Hindu thinkers in equating the divine noumenon with impersonal reality, in contrast to personal deities who are merely phenomenal. The personalist-dualist experience of I–Thou encounter between a human self and the transcendent Self, and the monistic or advaitic consciousness of oneness with infinite non-personal being, are alike experiences of divine phenomena. All that we can say of the divine noumenon is that it is the source and ground of all those experienced realities, as also of human minds which are aware of these different phenomenal forms.

Religious Differences

The thesis we are considering, then, is that religious experience is experience of the Transcendent, not however as divine noumenon but as divine phenomenon. The Transcendent as the phenomenal object of humans' religious experience is a joint product of the divine noumenon itself and the various human concepts of the Transcendent which have developed within different human cultures. These concepts have a common source in man's innate religiousness – that is, in our tendency to experience religiously, or in terms of the Transcendent; and the specific forms taken by the generic concept of the Transcendent arise from the manifold influences which have produced the varied ways of thinking and feeling that are characteristic of different human cultures.

But why are there these different human concepts of the Transcendent, correlated as they are with different forms of religious awareness, different kinds of cult, and different ways of living and worshipping? To answer this question in detail is the task of the historians, anthropologists and sociologists of religion, and is a task which they may or may not ever be able fully to discharge. But the general conclusion seems inevitable that concepts of the Transcendent are related to the conditions of human life in different ages and different parts of the world – in short, to different human cultures.

As earnest of more fully developed theories for which we may hope in the future, such suggestions as the following have been made:

In nomadic, pastoral, herd-keeping societies, the male principle predominates; among agricultural peoples, aware of the fertile earth which brings forth from itself and nourishes its progeny upon its broad bosom, it is the mother principle which seems important. Among Semitic peoples therefore, whose traditions are those of herdsmen, the sacred is thought of in male terms: God the father. Among Indian peoples whose traditions have been for many centuries, and even millennia, agricultural, it is in female terms that the sacred is understood: God the mother.[6]

I am not equipped either to criticize or to contribute to this work of relating the several kinds of religious experience and thought to the different circumstances of human life. But it seems clear that, whether or not we can successfully trace them, all manner of environing influences have gone into the formation of the different human cultures; and that many of these same influences must have affected the religions which are aspects, and indeed usually central aspects, of those cultures. And once a broad cultural stream is flowing, even the new revelatory experiences and insights of the great spirits who arise within it are bound to share the basic character of that stream. Thus, it is not surprising that Gautama (the Buddha) lived in India and Jesus in Palestine.

Cognitive Freedom

There is a very important difference to be noted between our awareness of the Transcendent and our awareness of our material environment, with our awareness of other human selves standing somewhere between these extreme cases. This is a difference within the dimension which has been thought of as the degrees of value and also as the degrees of reality or being – although in the Platonic tradition these two scales were seen as one. When we add that it is of the essence of human existence – whether as child of God or as divine spark – to be finitely free, we see that our relationship to that which is superior to ourselves in value or in fullness of being will differ in character from our relationship to that which is inferior to ourselves, with our relationship to that which is on the same level as ourselves falling between these two extremes. We are not diminished in our essential dignity or freedom by being aware of the existence of realities below ourselves in the scale of value or of reality. The power of storm and earthquake, or the strength of elephant or tiger, dwarfs my own strength; and the vastness of the universe around us shows us by comparison as microscopically small. But humanity nevertheless transcends the whole world of nature, with all its immensity of power, by our consciousness of it; as Pascal said, 'if the universe were to crush him, man would still be more noble than that which killed him, because he knows that he dies and the advantage which the universe has over him; the universe knows nothing of this'.[7] And in relation to other human beings, while many are more successful, or more intelligent, or more wealthy, or more powerful, and so on, yet they are still in the end only fellow mortals and thus ultimately on the same level as myself. But in relation to absolute value or absolute reality I am nothing, and can have no personal being and freedom in relation to it, unless the infinitely good reality allows me largely to shut it out of my consciousness. Accordingly, we preserve our freedom over against that which is infinitely superior to ourselves by being aware of it, not in its infinite fullness, but in terms of limited and limiting concepts.

In theistic terms, to be directly confronted by infinite goodness and love, infinite knowledge and power, infinite fullness of being and life, would deprive us of any independence. There would be no room for a free human response of faith and love, or of trust and obedience. Indeed, the disparity between our finite selves and the infinite divine reality would exclude our very existence as relatively autonomous centres of finite freedom. Therefore God has to be the hidden God, veiling himself by creating us at an epistemic distance in order that he may then progressively reveal himself to us in limited ways which respect and preserve our own human freedom as persons. Again, in non-theistic terms, it is the finite individual's relative ignorance (*avidya*) of Brahman that constitutes his own finite individuality. As he rightly exercises his freedom through the long process of *samsara*, separate individuality is eventually transcended and he becomes the infinite Spirit.

It has been suggested, for example by Bergson, that one function of the brain is to filter out the virtual infinity of information reaching us through our senses, so that what comes to consciousness is the relatively simple and manageable world which we perceive and can successfully inhabit. We also have a system for filtering out the Transcendent and reducing it to forms with which we can cope; for 'humankind cannot bear very much reality'.[8] This system is religion, which is our resistance (in the electronic sense) to the infinite Transcendent. In the earliest stages of humankind's development, the Transcendent was reduced in human awareness to the dimensions of our own image, so that the gods were, like human kings, often cruel and bloodthirsty; or to the dimensions of the tribe or nation, as the symbol of its unity and power; or again to the greater dimensions of the forces of nature, such as the life-giving and yet burning radiance of the sun, or the destructive power of storm and earthquake, or the mysterious pervasive force of fertility. And the response that was required, the way of life which such awareness rendered appropriate, was a communal response. For the anthropologists have shown us how closely knit primitive societies have been, and how little scope they offered for individual thought, whether in religion or in other aspects of life. As Robertson Smith wrote long ago, 'Religion in primitive times was not a system of belief with practical applications: it was a body of fixed traditional practices, to which every member of society conformed as a matter of course.'[9] It was with the gradual emergence of individuality, in what Karl Jaspers has called the axial period, particularly during the second half of the first millennium BCE, that higher conceptions of the Transcendent developed in correlation with a deeper sense of moral claim upon human life, and upon the individual as well as the collectivity.

For it was the emergence of the individual, and in particular of the religious individual, that made possible those great souls or mahatmas on whose consciousness the Transcendent impinged in new ways or with new intensity and power. The greatest of these became founders of religious traditions – Moses, Zoroaster (though he was much earlier than the axial age), Confucius, Gautama, Jesus, and later Muhammad. Others effected important developments within existing traditions – the Hebrew prophets, the writers of the Upanishads and of the *Bhagavad Gita*, Pythagoras, Socrates, Plato. Each of the great religious traditions has of course continued to develop in larger and smaller ways through the centuries, one form each of contemporary Buddhism, Christianity, Hinduism and Judaism being represented in the material prepared for this conference.

The broad hypothesis which I am suggesting, then, is that the Infinite Spirit presses in all the time upon the multiplicity of finite human spirits, and yet always so that our finite awareness of this encompassing reality is filtered through a set of human religious concepts and spiritual practices. When the developing human race produces a spirit who is able to respond to the Transcendent in a new and fuller way, his or her experience of the Transcendent overflows or breaks the system of religious concepts inherited from their culture, and they proclaim a new truth about God or about the meaning of the process of existence, bringing with it new demands for the living of human life.

Belief, and Experience of the Transcendent

All this is hypothesis, of the kind which we are led to develop when we accept as true the religious-experience reports of the mystics. But can we, and indeed can they, properly have confidence in those reports? Let us, in this last section, consider the question of the cognitive value of religious experience.

The central feature of the mystics' reports is that they speak of a divine reality other than the human mind and other than the material universe which is our present environment. This transcendent reality is experienced as the God of the theistic religions and as Brahman or Emptiness (*sunyata*) – an emptiness that is also, paradoxically, fullness – in the non-theistic religions; and I have suggested that these are all divine phenomena constituting forms in which the unknown divine noumenon impinges upon human consciousness. The status of these divine phenomena is thus comparable with that of the phenomenal world in Kant's critical philosophy. That world exists independently of the individual human consciousness, being common to a community of minds functioning in the same way – this community being, in the case of the phenomenal world, coextensive with the human race. But the perceived world, although thus objectively real in relation to ourselves, is still a phenomenon constituting the particular way in which the noumenal reality becomes the object of our finite human consciousness. In an analogous way, God, Jahweh, Allah, Brahman, Emptiness, in so far as these are objects of human religious experience, are divine phenomena constituting ways in which the unknown divine noumenon impinges upon human consciousness within different religious communities, with their different concepts of the Transcendent.

Our question now concerns the reality, over against our human consciousness, of God, Brahman and the other divine phenomena. Can we properly claim to know that God exists, or that Brahman is real?

We must be careful to pose the question rightly. Whenever we ask whether x exists – whether x be an electron, a tree, a house, a human consciousness, or Brahman, or God – we must not exclude ourselves, as the cognizing minds asking the question, from the picture. The apparently purely objective question, Does x exist? is always in reality the objective/subjective question, Do I know that x exists; Is the existence of x an item of knowledge, that is, *of my* knowledge? But even this reformulation is not yet quite right. For many philosophers have defined knowledge in ideal terms so that 'I know p' entails p, and there can thus be no knowing p except when p is in fact the case. This ideal definition has many advantages, but it also has the inconvenience that we are never entitled to certify definitely that we know, but only to register claims to know. We can claim to know that p, that is, claim that what we present as our well warranted belief that p corresponds with the facts. But this claim must necessarily be made from the perspective of our own finite range of data. And it is not open to us, having made that claim from our own particular and limited standpoint, to go on to certify it from an unlimited or ideal perspective. Only omniscience could know that a human being's claimed knowledge is indeed knowledge in the ideal sense. We have the data on the basis of which we claim to have knowledge, but we do not have further data, or knowledge that there are no further data, such as only omniscience could have. And therefore if we are to speak strictly, we must speak not of *knowledge* that the Transcendent exists, but of a well-grounded knowledge claim. I shall accordingly speak interchangeably of well-grounded beliefs and well-grounded knowledge claims. Our question is thus not properly formulated as 'whether the Transcendent exists' but 'whether there is well-grounded human belief that the Transcendent exists', or in other words in the reality of the Transcendent.

At this point we turn to the mystics, and above all to the great souls whose religious experience lies at the origin of the major world faiths. I shall put the argument in terms of the theistic experience of living in the presence of God; but a parallel argument will apply to the non-theistic forms of religious experience. In the theistic world, then, such a person as Jesus was as powerfully conscious of being in the presence of God as he was of the presence of other human beings and of his physical environment. And so let us ask: is it rational for such a person, experiencing in this way, to believe and to claim to know, on the basis of his own experience, that God is real?

I suggest that it *is* rational for him to make such a claim, and indeed that it would be irrational on his part not to. We have to trust our own experience, for otherwise we have no basis on which to believe anything about the world in which we find ourselves. Of course we also know that sometimes particular parts of our experience are delusory, so that experience is not *always to* be trusted. But we only know this on the basis of trust in the general veracity of our experience. We cannot go beyond our experience as a whole; for there is no 'beyond' for us to go to, since any further data that we may come to have must, when we have it, form part of our experience as a whole. And if some aspect of our experience is sufficiently intrusive and persistent, and coherent with the rest of our experience, then to reject it would be in effect to doubt our own sanity and would amount to a kind of cognitive suicide. One who has a powerful and continuous sense of existing in the presence of God *must*, as a rational person, claim to know that God exists; and she is as entitled to make this claim as she and the rest of us are to claim to know that the physical world and other people exist. In each case doubt is theoretically possible: a solipsism which reduces the world, or other minds, or God, to a modification of one's own private consciousness remains a logical possibility.

But we are so made that we live, and can only live, on the basis of our experience and on the assumption that it is generally cognitive of reality transcending our own consciousness. Indeed, what we call sanity consists in acting on the basis of our putatively cognitive experience as a whole. And this being so, the religious person, experiencing life in terms of the presence of God, is rationally entitled to believe what he experiences to be the case – namely that God is real, or exists.

But having said this one must immediately add certain qualifications.

For we cannot say that *all* religious and quasi-religious experiences, without exception, provide a good grounding for knowledge-claims. Just as there are illusions and delusions in other fields of experience, so also in religious experience. Suppose, for example, someone experiences his life in terms of astrology, or alchemy, or influences from extra-galactic intelligences who visit this earth in flying saucers, or in some other way which most of us regard as perverse or crazy. What are we to say about such a form of experience?

Let us suppose that the persons concerned make a knowledge-claim on the basis of their experience. Are we to hold that they are rationally entitled to make such a claim? The question, I would suggest, becomes the question whether we regard them as fully sane, sober and rational persons. If we do so regard them, we must also regard them as entitled to trust their own experience and to base knowledge-claims upon it. And our judgement as to whether someone is fully sane, sober and rational will have two dimensions. One will be our estimate of the person him- or herself; and here our assessment is partly psychological and partly moral. The criteria for such judgements are of course very hard to formulate; and yet it is clear that we are accustomed to make judgements in this area almost every day of our lives. The other dimension concerns the content of the knowledge-claim. It can only be rational to base a knowledge-claim upon some aspect of our experience if that claim is consistent with our other knowledge, based as this is upon the rest of our experience. And it may well be that knowledge-claims about the truth of witchcraft, or astrology, or alchemy, or about the existence of extra-galactic intelligences who visit the earth in flying saucers, fail to cohere with what we know on the basis of our experience as a whole. In particular, such claims may clash with our scientific knowledge. In that case the wider experience will, in a rational person, provide a context within which the special experience is criticized, and bracketed as peculiar and suspect. And when, in hearing reports of astrological or other eccentric experience-reports, we judge the beliefs based upon such experience to be incompatible with public scientific knowledge, we shall probably hold that the person holding the belief is irrational or eccentric and that their special form of experience is not to be relied upon. For it is only if we can accept both that the special beliefs *may* be true and that the individual is a sane and well-balanced human being, that we feel obliged to take their experience-reports seriously.

How does all this apply to the religious case? It means that a rational person will only trust their own religious experience, and will only trust the religious-experience reports of others, if the beliefs to which they give rise are beliefs which they judge *may* be true. In the theistic case, the existence of God must be judged to be possible if the 'experience of living in God's presence' is to be taken seriously. This is where philosophical theology, or natural theology, comes into its own. Its office, I would suggest, is not to prove that God exists, or even that God's existence is probable; but to establish the possibility of divine existence. Without arguing the matter here I believe that reason can ascertain that it is *possible* that there is a God; and in that case theistic religious experience has to be taken seriously. But whether experiences in terms of witchcraft, astrology, alchemy, flying saucers, and the rest, are to be taken seriously depends upon a corresponding rational scrutiny of the content of the knowledge-claims to which they give rise.

The final question that I must briefly raise is this: suppose, for the sake of argument, that we accept the right of the great theistic mystics to believe in the reality of God on the basis of their own religious experience. We shall then be prepared to acknowledge that such a person as Jesus or St Paul or St Francis or Martin Luther, or again Muhammad, or Ramanuja, or Guru Nanak, have been entitled, as rational persons, to claim on the basis of their own experience to know that God exists. But what about ordinary religious believers, who do not enjoy the same overwhelmingly powerful forms of theistic experience? Does our line of thought point to any justification for belief in the existence of God (or the reality of Brahman) on the part of ordinary people? Not, I would say, if they do not experience religiously in any degree whatever. For the absolutely un-mystical – if such there are – there can be no good grounds for religious belief. However, ordinary believers do have some at least remote echo within their own experience of the much more momentous experience of the great religious figures. And it is this that makes them take their reports seriously. If one experiences one's own life religiously at least sometimes and to some slight extent, this makes it possible, and I would suggest reasonable, to be so impressed by the reports of the great souls as to come to share their belief in the reality of the Transcendent. Such belief is not *as* well-grounded as theirs is. But I would suggest that it is well enough grounded for it to be reasonable to proceed in faith in the footsteps of a religious leader, anticipating the full confirmation which this faith will ultimately receive if it does indeed correspond with reality.

Notes

1 See Meister Eckhart, Sermon 27.

2 Rudolf Otto, *Mysticism East and West*, New York: Meridian Books, 1957, p. 14.

3 Paul Tillich, *The Courage to Be*, New Haven: Yale University Press, 1952, p. 189.

4 A. N. Whitehead, *Process and Reality*, New York: Macmillan, 1929, pp. 523–4.

5 Gordon Kaufman, *God the Problem*, Cambridge, MA: Harvard University Press, 1972, p. 86.

6 Trevor Ling, *Religion East and West*, London: Macmillan, 1968, p. 27.

7 Pascal, *Penseés*, no. 347.

8 T. S. Eliot, from 'Burnt Norton'.

9 W. Robertson Smith, *The Religion of the Semites*, 3rd edn, London: A&C Black, 1927, p. 20.

3

The Religious Meaning of Life

The notion of the meaning of life is initially extremely vague. In order to be useful, it has to be specified further, and different people will quite reasonably do this in different ways. I must therefore begin by saying in what sense I shall be using the expression here.

Practical Meaning

First, then, not semantic meaning, the meaning of words and sentences, but what for want of a better term I shall call practical meaning, that is to say, meaning that makes a difference to the way in which, actually or potentially, we act and react in the world. And by the practical meaning for us of a thing, event, or situation – including our situation as part of the universe – I mean the dispositional state it evokes in us as a result of our identifying, or misidentifying, it as being that particular kind of thing or event or situation.

So an object's meaning for us consists in the actual or potential difference that it makes for us – it consists in what in relevant circumstances we find it appropriate to do or avoid doing in relation to that object. To take a trivial example, I believe that what I am holding is a tennis ball if it is true of me that I will treat it, in circumstances in which the issue arises, as a tennis ball rather than, say, as a cricket ball or a hand grenade or anything else. Its meaning for me is such that I will treat it in this way.

This practical meaning is always both species and culture relative: a kitten might see the tennis ball as something to play with, and a stone-age person, translated here in a time-machine, would not have the concepts of tennis or tennis ball and would accordingly see the same object as something quite different. So already a basic epistemological truth, classically propounded by Immanuel Kant, comes into view, namely that perceivers contribute significantly to the meaning that their environment has for them.

Let us now move on from the meaning of objects, such as a tennis ball, to the meaning of situations. A situation is a complex of objects which has its own meaning over and above the sum of the meanings of its constituent objects. A situation is formed by selective human attention operating on a higher level than in object-awareness – higher in the logical sense that it presupposes object-awareness – and human life is ordinarily lived on this higher level of situational meaning. To take an example, the meaning for us of being at a session of an academic conference is such that we behave in ways that are appropriate. Its accepted meaning within our culture is such that I read aloud my paper, and you politely listen while thinking up difficult questions to raise in the discussion period. But the stone-age persons whom I mentioned earlier, if suddenly materialized among us, would not find the same meaning in this physical configuration. For them it would constitute a very different situation, because they would not have such concepts as conference, university, academic paper, philosophy, and so on that are familiar elements of our own cultural world.

I want in due course to move from limited situations such as this to the unlimited situation of our existence in the universe. But first I want to stress again a basic point that has already emerged, namely the contribution of the perceiver to all our awareness of meaning. During the two centuries since Kant this has become an increasingly widely accepted idea, and has in our own time been further reinforced by the development of cognitive psychology and the sociology of knowledge. Its significance for the epistemology of religion was first suggested to me by Wittgenstein's disciple John Wisdom, in his lectures in Cambridge in the early 1950s, after Wittgenstein's death in 1951 – although neither he nor Wittgenstein would necessarily have approved of the use that I want to make of it. But in the *Philosophical Investigations* (part II, section xi), Wittgenstein discusses what he called 'seeing as' – as when you see an ambiguous picture first in one way and then in another. It seems natural to expand this into the concept of experiencing-as, which we need if we are to apply the basic idea to situations. But John Wisdom took this further. Attending his lectures was a strange experience. One would listen to his apparently formless and unprepared meanderings, bored stiff, for weeks on end, and then suddenly he would say something so excitingly illuminating that one had to come back for more. For example, he once spoke of doing metaphysics as being like seeing the pattern in a puzzle picture. As was typical with Wisdom's lectures, this was a tantalizingly suggestive throw-out remark which he never, so far as I know, developed further. But to me it was a clue to the nature of religious awareness and hence of the religious understanding of the meaning of life. The general point, then, thus far is that consciousness of our environment is an interpreted awareness of it as having practical meaning for us. Here 'interpretation' is not of course theoretical interpretation, as when we interpret a text or a detective interprets the clues, but the perceptual interpretation that is taking place all the time in our continuous awareness of a meaningful environment within which we are able to act and react in ways that we take to be appropriate.

Physical, Moral and Aesthetic Levels of Meaning

I now want to take note of the different levels of meaning that we discern in human situations. These are the physical, the social or ethical, the aesthetic, and the religious; and I refer to them as *levels* of meaning because the ethical and the aesthetic presuppose and are mediated through the physical, while the religious can presuppose and be mediated through each or all of the others, whereas the reverse does not hold. We are primarily interested here in the religious meaning both of limited situations and of the unlimited situation of our presence in the universe; but the same epistemological structure runs through the whole hierarchy of forms of awareness.

Religious Meaning

Here I must move quickly through the meaning of particular sacred objects and places and of the situations that consist in the enactment of religious rituals. Sacred objects include totems, and the clay, wood or stone figures of Hindu deities, of the Buddha and Bodhisattvas, of Christ, the Virgin Mary and Christian saints, and so forth; and such sacred writings as the Torah scroll, the Bible, the Qur'an, the Adi Granth; and such symbolic images as the cross, the crucifix, the Islamic crescent moon, Hindu and Buddhist mandalas, and so on; and again, sacred buildings include stone circles, synagogues, churches, chapels, cathedrals, mosques, gurudwaras; and sacred places include Benares, Jerusalem, Mecca, and so on; while religious events include the ancient Vedic rituals, the Christian Eucharist, the Muslim *salat*, and solemn processions and sacred dances. All of these are designed, or more often have evolved, to evoke a dispositional response which is, generically, a move toward the centring of the life of the individual and the community in the sacred, the divine, the transcendent in the particular form selected by this symbolic object or event – thus reinforcing communal dedication to a local deity or producing a greater degree of devotion to Vishnu or to Shiva, or to the Adonai of rabbinic Judaism, or to Christ, or to the Holy Trinity, or to Allah, or a greater degree of inner transformation in response to the Dharma or the Tao (or Dao).

But our concern now is with a larger and more general form of practical meaning, the meaning of life, the religious meaning of our existence in the universe. We are concerned with religious ways of experiencing our total environment, and with our correlative dispositional responses.

The way in which we inhabit the universe – not necessarily from day to day but in the overall tenor of our lives – is a reflection of the character that we conceive and hence experience it to have. And so the meaning-of-life question is: What is the nature of this universe in which, and as part of which, we find ourselves? Above all, is its ultimate nature, so far as we humans are concerned, benign or hostile or indifferent? I say 'so far as we humans are concerned' because we are minute fragments of the universe, and it seems very unlikely that we have the conceptual equipment to comprehend the nature of reality as a whole. We may however be able to comprehend in our own human terms what its nature is in so far as it affects us. As John Stuart Mill said,

> If to know authentically in what order of things, under what government of the universe it is our destiny to live, were not useful, it is difficult to imagine what could be considered so. Whether a person is in a pleasant or in an unpleasant place, a palace or a prison, it cannot be otherwise than useful to him to know where he is.[1]

Each of the great world religions offers a comprehensive conception of the nature of the universe; and in so far as such pictures are believed, and are thus built into our dispositional structure, they automatically affect the way in which the believer experiences the universe and lives within it. In other words they determine what the overall meaning of life is for us. We are of course talking here about genuine beliefs, belief on which we are prepared to act – what Cardinal Newman called real as distinguished from notional assents.[2]

As a relatively trivial example of the fact that the way in which we experience our environment affects our dispositional state, consider the following imagined situation. I am in a strange building, and walking by mistake into a large room I find that a militant secret society is meeting there. Many of the members are armed, and as they take me for a fellow member I think it expedient to acquiesce in this role. Plans are being discussed for the violent overthrow of the constitution. The whole situation is alarming in the extreme. Its meaning for me is such that I am extremely apprehensive. Then I suddenly become aware in the dim light above us of a gallery in which there are silently whirring cameras, and I realize that I have walked by accident onto the set of a film. This realization consists in a change of interpretation of my immediate situation. Until now I had automatically interpreted it as 'real life' and as demanding considerable circumspection on my part. Now I experience it as having a quite different significance. But at ground level there is no change in the course of events; the meeting of the secret society proceeds just as before. And yet my new awareness of the more comprehensive situation alters my experience of the more immediate one. It now has a new meaning for me, such that I am in a different dispositional state in relation to it. For example, if one of the 'conspirators' noticed my arrival and threateningly pointed his gun at me, I might pretend to be terrified but would not be so in fact.

This is not an adequate analogy for our religious situation, because the cameras and their operators in the balcony are only more of the same kind of reality as the set and the actors and extras at ground level. But it does nevertheless perhaps help to make intelligible the suggestion that the religious understanding of our lives as taking place in the presence of, and as grounded in, the Divine, the Transcendent, the ultimately Real, can make a profound difference to our understanding of the meaning of our life now.

Religion as Cosmic Optimism

Let me now put to you the hypothesis that the great world religions are different forms of what I shall call cosmic optimism. 'Cosmic optimism' is not a term that figures in the distinctive vocabulary of any of them. But my suggestion is that it is a generalization of their distinctive affirmations about the ultimate character of reality as this affects us human beings. Concerning that reality, the great monotheisms affirm, in the case of Judaism, that 'as the heavens are high above the earth, so great is [the God of Israel's] steadfast love towards those who fear him' (Psalm 103.11); or that the heavenly Father of the New Testament is a limitlessly loving God; or that the Allah self-revealed in the Qur'an is ever gracious and merciful. Most Hindus are also theistic, but turning to the great non-theistic faiths, advaitic Hinduism affirms that in our deepest nature we already are the *saccidananda*, being-consciousness-bliss of

Brahman, but have yet, so to speak, to become what we are; or again, that our true nature is the universal Buddha – the dharma-nature of the universe which is reflected within human experience as the limitless compassion of the Buddhas – and again we have to become what in a sense we already are. In each case they teach that we can, whether suddenly or gradually, whether on earth or in heaven, whether in this life or through many lives, receive or achieve the salvific transformation to a new relationship or a newly discovered identity with that ultimate reality.

Each tradition draws a radical distinction between, on the one hand, the state from which we desire to be saved or released or from which we need to awaken, and on the other hand the limitlessly better state to which it shows the way. There is a deeply pessimistic view of our present predicament, combined with a highly optimistic view of what is ultimately open to us. The pessimism is an understanding of ordinary human life as fallen into sin and guilt, or lived in disobedience and alienation from God, or as caught in the unreality of spiritual blindness (*avidya*) and the consequent round of suffering existence (*samsara*). But there is also the affirmation of a limitlessly better possibility which is available to us because the Ultimate is benign from our human point of view. By divine grace, or divine mercy, or by a gradual transcending of the ego point of view and a realization of our own deepest nature, we can attain or receive the highest good, variously conceived as heaven, paradise, unity with God, harmony with the Tao, absorption into Brahman, nirvana. In so far as this limitlessly better state is said to be available to everyone, the message of each of the great religions constitutes good news.

I mean, then, by the cosmic optimism of the world religions that in each case, if their conception of the nature of the universe is basically correct, we can be glad to be part of the universe and can rejoice and be thankful for our present human existence. That is to say, the meaning of life is such that we can have an ultimate trust and confidence, even in life's darkest moments of suffering and sorrow.

However, I think that we have at this point to draw a distinction like that which Cantwell Smith draws between what he calls faith and what he calls the cumulative traditions.[3] I do not personally think that his term 'faith' is the best word for what he is referring to, namely the actual response to God, or to the Transcendent, that informs an individual's life. And so, although this may not be the best term either, I shall speak of life responses to the Transcendent, distinguishing these from religion in the sense in which that is studied by anthropologists, sociologists and historians. For it makes no difference to work in these disciplines whether or not God exists or whether or not there is, more broadly, a higher and ultimate spiritual reality. It is sufficient, for the scientific study of religion, that individuals and communities have believed that there is. In other words, the scientific or objective study of religion is the non-religious study of it. This is entirely legitimate, and indeed extremely valuable; but I want to insist that the religious study of religion is no less legitimate. The two, although importantly different, are only rivals if the methodological naturalism of the scientific approach is treated as a dogmatic naturalism. Otherwise not. And from the point of view of a religious interpretation of religion, responses to the Transcendent are to be distinguished from the institutions and practices of the cumulative traditions. At the same time, although they are to be distinguished, in practice they are mingled together; for religious responses to the Divine are normally expressed in and through the religious practices, organizations and belief systems constituting the historical traditions. But the distinction enables us to recognize that these traditions do not always or everywhere or fully embody a response to the Transcendent. They have their own autonomous existence, in virtue of which they can be the subject of scientific study. And sometimes they can proceed on through history even when largely devoid of any response to the Transcendent – like an aeroplane that continues its flight after the pilot has bailed out!

There is generally a wide gap between the meaning of life as taught by our religion and the immediate concrete meanings in terms of which we live our daily lives. It does not follow from the fact that our religion teaches a form of cosmic optimism that we, as believers, are always in a cheerful and optimistic frame of mind! Nor does the belief that human existence is ultimately good mean that our present self-centred, unre-deemed, illusion-bound existence is good, even though there is a great deal that is good within it. Pain and suffering, starvation and disease, war and genocide, repression and exploitation are real, and they effectively blot out the ultimate goodness of human existence for very many people for much or even most of their lives. That human existence is good means that it is a process or project, leading to a wholly good conclusion. But although the religions explicitly teach this, the majority of men and women of each faith live much of their daily lives without any such thought. Belief in the goodness of the Ultimate from our human point of view is probably for most people most of the time a notional rather than a real belief – although it is one that may come vividly to life in some moment of crisis.

Further, even the teachings of the great traditions contain elements that conflict with belief in a wholly good outcome of the human project, so that the cosmic optimism hypothesis has to be carefully qualified. We have to consider to what degree the great ethnic religions, Hinduism and Judaism, are optimistic only concerning their own community but pessimistic concerning the rest of humankind; and in the end the answer of most Hindus and most Jews is that salvation is *not* confined to their own community. Again, it has been believed within the monotheistic faiths, and strongly so in the medieval period, that the large majority of the human race are destined to an everlasting hell – either because they are outside the Church or because they are infidels, not of the 'people of the book'. And within each religion there is today a large fundamentalist wing that retains that medieval view; and we have to say that in so far as any tradition teaches the exclusion of a proportion of men and women from the fulfilment of the human project, to that extent it is a form of cosmic pessimism rather than of cosmic optimism. Within each theistic tradition wicked individuals who die unrepentant have been believed to be consigned to an eternal damnation, so that for them no redemption is then ever possible; and we have to distinguish – though how much we should make of the distinction is a difficult question – between being excluded from the ultimate good fulfilment by the structure of the universe and being self-excluded by one's own free actions. And so the situation is complex, and we shall find in the history of religions the picture offered by each tradition has been a mixture of good news and bad news concerning the ultimate destiny of humankind as a whole.

It must also be made clear that when we speak of the ultimate goodness of the universe from our human point of view, we are talking about the total character of a reality which far exceeds anything that we can presently see or that the physical sciences can ever discover. For it is clear from the evils that afflict humanity, and from the equally evident fact that the realization of the human potential is seldom fulfilled in this present life, that if the process is ever to reach its completion, it must be continued beyond this life. The faith that, in the words of the Christian mystic Julian of Norwich, 'all shall be well, and all shall be well, and all manner of thing shall be well' presupposes a conception of the ultimate structure of reality that makes this possible.[4]

The great traditions and their sub-traditions have developed different pictures of this structure and of the final fulfilment as heaven, paradise, union with God, the beatific vision of God, an absorption into Brahman in which separate ego existence has been transcended, nirvana, the universal realization of the Buddha-nature of all things, and so on. But it is important to note that the idea of a good outcome of the life process does not require that any one of these specific conceptions of it will turn out to be accurate. Indeed, thoughtful people within each tradition have always been aware that the scriptural accounts of heaven/paradise are presented in a poetic imagery which points beyond the range of our present imagination; or in the Eastern faiths that the final unity that is sought is, once again, not thinkable in any earthly terms.

There are, then, two closely related conditions that qualify a religion as a form of what I am calling cosmic optimism. One is that it conceives of that which is ultimately real as benign from our human point of view; and the other is that it conceives the structure of the universe to be consonant with this.

The next step, if there were space, would be to look at each of the great world religions to see whether or to what extent they fulfil these two conditions. I only have space, however, to do this for one sample case, for which I have chosen Buddhism.

Buddhist Cosmic Optimism

Buddhism is not of course a single uniform entity, as our modern Western reifying name might suggest, but a history of experience and thought launched in northern India some 25 centuries ago, and developing since within different cultures to form a distinctive family of traditions. In its early centuries the Buddhist movement was strongly influenced by the pervasive Hindu outlook of India, although also reacting against some central aspects of it; for the Buddha's *anatta* teaching rejected the idea of an eternal unchanging Atman, and the Buddhist community, the *sangha*, rejected the hierarchical caste system of India. When Buddhism moved north, early in the Common Era, the Mahayana Buddhism of China, Tibet, Korea, Thailand, Japan and Vietnam took forms that are in some ways different from the southern Theravada (or Hinayana) Buddhism of Sri Lanka and Southeast Asia. Very roughly, the more world-denying ethos of religious life in India gave way in China to a more earthly and world-affirming outlook, with the discovery that nirvana and *samsara* are identical: that is to say, earthly life in its full concrete particularity becomes nirvana in the experience of those who have entirely transcended the ego point of view.

The terms enlightenment, liberation, awakening, nirvana, *sunyata* ('emptiness'), Dharmakaya and so on range in connotation between the psychological and the metaphysical. Some Westerners, usually in reaction against what they see as the anthropomorphism of the

Christian conception of God as a greatly magnified person, have responded eagerly to Buddhism, seeing it as a psychological technique for attaining inner peace and serenity without involving any notion of a transcendent reality. This particular Western appropriation of Buddhism parallels the contemporary non- or anti-realist versions of Christianity, according to which God is not a transcendent (as well as immanent) reality but an imaginary personification of our human ideals. But, while there are Buddhists – particularly in the West – who adopt a non-realist epistemology, it seems to me impossible to sustain such a picture from the Pali scriptures.

The Buddha taught the insubstantiality of the world, as a single universal interdependent process of ceaseless change (*pratitya samutpada*) in which each movement in some degree conditions and is conditioned by every other in a vast network of dynamic mutuality. Everything is compounded of elements with only a fleeting momentary existence; and the appearance of solid enduring entities, including the human self, is illusory. Indeed it is the deep realization of this that can free us from the self-centred outlook that makes our experience of life so often one of anxious craving, sorrow and joylessness – in Buddhist terms *dukkha*.

The Pali *nibbana* (or in Sanskrit, nirvana) means, literally, 'blowing out', as in the blowing out of a flame. However, this is not a ceasing to exist, but the blowing out, or destruction, of illusion and its fruits. The Buddha taught, 'The destruction of lust, the destruction of hatred, the destruction of illusion, friend, is called Nibbana.'[5] And this is not only an individual psychological state, but a reflection in a particular momentary occasion of the ultimate universal reality that is variously referred to as nirvana, the Dharmakaya, *sunyata*, the Buddha-nature of the universe. Thus nirvana is described in the Pali scriptures as an eternal reality, 'the unborn . . . unageing . . . undecaying . . . undying . . . stainless'.[6] In a famous passage the Buddha teaches, 'Monks, there is a not-born, a not-become, a not-made, a not-compounded. Monks, if that unborn, not-become, not-made, not-compounded were not, there would be apparent no escape from this here that is born, become, made, compounded.'[7] The contemporary Theravadin scholar Narada Mahathera accordingly speaks of nirvana as 'the permanent, immortal, supramundane state which cannot be expressed by mundane terms'.[8] And Takeuchi Yoshinori, of the Kyoto school of philosophy, quotes with approval Friedrich Heiler's words,

Nirvana is the equivalent of what Western mysticism understands as the 'Being of beings', the supreme and one reality, the absolute, the divine . . . Nirvana is the infinite, the eternal, the uncreated, the quality-free, the ineffable, the one and only, the highest, the supreme good, the best, the good pure and simple.'[9]

Again, Edward Conze, a leading Western authority, says that

> It is assumed first of all [in Buddhism] that there is an ultimate reality, and secondly that there is a point in ourselves at which we touch that ultimate reality. The ultimate reality, also called Dharma, or Nirvana, is defined as that which stands completely outside the sensory world of illusion and ignorance, a world inextricably interwoven with craving and greed. To get somehow to that ultimate reality is the supremely worthwhile goal of the Buddhist life. The Buddhist idea of ultimate reality is very much akin to the philosophical notion of the 'Absolute,' and not easily distinguished from the notion of God among the more mystical theologians, like Dionysius Areopagita and Eckhart.[10]

However, the focus of Buddhist attention is always upon the present life and indeed upon the present moment. The dharma is wholly practical, a way to liberation. Gautama said, 'As the great ocean is saturated by only one taste, the taste of salt, so this teaching and system is saturated by only one taste, the taste of salvation [i.e. liberation].'[11]

The Buddha strongly discouraged philosophical speculation because it can so easily become a substitute for the spiritual quest. But this exclusion of speculation occurred within the context of the belief, continuously affirmed or assumed, that the karmic project of which we are each the present incarnation progresses through many lives until enlightenment/liberation/awakening is at last attained. Thus it is taken for granted that the structure of the universe is such that human existence is moving, on a vast time-scale, towards a limitlessly good fulfilment. This is not however thought of (as generally in Western religion) as the perfecting of the individual self or community of selves, but as a state lying beyond the range of our present conceptualities.

Normative Buddhism, then, offers a picture of the universe as structured towards the 'nirvanization' of all life. Different schools of thought hold that enlightenment (*satori*) is possible either in this life for all who seek it with all their heart and mind, or in this life only for those who have already approached it through many previous lives; that it occurs suddenly, that it occurs in stages; that when it occurs it liberates us *from* the material world and that when it occurs it liberates us *for* the material world. There is thus immense variety within Buddhism. But in all its forms it holds that none are excluded from the ultimate fulfilment of the human project. Buddhism is thus unambiguously a form of cosmic optimism.

Given this Buddhist worldview, what is its correlative dispositional response? How are Buddhists taught to pursue enlightenment/liberation/ awakening/nirvana? The Buddha teaches a practical way to release from *dukkha*, the pervasive anxiety and insecurity of ordinary human life as we encounter pain, sorrow, grief, despair, frustration, sickness, ageing and death. Life has for us this *dukkha* quality, he taught, because we experience the world as centring upon ourselves. I experience everything in its relation to *me*, as welcome or unwelcome, propitious or threatening, as likely to satisfy or frustrate my desires; and this way of experiencing life creates a basic *angst* which is sometimes conscious and sometimes unconscious. Liberation from this is achieved by transcending the ego point of view in order to participate in a more universal perspective.

There is, incidentally, an interesting analogy between the role of the universal point of view in Buddhism and in the Kantian ethic. According to Kant, morally right action is action that is best, not in the private interests of the agent, but from a universal and impartial point of view in which every individual is valued equally as an end in him- or herself. This point of view is achieved, according to Kant, by applying a 'universalization' criterion. Can we perhaps say that Buddhism teaches the inner spiritual attitude of which the Kantian ethic teaches the practical application?

The way to this inner spiritual attitude is the 'Noble Eightfold Path', which is both ethical and spiritual. Ethically it consists in developing a universal compassion (*karuna*) and loving-kindness (*metta*). There are concrete steps to this. We are enjoined to practise right speech – not lying or slandering or maliciously gossiping; right action – not stealing or acting dishonestly, not taking life, not indulging in illegitimate sex; and right livelihood – not earning one's living in ways that harm others such as by dealing in armaments or in harmful drugs. Thus within Buddhism – as within the other world faiths – the religious meaning of our situation in the universe presupposes its ethical meaning, which in turn presupposes its physical meaning. Spiritually the way to enlightenment is that of prolonged meditation producing a realization of the insubstantial and fleeting nature of the self, leading to an eventual detachment from the ego point of view. This is a transcendence both from egoity and to – and here I offer a variety of terms – enlightenment, liberation, awakening, nirvana, *sunyata* ('emptiness'), conscious participation in the Dharmakaya or in the universal Buddha-nature. What the ultimate reality is with which we become one in enlightenment cannot be stated in human concepts. For it is for us *sunyata* – empty of everything that the human mind projects in its activity of awareness.

All who have an inkling of this state will seek it in this present life. For 'Above, beyond Nibbana's bliss, is naught';[12] and again, 'He that doth crush the great "I am" conceit – this, even this, is happiness supreme.' In the *Dhammapada*, a collection of the Buddha's sayings which constitutes for many a Buddhist Bible, there is a continual stress upon the blessedness of approaching the nirvanic state now:

> happily do we live without hate among the hateful . . . happily do we live without yearning among those who yearn . . . happily the peaceful live, giving up victory and defeat . . . there is no bliss higher than Nibbana . . . Nibbana, bliss supreme . . . Nibbana is the highest bliss . . . the taste of the joy of the Dhamma.[13]

And so, because the nirvanic state is limitlessly good, and is open without restriction to everyone, the message of Buddhism is clearly a form of cosmic optimism.

Other Cosmic Optimisms

I believe that an analogous case can be made for the cosmic optimism of Christianity, Judaism, Islam and Hinduism. There has only been space here to spell the case out in one instance, and I chose Buddhism because it is in many ways so different from the Christianity within which I myself live. But I can now in closing indicate the broad outline of the argument in relation to the other great traditions.

Christianity presents itself as a gospel, good news. In Jesus' teaching there is a very clear affirmation, expressed in parable after parable, of the goodness and love of God. Although his mission was primarily to his fellow Jews, there are several indications that he did not see God's saving love as confined to them. On the contrary, 'many will come from east and west and will eat with Abraham and Isaac and Jacob in the kingdom of heaven, while the heirs of the kingdom [that is, the children of Israel] will be thrown into the outer darkness' (Matt. 8.11–12). This saying does however also remind us of the doctrine of hell, which I have recognized above as undermining religious cosmic optimism. Hell has played a prominent part in Christian belief, particularly in the pre-modern period; and Jesus certainly spoke vividly of dire consequences beyond death for evil-doers, the criterion of judgement being always moral rather than theological. However, I do not think that it can be shown that he taught an *eternal* and therefore necessarily unredemptive punishment. The relevant passages are sparsest in the earliest Gospel, that of Mark, and most prominent in the latest, that of John. But in the majority of the parables of judgement the punishment to come is clearly limited; for example, 'until you have paid the last penny' (Matt. 5.26), 'until he should pay his entire debt' (Matt. 18.34). And when the word eternal (*aeonion*) is used, it does not necessarily mean 'for ever and ever' but can mean until the end of the aeon, or age.[14] Thus a Christianity that emphasizes Jesus' teaching of divine love and God's gracious forgiveness of the truly penitent – as in the Lord's Prayer and in the parable of the prodigal son – is indeed good news for all, a form of cosmic optimism.

Judaism's cosmic optimism consists in a special covenantal relationship between the people and their God, who is both gracious and just, and in a faith in the people's future welfare and ultimate fulfilment within the divine kingdom. Toward the end of the biblical period the idea of the world to come (*olam ha-ba*) became part of Jewish thinking, developed within rabbinic Judaism – particularly in the medieval period – in terms first of bodily resurrection and later of the continuing life of the soul. Further, the rabbis concluded that redemption is not confined to Israel, and that non-Jews do not have to obey the many laws of the Torah to be accepted by God but only the basic moral principles believed to have been revealed to Adam and Noah. Thus while Jewish thinking has been compelled by history to be focused on the survival and welfare of the Jewish people, it is in principle universal in scope. In affirming both the loving-kindness of God and the reality of the world to come, Judaism too constitutes a form of cosmic optimism.

As a form of cosmic optimism Islam exhibits essentially the same structure as the other 'religions of the book'. That is to say, there is an affirmation that the Ultimate is gracious and merciful toward humanity, and that God's good purpose for all who seek him will finally be fulfilled in the life of paradise. Every sura of the Qur'an (except one) begins with an invocation of *Allah rahman rahim*, God gracious and merciful. And the divine mercy is not restricted to the Muslim community: 'Surely the believers [that is, Muslims] and the Jews, Nazareans [Christians], and the Sabians, whoever believes in God and the Last Day, and whosoever does right, shall have his reward with his Lord, and will neither have fear nor regret' (2.61). Islam teaches the unqualified unity and the absolute sovereignty of God, the sole ultimate reality, so that our appropriate human response to God is one of total submission and of trust in the divine goodness and mercy. The final judgement is strongly emphasized, and in the mainstream of the tradition it has been assumed – as in traditional Christianity – that many will forfeit paradise. But Islam contains great internal diversity: some of the Sufis thought that hell might be empty![15] It would seem, then, that Islam is a form of cosmic optimism in the same sense – admittedly qualified in much of their histories – as Christianity and Judaism.

Hinduism – that is to say Indian religiousness in its wide variety of forms – sees human existence, both in this life and beyond it, as a journey. On the large scale it is a journey through many lives in which souls (*jivas*) are gradually moving towards their final liberation (*moksha*): 'After a number of births, perfected, he reaches the highest goal' (*Bhagavad Gita* 5.45). This goal is differently conceived within the theistic and non-theistic strands of Hindu religion. According to the Advaita Vedanta of Shankara and others, our surface personality, or conscious ego, is only a fleeting material individuation of the universal Atman, which is ultimately identical with the universal Brahman, beyond the limitations of personality. On the other hand, according to the great theistic philosopher Ramanuja the material universe, including human selves, constitutes the 'body' of God, and the final state is life within the eternal divine life. It is also the case that within the Hindu pictures of the structure of the universe there are many hells and many heavens. But these are not in the same category as the standard heaven and hell of Western monotheism. They are levels of existence in which *jivas* spend limited periods of time. But the ultimate state is eternal and is ultimately for all, whether as union with Brahman in which individual egoity has been entirely transcended, or as life within the life of God. Such a worldview clearly constitutes another form of cosmic optimism.

To summarize, then, the meaning for us of our human life depends upon what we believe to be the nature of the universe in which we find ourselves. The great world religions teach that the process of the universe is good from our human point of view because its ultimate principle (as some would say) or its governor (as others would say) is benign – again, from our human point of view. This is basically a very simple and indeed, I would think, obvious suggestion – though not necessarily any the worse for that.

Notes

1 John Stuart Mill, *Nature and the Utility of Religion and Theism*, London: Longmans, Green, 1875, p. 69.

2 John Henry Newman, *A Grammar of Assent*, 1870; New York and London: Longmans, Green, 1947, ch. 4.

3 Wilfred Cantwell Smith, *The Meaning and End of Religion*, 1962; Minneapolis: Fortress Press, 1991.

4 Julian of Norwich, *Showings*, Long Text, ch. 27.

5 *Samyutta Nikaya*, IV.250, trans. Frank L. Woodward, in *The Book of the Kindred Sayings*, London: Luzac, 1956, pt. 4, p. 170.

6 *Majjhima Nikaya*, I.163, trans. I. E. Horner, in *The Collection of the Middle Length Sayings*, London: Luzac, 1954, vol. 1, pp. 206–7.

7 *Udana*, 80 (iii), trans. Frank L. Woodward, in *The Minor Anthologies of the Pali Canon*, London: Oxford University Press, 1948, pp. 97–8.

8 Narada Mahathera, introduction to *The Dhammapada*, 2nd edn, Colombo: Vajiranama, 1972, pp. 24–5.

9 Takeuchi Yoshinori, *The Heart of Buddhism*, trans. James Heisig, New York: Crossroad, 1983, pp. 8–9.

10 Edward Conze, *Buddhism, its Essence and Development*, New York and London: Harper & Row, 1975, pp. 110–11.

11 *Vinaya Pitaka, Cullavagga*, 9, 238, trans. I. B. Horner, in *The Book of the Discipline*, London: Luzac, 1963, vol. 5, p. 335.

12 *Therigatha*, 476, trans. C. A. F. Rhys Davids, in *Psalms of the Early Buddhists*, London: Luzac, 1964, p. 169.

13 *The Dhammapada*, trans. Narada Mahathera, Colombo: Vajiranama, 1972, ch. 15.

14 For a fuller discussion of both the biblical evidence and the philosophical issues, see my *Death and Eternal Life*, London: Macmillan, 1985 and Louisville, KY: Westminster John Knox Press, 1993, ch. 13.

15 For example, Rumi, *Masnavi*, Bk. 5, 432.

4

On Being Mortal

(A sermon delivered at Great St Mary's Church, Cambridge, in 1967)

As Christians we believe that we human beings are living a double life – a mortal life and, overlapping with it and interpenetrating it, an eternal life. This Christian claim is certainly a tremendous one, not only hard to believe but also hard to understand. And yet even apart from any religious teaching it is clear that we do have a double status which is unique among the creatures of this world. On the one hand we are animals, formed out of the long, slow evolutionary process. We have emerged out of the lower forms of life and we constitute part of the continuous realm of nature. And as animals we are mortal, made (as the book of Genesis says) out of the dust of the earth and destined to return to that dust. We have a normal life span of some eighty or more years. And then, in our seventies or our eighties or at most our nineties, we shall die, and this living body, then lifeless and cold, will begin to disintegrate and return to the dust of the earth. This on the one hand is true.

But on the other hand, while we are part of nature, in a quite precise sense we transcend nature. For we are possessed of reason, which is the power to contemplate and understand nature, including our own nature, from an intellectual vantage point outside it. As physicists and chemists, astronomers and cosmologists, psychologists, sociologists and historians, as poets and philosophers we transcend the natural order of which we are part. For while the physical universe goes blindly on its way in a stream of unconscious cause and effect, we are centres of self-consciousness and freedom. Around these centres there has developed a moral conscience and a sense of values and of responsibility in virtue of which we are rational and moral persons. And Christianity adds that as rational and moral persons we are made 'in the image of God' as beings to whom he (or she) can give eternal life. And so we have this double status as mortals to whom God is giving the gift of immortality. We are animals, and yet animals made as rational and personal in the image of God for eternal fellowship with him. And this morning I should like to think a little about this peculiar dual existence of ours with its inter-weaving of the threads of mortality and immortality.

First, two thoughts about being mortal, one addressed particularly to those who are young and the other to those who are old.

If you are young – in your teens or twenties – you probably haven't yet realized that you *are* mortal! Of course you know that all humans are mortal, and that you are human; and you draw the logical conclu-sion. But this is not the same as being conscious with your whole being, and as a fact to be reckoned with, that you personally are in due course to die. It is possible when young even to go through a great war without really believing in your own mortality. I had my own 22nd birthday on a troop ship that was being attacked by submarines just outside the Straits of Gibraltar; but neither then nor at any other time during those war years did I *feel* mortal. And it is I believe very commonly only when we are approaching the half-way point of life that we become con-sciously mortal. This is no doubt one of the factors that tends to set a gulf between the older and younger age groups – for what bigger differ-ence could there be than that one group consists of immortals and the other of mortals? And yet strangely enough even this communication barrier need not be insuperable; for we who are now mortal can remem-ber the time when we were immortal, and should be able to converse with those who are still in that paradisal state.

And then an observation addressed more to those who are old, those who in the UK are called old-age pensioners but who in the United States of America have the much nicer title of senior citizens. It may be worth saying to some that the experience of dying is – so far as observa-tion can tell – not usually anything to be dreaded. It is generally, often because of drugs, pain-free, and when it comes at the natural end of the life span, when the organism is wearing out, death is usually not unwel-come. For the dying person, their bodily frame having done its work, is usually at that stage so tired and so reduced in vitality that in the end he or she slips thankfully away from consciousness and from this life with the relief of an utterly exhausted person dropping gratefully to sleep. At that last stage death, so far from being feared or resisted, is welcome. When death is close at hand in the natural course of nature it has often ceased to appear as an enemy and is accepted as a friend. This, as I said, is generally the case with death in old age. But of course when, at any age, death is caused by a painful disease or a terrible accident or violence our situation is very different. (It then gives rise to the increasingly openly debated question of medically assisted suicide and of legally binding Advance Decisions.)

However, let us turn from that last phase to the middle years of life, in which I suppose most of us here now are. What is the Christian attitude to our mortality, and to the mortality of those whom we love?

It is here that God's gift of eternal life can affect and colour the sense of our mortality. Death is still to be sure a solemn matter. As entry into the unknown, into 'that undiscovered country from whose bourne no traveller returns', it will always be met with a certain profound and solemn awe and apprehension – awe and apprehension in face of a great mystery. But it should not evoke the sickening fear with which we face that which we know to be evil. For the one thing that as Christians we do know about that which lies on the other side of death is that it is not evil but good. It is a fuller stage in the outworking of the Creator's loving purpose for his children.

Of course we know nothing concrete about the conditions of our existence after death. We have a few hints, on the basis of which we can speculate – hints suggesting continued individual identity, in some kind of re-embodied state, and of the further unfolding, possibly through many lives, of the immense potentialities of our human nature. Amid the hints, what we have firmly and clearly is the promise given by Jesus, chiefly in parables, that beyond death there lies ultimately the fulfilment of God's good purpose for his children. This fulfilment is called in the New Testament the kingdom of God, and it is pictured in very earthly terms as a great banquet in which all and sundry rejoice together in dancing and gladness. The meaning does not of course lie in the details of the picture of the messianic banquet, for they are simply pointers to something beyond our present experience. The meaning lies rather in the basic character of the kind of picture that Jesus chose to use. He did not, like some of our hymns and prayers, use symbols suggesting that eternal life is negative, static and boring. He used symbols pointing to eternal life as limitlessly enhanced life, as a state of being more intensely alive in an existence which is both perfect fulfilment and yet also endless activity and newness. If death leads eventually to *that*, then although we shall still think of it, both for ourselves and for others, with trembling awe and apprehension, yet it will not evoke terror or despair; for beyond death we and they will not be less alive but more alive than we are now.

But let me ask this question, which is provoked by what I have just been saying: If God's gift to humanity is not only life but unlimited life, what is the purpose of death? Why should we die at all, if it is only to live again beyond death? Why our animal mortality, if we are really to enjoy eternal life?

Well, here is a suggestion. Perhaps death serves, but in a bigger way, a function like that of sleep. Sleep cuts life up for us into small manageable sections. Even if we did not need sleep for physical rest we should still need it to divide life into parts that we can cope with. We could not face an endless continuity of consciousness, an unceasing bombardment of sense impressions, continual activity without respite. Life would be intolerably intense if we did not after 18 or so hours relapse into unconsciousness, and then begin again the next day. Without that periodic disengagement in sleep we should be so continuously up against the world and one another, and all life's complexities and problems, that we might well break down under the unremitting pressure. Sleep is indeed a beneficent provision of nature. As so often, Shakespeare has perfectly expressed it:

Sleep that knits up the ravell'd sleave of care,
The death of each day's life, sore labour's bath,
Balm of hurt minds, great nature's second course,
Chief nourisher in life's feast.[1]

– chief nourisher because it gives us an ever renewed appetite for life's feast.

Now perhaps the dividing-up function of sleep suggests a similar function for death in dividing up our immortal existence. Perhaps we could not at present face an endless vista of life, but need the termination of death to circumscribe our life and make it manageable. Perhaps the function of death is to give us, at the present stage of our spiritual growth, a portion of life that we can cope with. In his play, *Back to Methuselah*, George Bernard Shaw's Adam, before the fall, contemplates the prospect of an unending continuance of life, and is appalled by it:

It is the horror of having to be with myself for ever. I like you [he says to Eve]; but I do not like myself. I want to be different; to be better; to begin again and again! to shed myself as a snake sheds its skin. I am tired of myself. And yet I must endure myself, not for a day or for many days, but for ever. That is a dreadful thought.[2]

I think Shaw was right. We should not want to live for ever and ever, as we now are. It is better to have the limited period of our earthly life, in which we strive as best we can, and then for God to end it and move us on to another and different stage. The boundary of death gives us this present finite life to concentrate upon without being able to look beyond it. It sets a task before our eyes and under our hands. Our mortality presents us with an enclosed horizon, a limited vista of existence, some seventy to ninety years or so – long enough for the largest human plans and achievements, and yet short enough for life to have a shape, a direction, an urgency. Because time is limited it is precious. Because we do not live in this world for ever we have to get on with whatever we are going to do.

So if this is the purpose for which God has established our mortality, how should we respond to that purpose? How should we taste our mortality? We are made mortal so that this earthly life shall have its full weight and value and urgency; so let us therefore live it to the full as the time that God has given us to concentrate upon. Let us accept the circumscribing horizon which death creates and live wholeheartedly within it, seeing each day with its new tasks and opportunities as something precious to be seized before it is gone. Let us accept our mortality not as a limitation but as a means of concentration, and live in the present moment that God has given us, that extended moment whose duration is the duration of a human life. Although as Christians we know that this life will be caught up into eternity, we should live it as though it were complete in itself, with nothing else beyond it. We are not to try to peer past it, seeking to gain rewards or to avoid penalties beyond the frontier of death. This life is meant to stand validly on its own earthly feet.

We should then fully accept our mortality as something that God has ordained in his wise love, and so live that, like the good pagan – or the good humanist – we can say: I don't at present *mind* whether there is an afterlife or not; I don't need one to make this life acceptable, for it is acceptable already in its own right. And if we have been at all fortunate in the circumstances of our lives we can readily say this. I think that if I believed that death is annihilation I should still be profoundly pleased to be alive. And indeed I often do more than half believe that death *is* annihilation, but am nevertheless very glad to be alive. But one must add that there have always been those who bear much more than their share of the world's suffering, to whom this life is only a very qualified blessing, and for whom it is no doubt in order to dwell upon the life to come. But for most of us God's gift of immortality is to remain during this life a hidden blessing, a future bonus, a background thought that does not obscure the immediacy and importance and vividness of the present moment.

For in giving us our present mortal life God has appointed *this* as the place and time of our salvation. It was into this world and this earthly life that Christ the saviour came. Here and now God is present though unseen, seeking our response. The call to respond to God by serving his purpose on earth, which is the purpose that we must each find for ourselves by giving ourselves in service to our neighbour, this call is immediate and urgent – not because the doors of salvation are going to be shut at the moment of death, but because our salvation is our highest good. We need no further reason, and no later day, to accept our highest good as God's gift.

Notes

1 William Shakespeare, *Macbeth*, Act I, scene ii.

2 George Bernard Shaw, *Back to Methuselah*, 1921; Harmondsworth: Penguin, 1939, p. 71.

5

Reincarnation

In *The Gay Science* and *Thus Spake Zarathustra*, and the posthumous *The Will to Power*, Nietzsche puts forward the idea of eternal recurrence, the endless repetition in every detail of the entire history of the universe, including our own lives, and including this present moment. 'This life [he says] as you now live it and have lived it you will have to live once again and innumerable times again; and there will be nothing new in it, but every pain and every joy and every thought and sigh and everything unspeakably small or great in your life must return to you – even this spider and this moonlight between the trees . . .'[1] I am not concerned here with Nietzschean exegesis and the question whether eternal recurrence was intended by him as a serious scientific theory or more likely, as I think, a metaphorical or poetic way of presenting a profound personal challenge.

It is true that he does at one point offer an argument for it as scientific cosmology, based on the principle of the conservation of energy. The universe, he says, consists of a finite number of quanta of energy which, churning about randomly, must sooner or later, in infinite time, fall into the pattern which constitutes our universe, and must sooner or later repeat that pattern again and again an infinite number of times.[2] However, this does not occur in anything that he published himself but only in the collection of notes which his sister later put together and published after Nietzsche's death under the title *The Will to Power*. In his own books the idea comes as the most penetrating possible question about the value of each individual's life and of human life generally. Has your life thus far been such that you would want to live it again and again endlessly, exactly the same in every minute detail? And would you want human history as a whole to be repeated endlessly, just as it has been? To say Yes is, for Nietzsche, the ultimate affirmation of life by his ideal type, the Over- or Higher- or Superman, who however does not yet exist except in his imagined Zarathustra. He sees the challenge to accept life as it is in this full sense as a burden which present-day humans cannot bear. But to affirm life unreservedly in all its mixture of good and evil, happiness and pain, beauty and ugliness, pleasure and horror, triumph and tragedy, would not be to judge it good, or more good than bad, but would be to go beyond good and evil to a sheer act of self- and life-affirmation.

Now there are writers by whom one can be deeply moved and influenced while actually believing very little that they say, and for me Nietzsche is one such. I appreciate his penetrating psychological and social insights. But his training was in philology, not philosophy, and we can best reap the rewards of reading him by overlooking the fact that both the challenging question and the Higher Man's response to it are logically null and void. For if there is eternal recurrence, everything, including our affirmation or non-affirmation of it, is happening exactly as it has happened an infinite number of times before, and we do not have the freedom this time round to vary it. For eternal recurrence entails total determinism, including becoming or not becoming an Overman, and including our present response to the challenge to affirm eternal recurrence.

But having noted this, as in duty bound, let us forgive and forget it. Let us turn to David Hume, who asks the same challenging question but, as the cool and lucid thinker that he was, without the poetic extravagance of eternal recurrence. He has one of the characters in his *Dialogues*, Demea, say, 'Ask yourself, ask any of your acquaintance, whether they would live over again the last ten or twenty years of their life. No! but the next twenty, they say, will be better.'[3] For however satisfying our life as a whole may have been during the last ten or twenty years, we can all think of innumerable points at which it could have been better, so that, if we are comparing the way it has been with the way it might have been with these improvements, we would say No to the actual in comparison with the improved version. But we must eliminate this comparison in our thought experiment. I have to try to look back on my life as a whole during the last ten or twenty years and ask whether I would wish to live it again just as it has been, not changed or improved in any way, and without knowing that it had all happened before. It would be exactly as though one were living it for the first time, with the alternative being not having existed at all.

Setting the question up in this way I think that Hume (though not the Demea in his *Dialogues*), and also Nietzsche, and indeed almost all of us would opt to live it again. Only very few very unhappy people living in deep depression or in utterly unbearable circumstances of some kind would, I think, wish not to have existed. I suspect that even the millions in our world now living in dire poverty, anxiety and danger hope, with

Demea, that the next years will be better and will thus make the past span of life worthwhile, not in itself but because it will have led on to that better future.

But on the other hand, still focusing on those millions who have lived in hope that life would in the future become better for them, or perhaps for their children, when we look back over human history we see that in a very large proportion of cases that hope was not in fact fulfilled. And so we have to ask whether we would want that entire history to be endlessly repeated in an eternal recurrence, or indeed in a single recurrence. If we think of ourselves simply as individuals, I would say Yes, as one of those who have been fortunate in the lottery of life. But should I say Yes on behalf of humanity as a whole, including those many who have been desperately unlucky in that lottery? Would I want those who have lived in miserable slavery, or in constant fear and anxiety, or with debilitating and painful diseases, to have to live that life again and again without knowing, as they did not, that their situation was never in fact going to change for the better? Would I want those who have become sadistic monsters, from serial rapists and murderers to evil dictators, to live again and again? Would I want all the wars, persecutions, tortures, murders, rapes, cruelties and all the famines, droughts, floods, earthquakes and diseases to happen again and again? This is a challenge to the world religions, because each of them is in its own way a form of cosmic optimism, affirming the positive value of the totality of the process of which human history in this world is, according to them, a phase.

At this point I want to bring in Jean-Paul Sartre. He makes the very important point that the meaning or significance of a present event in our lives depends upon what it turns out to have led to in the future. For example, speaking of adolescent love, he says, 'The adolescent is perfectly conscious of the mystic sense of his conduct, and at the same time he must entrust himself to all his future in order to determine whether he is in process of "passing through a crisis of puberty" or of engaging himself in earnest in the way of devotion.'[4] And in general the significance of our present choices depends upon the larger pattern of our lives to which they contribute as this develops over the years. And it is true of us collectively, as societies and nations, that the meaning or significance of what we do now is determined in part by what comes out of it in the future. We can all recall career decisions, personal relationship decisions, commitments of many kinds, deliberate and accidental actions and inactions, whose significance both positive and negative has been determined retrospectively. I want to project this principle onto a much larger scale. I shall argue that, for the great religions, our present life receives its ultimate meaning from the eschatological future which they all in their different ways affirm. There are, to use visual imagery, widening circles of meaning, from the immediate meaning inherent in each present moment of experience, to that same moment as it takes its place in the larger context of a further, say, ten years of living, to the further, sometimes different, meaning that it takes on after another period of years, and so on as our life develops, to its final meaning in the light of the all-encompassing eschatological future.

For Sartre there is no such final all-encompassing circle, no state that, in his terms, has its value in-itself-for-itself. Death is an absolute end and there is no possibility of further life within whose enlarging pattern our present life could become a stage on the way to an all-justifying good. And so we are about to enter the culturally forbidden territory of speculation about death and the possibility, affirmed as more than a possibility by all the great world religions, that our present life is only a very small part of our total existence.

However, thoughts of a life after death are all alike ruled out by the naturalistic assumption that nothing exists but matter. For if we think, in traditional Christian terms, of a further resurrected life, there must presumably be a disembodied phase corresponding to the 'sleep' before the general resurrection, or the purgatory of Catholic doctrine; or if we think in Tibetan Buddhist terms, there is the between-lives period described in the *Bardo Thodol*, and all of these possibilities are incompatible with physicalist naturalism. Physicalist or materialist naturalism assumes either consciousness–brain identity, according to which mental events literally are electro-chemical events in the brain, or epiphenomenalism, according to which consciousness is not itself a physical object or process but a non-physical by-product temporarily generated by the functioning of the brain and having itself no executive power. Whether either of these theories – for they are theories – is sustainable is today the hottest point in the whole science/religion debate. Practising neuroscientists themselves are generally not very interested in such theories, because it makes no practical difference to their work whether, in mapping brain activity in ever greater detail, they are mapping the neural correlates of thought or thought itself. However, those of them who have discussed the question, and these are among the most eminent within the profession, have had to conclude that the nature of consciousness and its relation to neural activity remains a mystery. All I have time to do at the moment is to quote a few of them. Thus V. S. Ramchandran of the Center for Brain and Cognition at the University of California at San Diego says, 'despite two hundred years of research, the most basic questions about the human mind . . . remain unanswered, as does the really big question: What is consciousness?'[5] Roger Penrose, of Oxford, who advocates an emergent property theory, adds that 'conscious actions and conscious perceptions – and, in particular, the conscious phenomenon of *understanding* – will find no proper explanation within the present-day picture of the material universe, but require our going outside this conventional framework to a new physical picture . . . whose mathematical structure is very largely unknown'.[6] Steven Rose, Director of the Brain and Behaviour Research Group at the Open University, concludes that 'the issue of consciousness lies beyond mere neuroscience, or even psychology and philosophy'.[7] Wolf Singer, Director of the Max Plank Institute for Brain Research in Frankfurt, believes that self-awareness and the subjective connotations of qualia 'transcend the reach of conventional neurobiological approaches'.[8] Benjamin Libet of the University of California at Los Angeles says that, 'There is an unexplained gap between the category of physical phenomena and the category of subjective phenomena.'[9] Antonio Damasio, Head of the Department of Neurology at the University of Iowa College of Medicine, says,

> If elucidating the mind is the last frontier of the life sciences, consciousness often seems the last mystery in the elucidation of the mind. Some regard it as insoluble . . . [A]t the moment the neurobiological account is incomplete and there is an explanatory gap.[10]

But there is, surely, more than just a gap that a more complete knowledge of the brain may one day fill, because no knowledge of the workings of the neural networks, however complete, can convert correlation into identity. Damasio himself is clear that he and his colleagues are researching the 'neural underpinnings'[11] of consciousness, 'the neural architecture which supports consciousness',[12] but not consciousness itself.

Once this is accepted, the door is open to a huge range of possibilities that were automatically excluded by the widespread naturalistic assumption. That assumption has long been, for us in the industrialized West, a paradigm so firmly fixed in our minds that we do not so much see it as see everything through it. However, if we have to accept that the universe includes the non-physical reality of consciousness, and no doubt also a huge range of unconscious mental life, as well as the physical reality of matter, then the materialist or physicalist assumption becomes a ghost to be exorcized. This does not of course entail a religious interpretation of the universe, but it does show that such an interpretation is an open possibility, not to be excluded on the mistaken ground that it has been ruled out by the sciences. And any re-formed naturalism will have to be much more complex and sophisticated than the old version.

Moving now within the realm of religious possibilities, and still on the culturally forbidden subject of death, we are confronted by two very different options. Most Westerners, whether they accept, or more often reject, the idea of a life after death, think in terms of an eternal heaven and hell. For most Easteners, on the other hand, what they either accept or reject is the idea of a journey through many lives. Which of these options is for us the standard idea to be either accepted or rejected depends in the great majority of cases on where we were born. However, philosophy, in contrast to theology, tries to transcend this global postcode lottery. And it seems to me that, given the possibility of more life than the present one, then from a religious point of view the Eastern model is to be preferred. For at the end of this short life very few, if indeed any, are ready for either eternal bliss or eternal punishment. But on the other hand all are ready for further growth and development. And if such a process is indeed taking place, we are all clearly at an early stage in it. If it is to proceed it requires further interactions with others within a common environment. It seems that this must take the form of further mortal lives, lived within the boundaries of birth and death, because it is the inexorable pressure of these boundaries that gives life the urgency that an unlimited horizonless future would lack. The cosmic scenario that best meets these requirements is some form of the concept of rebirth or reincarnation. So this is the option that I now want to explore a little.

Let me bring in at this point Milan Kundera's strange but striking novel *The Unbearable Lightness of Being*. At one point he has his central character Tomas reflect as follows:

Somewhere out in space there was another planet where all people would be born again. They would be fully aware of the life they had spent on earth and of all the experiences they had amassed here. And perhaps there was still another planet, where we would all be born a third time with the experience of our first two lives. And perhaps there were yet more planets, where mankind would be born one degree (one life) more mature . . . Of course we here on earth (planet number one, the planet of inexperience) can only fabricate vague fantasies of what will happen to man on those other planets. Will he be wiser? Is maturity within man's power? Can he attain it through repetition? Only [Kundera says] from the perspective of such a utopia is it possible to use the concepts of pessimism and optimism with full justification: an optimist is one who thinks that on planet number five the history of mankind will be less bloody. A pessimist is one who thinks otherwise.[13]

This points very well to the sense in which, within the multiple lives option, religion involves the cosmic optimism which believes that through a series of lives in which any moral/spiritual maturing achieved in one is carried forward to the next, human existence will eventually be perfected. Each life story, and the human story as a whole, will lead eventually to a limitlessly good state. This cosmic optimism anticipates an end state that has a value in itself so great as to make worthwhile the long path that has led to it, so that in retrospect we will all be profoundly glad to have travelled it.

In Kundera's imagined scenario he looks forwards from human life as it now is to a supposed better future. But let us try the thought experiment of thinking back from that imagined future better state. Suppose that on the fifth planet human beings have become distinctly more caring towards one another, distinctly more inclined to be concerned for their neighbour as much as for themselves, no longer able to be stirred to communal hatreds and wars, sharing the earth's resources equitably – by no means perfect beings in a perfect society but manifestly having moved in that direction. If we were part of that future world, and could see the emerging trajectory, would we think that the earlier stages are now justified retrospectively by the increasingly better states to which they have led? We know what pain and suffering and despair and unhappiness there is in the world today. Would even this be justified within Kundera's imagined scenario?

I think that most of us, perhaps all of us, including those who now suffer most, would say Yes. We would all think that if that is indeed what is going on then we are glad to exist rather than not exist as part of this process. It is not a matter of a balancing compensation in the hereafter for pain suffered in this life but of the ultimate fulfilment of the human potential. In the course of this some may well have suffered much more than others – at any rate this is certainly the case within any one particular lifetime – and yet all will have come by their own individual paths to the same end. Some may well have had a harder journey than others, and in this respect life may very well not be fair. It may be more like the situation in Jesus' parable of the workers in the vineyard who all receive the same reward even though some have laboured for much longer than others. Further, in the scenario we are considering, it is not the case that the particular experiences which happen to each individual were specifically necessary to lead them to the future great good, or that the events of each person's life had to be just as they are, nor that the course of our lives is planned or directed by an omnipotent and loving God. Rather what happens occurs through the unpredictable interactions of very imperfect free beings. Remember that much the greater part of human suffering is caused by human actions or inactions. But whatever may be the largely accidental course of our life, or our many lives, it can – according to the religions – become the path by which we shall eventually have arrived at what John Bunyan symbolized in Christian terms as the Celestial City.

In both East and West the rebirth or reincarnation idea is popularly understood in an unsophisticated way as the present conscious self being born again in this world, including even sometimes being born in lower forms of animal life. But this popular picture is far from the conceptions found in some of the Buddhist and Hindu philosophies. These are themselves diverse, and there is no one official doctrine. But three major differences from the popular idea are fairly standard. The main one is that it is not the present conscious self that is re-embodied, not the *persona* gradually formed by the set of circumstances into which we are born – by our genetic inheritance, our various innate gifts and limitations, the family of which we are part, our short or long span of life, the region of the world and the society and culture and historical epoch in which we find ourselves, and the way things go in the world around us. That which is re-embodied in a future new conscious self is a deeper unconscious dispositional structure which Hindu philosophers speak of as the *linga sharira*, or subtle body – though this has to be understood within a whole philosophical framework in which it is not a body at all in our ordinary sense – and which Buddhist philosophers speak of as a karmic bundle or complex. For them the conscious self is entirely evanescent, not an enduring substance. I suppose the most obvious Christian term for the deeper ongoing self would be the soul. It is an aspect of our nature that exists far below the level of consciousness. All of the various factors in terms of which we live our conscious lives constitute, so to speak, the hand of cards which this deeper self has been dealt in this particular life, the stream of challenges and opportunities, capacities and limitations, with which life presents us. A major question, which I do not take up here, is whether or not some automatic process provides the reincarnating 'soul' with a 'hand of cards' appropriate to its need for further development. But what both affects and is affected by this basic dispositional structure is what the conscious personality does with these cards. We are all the time both expressing and forming our deeper self by our responses to the circumstances, both agreeable and disagreeable, in which we find ourselves. And it is this cumulative quality of response that is built into the basic moral/spiritual character that will be re-embodied in another conscious personality.

Another difference from the popular conception is that our future lives may well not be lived on this earth but, as in Kundera's picture, on other planets of our solar system, or even in other galaxies of our universe, or perhaps in the quite other spheres of existence of which Hindu and Buddhist philosophies speak. Or some of our lives may be lived in this world and some elsewhere. Each successive Dalai Lama, for example, is supposed to be a reincarnation of his predecessor, born not only in this world but specifically in Tibet. But Buddhism also speaks of other spheres of existence within which life is carried on. If we ask where these realms are, meaning where in the only universe that we know, the answer is nowhere. The idea of other spaces has generally seemed in the West to be pure gratuitous imagining, but we may have to get used to the idea that there are things that are real although they don't exist in our customary sense. For the more we read those scientists who are trying to communicate with the rest of us, the more we are led to suspend many of our inherited assumptions. Sir Martin Rees, formerly the Astronomer Royal, who is not himself a religious believer, in his book *Our Cosmic Habitat*,[14] argues for the currently canvassed cosmological theory that this universe, beginning with its own big bang some 13 billion years ago, is one of innumerable universes, among which there may well be many that sustain life, some more and some less advanced than the life on our own planet. He claims that 'the multiverse concept is already part of empirical science'.[15] Indeed the range of responsible scientific speculation is now greater and more exciting than it has ever been, and the possibilities that it opens up are much more mysterious and surprising than even a decade ago. Stephen Hawking's account for lay readers of current scientific cosmology in *The Universe in a Nutshell*[16] is far less dogmatic, far more conscious of surrounding mystery, than both the mainstream Christian theologies and the dogmatic naturalism of our time.

Returning to the multiple lives idea, yet another difference from the popular conception is that in the more philosophical Eastern doctrines of reincarnation, or rebirth, there is generally no conscious memory of previous lives, even though such supposed memories abound in popular folklore. As Gandhi wrote, 'It is nature's kindness that we do not remember past births. Where is the good of knowing in detail the numberless births we have gone through? Life would be a burden if we carried such a tremendous load of memories.'[17] A latent memory of the totality of our experience is however integral to the dispositional or karmic continuant which is expressed in each successive new conscious personality. There may or may not, as some claim, be occasional leakages of fragments of this complete memory into someone's consciousness, though normally not. However, the full accumulation of memory nevertheless exists beneath normal consciousness. According to the traditional story, when the Buddha attained to full enlightenment during his night of deep meditation under the Bo tree at Bodh Gaya, he remembered the complete succession of his previous lives. It is in virtue of this normally inaccessible thread of memory that the many lives are different moments in the same life project.

Returning now to Kundera, in his imagined scenario we do not now, in the first world, know what the future holds. Suppose however we had come to the belief that we are in fact taking part in a journey from world number one to world number five and then to yet further worlds beyond. Would not this change the way in which we experience and engage in our present life in world number one, the world as he says of immaturity? Would it not give a new and different meaning to what is now happening? Borrowing John Bunyan's image of life as a pilgrimage towards the Celestial City, the events on the journey, both its pleasant and joyful moments and its unpleasant and its terrible moments, have different meanings for the pilgrim who lives in faith in the reality of the Celestial City from that which it has for those who have no such faith. The cosmic optimism of the world religions consists in their picture of a larger process of which we are a part, such that we can live now in trust that, in Julian of Norwich's famous words of Jesus in her vision, 'All shall be well, and all shall be well, and all manner of thing shall be well.'[18] And in her vision Jesus adds, 'Accept it now in faith and trust, and in the very end you will see truly, in fullness of joy.'[19] An important aspect of religious faith within the great traditions consists in living now in trust of what Julian calls the 'fullness of joy' to which we are moving. More generally, to quote a contemporary scholar, Mark Webb, 'nearly all religious experiences result in the belief that the universe is an essentially friendly place; that is, that we shouldn't worry about the future'.[20] Needless to say it is also true that, despite occasional vivid awarenesses of the essential friendliness of the universe in its totality, the ordinary religious person often gets caught in Bunyan's Doubting Castle, and falls into the Slough of Despond, and is bothered by both Mr Formalist and Mr Discontent, and gets waylaid in Vanity Fair, and indeed falls at some time into all the other dangers that meet us on life's pilgrimage.

And so the hypothesis before us is that we are presently engaged in one phase, probably not the first, of a multi-life process of moral and spiritual growth within a universe which is, as the world religions affirm, ultimately benign or, speaking metaphorically, friendly. But how can it be said to be benign when it involves all the suffering, all the agony and despair, all the cruelty and wickedness that exist around us? Only, I think, if we grant the very high value of moral freedom and the consequent principle that goodness gradually created through our own free responses to ethically and physically challenging situations is enormously, we could even say infinitely, more valuable than a goodness implanted in us without any effort on our part. Putting this in the terms in which it appears in the intra-Christian theodicy debates, this is the Irenaean suggestion (as distinguished from the Augustinian theology) that God created humanity, not as already perfect beings who then disastrously fell, but as spiritually and morally immature creatures who are able to grow, through their own free decisions within a world that functions according to natural law and is not designed for our comfort, so that there are pains as well as pleasures, hardships to be endured, problems to be solved, difficult choices to be made, the possibility of real setbacks and accidents and of real failure and tragedy. The creative value of what is from our human point of view a very imperfect world is that only in such an environment can the highest human virtue come about of a love that is able to make sacrifices for others, the valuing of others equally with oneself. In a paradise in which there was no pain, in which nothing could go wrong, no one would be able either to help or to hurt another and there would consequently be no such thing as wrong action, and therefore no such thing as right action. But a world in which we can hate as well as love, wage wars as well as creating peace, persecute and enslave as well as working for social justice, ignore one another as well as caring for one another, is a world in which moral choices are real and in which moral growth is possible and does in fact often occur. But – to voice the obvious objection – surely a loving God would not allow the extremities of human, and also animal, suffering that actually occur. The intra-Christian debate involves at this point the question whether God could intervene to prevent 'man's inhumanity to man' or nature's perils without infringing either human freedom or the autonomy of the physical world. But since I am not postulating an omnipotent loving personal God, I leave that debate aside. I am postulating instead a cosmic process of which we are part, which we do not understand, which we often find to be harsh, sometimes extremely harsh, which we find to involve both great happinesses and great miseries, but which is nevertheless found in mystical experience within each of the great religions to be, from our human point of view, ultimately benign. And our reason tells us that this benign character must involve further living beyond our present life.

Notes

1 Friedrich Nietzsche, *The Gay Science*, trans. Josefine Nauckhoff, Cambridge: Cambridge University Press, 2001, p. 194.

2 Friedrich Nietzsche, *The Will to Power*, vol. 2, trans. Anthony Ludovici, London: Allen & Unwin, 1910, p. 430.

3 David Hume, *Dialogues concerning Natural Religion*, Part X, ed. Norman Kemp Smith, Oxford: Clarendon Press, 1935, p. 243.

4 Jean-Paul Sartre, *Being and Nothingness*, ET, New York: Philosophical Library, 1956; London: Methuen, 1957, p. 527.

5 V. S. Ramchandran, *Phantoms in the Brain*, New York: William Morrow, 1998, p. xvi.

6 Roger Penrose, in Steven Rose (ed.), *From Brains to Consciousness?*, London and New York: Penguin, 1999, pp. 176–7.

7 Steven Rose, in Rose, *Brains to Consciousness?*, p. 14.

8 Wolf Singer, in Rose, *Brains to Consciousness?*, p. 245.

9 Benjamin Libet, in Benjamin Libet, Anthony Freeman and Keith Sutherland (eds), *The Volitional Brain*, Thorverton: Imprint Academic, 1999, p. 55.

10 Antonio Damasio, *The Feeling of What Happens*, New York and London: Harcourt, 1999, pp. 4, 9.

11 Damasio, *Feeling*, p. 8.

12 Damasio, *Feeling*, p. 15.

13 Milan Kundera, *The Unbearable Lightness of Being*, trans. Michael Heim, London: Faber & Faber, 1995, p. 218.

14 Martin Rees, *Our Cosmic Habitat*, London: Weidenfeld & Nicolson, 2001.

15 Rees, *Cosmic Habitat*, p. xvii.

16 Stephen Hawking, *The Universe in a Nutshell*, London and New York: Bantam Press, 2001.

17 Mahatma Gandhi, *The Selected Works of Mahatma Gandhi*, vol. 5, Ahmedabad: Navajivan, 1968, p. 363.

18 Julian of Norwich, *Showings*, Long Text, ch. 27.

19 Julian, *Showings*, Long Text, ch. 32.

20 Mark O. Webb, 'Religious Experience as Doubt Resolution', *International Journal for Philosophy of Religion*, vol. 16, nos 1–2 (1985), p. 85.

6

Believable Christianity

The headline thought that I would like us all to keep in mind is 'The 10 per cent and the 90 per cent', meaning those who go to church – any of the churches – and those who don't. These figures are only approxima-tions. The actual figure for church attenders, according to a national poll in 2001, was less than 10 per cent. It was 7.9 per cent. And the 90 per cent of non-church attenders includes people of other faiths, many of whom worship in other than churches, amounting to, say, 3 per cent, about whom I shall have more to say later. But to focus attention let us use the headline: The 10 per cent and the 90 per cent.

Now I believe that a great many – no one knows how many – of the non-church attenders who are also not of other faiths are nevertheless religiously or spiritually concerned. There are several kinds of evidence for this. One is the numbers of young people in schools and universities who opt for religious studies even though they are typically sceptical about the churches and what they teach; another is the enormously flourishing and very various New Age movements – if you look in the bookshops you will find many more about them than about orthodox Christianity; yet another is the popularity of the more spectacular TV programmes and books about religion, including such widely read books as Dawkins's *The God Delusion*, and the ridiculous *Da Vinci Code*. So the 90 per cent include a lot of people who are genuinely inter-ested in religion, concerned about the meaning of life, why we are here, how to find the way to a good life, a life that is good for others as well as for ourselves, and what happens after death.

But the remaining small minority of church attenders are generally happy with the message they receive from the liturgies, sermons, hymns and prayers, and enjoy meeting their friends there Sunday by Sunday. Many church people are basically content with this. They see the Church as destined always to be a small minority, but one that exerts a major influence on society as a whole. They see it as the salt of the earth, which must not lose its savour because it is for the good of the world, and they believe that this is an OK situation. It means that we are where we should be within our comfort zone. But is this the right way to think?

Personally I don't think so. As the salt that the world needs, the existing Church is 'not fit for purpose'. It is more like – to continue with biblical metaphors – a lamp hidden under a bushel, the bushel being the wall of unbelievable beliefs accumulated over the centuries. At least, this is what I'm going to argue.

But a curious feature of the situation is that among church attenders today there is an amazingly wide range of beliefs. I suspect that if you could look into the minds of a typical congregation on any Sunday you would find almost as many varying conceptions of God, different understandings of what we mean by God, as there are worshippers. And to add to the confusion – and here is something rather startling – two sociologists, reporting their research in the journal *Sociology of Religion*, found that about 25 per cent of British people profess to believe in reincarnation, though they say this is generally more a gut feeling than a fully articulated doctrine. Another researcher has concluded that as many Anglicans believe in reincarnation as believe in heaven and hell.

So by no means everyone in church has anything like an orthodox set of beliefs. This was brought home to me thirty years ago now when the book *The Myth of God Incarnate* was published in 1977 and caused an uproar. Some of you may remember it. The national newspapers were discussing it and it had to be rapidly reprinted several times, going quickly to 30,000 copies. The book was by seven authors, including some of the leading theologians and biblical scholars of the day. The most significant were the leading Anglicans Maurice Wiles, the Regius professor of divinity at Oxford; Dennis Nineham, Warden of Keble College, Oxford, and former Regius at Cambridge; and Leslie Houlden, Principal of Cuddesdon Theological College, Oxford. So the prominence of some of the Anglican authors, and the then profoundly shocking title, caused, as I say, a great stir. And yet the central message of the book was that the historical Jesus of Nazareth did not teach or apparently believe that he was God, or God the Son, second person of a Holy Trinity, incarnate, or the Son of God in a unique sense. There was nothing new in this. It had been known for decades by New Testament scholars. What was new was that it was now being said publicly by people who could not be ignored. The uproar showed how little church teaching had prepared church people for the results of modern New Testament scholarship.

As editor as well as one of the contributors to the book I received numerous letters. Some of course were distinctly hostile. I was informed, for example, that I was only a heartbeat from hell. Since I am still alive, I don't yet know – though I am inclined to doubt it. But I also received a number of letters from clergy saying, Thank you for this. It's what I have long believed, but of course I can't tell my people; and others from lay people saying, Thank you for this. It's what I have long thought must be the case, but of course I can't tell my priest or minister. In other words, there was a good deal of double bluff going on; and I suspect that it is still going on today to much too great an extent.

So this brings me to what is probably the most important reason why so few people go to church today. I think it is because they find incredible what they know, or think they know, about what is taught in the churches. This is not necessarily because the basic ideas themselves are incredible, depending on how they are understood, but because of the way they are formulated and presented.

What is presented is that Jesus of Nazareth is the only saviour of the whole world, and Christianity the one and only true religion, based on the deity of Jesus as God (or God the Son) incarnate, the Holy Trinity, atonement for the sins of the world through Jesus' sacrificial death on the cross, and his bodily resurrection and ascension.

All of these beliefs seem incredible to most non-churchgoers. If there is a believable Christianity, what the churches officially teach is not it.

Now obviously the vital question is not whether an idea is believable to the modern mind but whether it is true. If it is true, then we must stick with it, whether others find it believable or not. But are these traditional doctrines rightly believable by us? Or do they need to be reinterpreted, understood in a new way? Let us look at them.

First, because all Christian thinking goes back to the Bible, we must start with some of the basic findings of the modern historical study of the New Testament. The scholars differ about a great many things, but on certain basics there is a broad consensus among them. I know that many of you here are familiar with all this, though probably some not; so I'll go through it rather quickly. First, although the four Gospels read at first sight as though they are eyewitness accounts of Jesus' life and teaching, none of them was written by any of the twelve apostles, and none of them was written earlier than forty years after Jesus' death. The earliest was Mark's, written around the year 70. Matthew and Luke followed in the 80s, using Mark as their main source but supplemented by sources of their own and possibly by another common source called Q, although some major scholars dispute this. Then the Gospel of John came in the 90s up to the end of the century.

Matthew, Mark and Luke are called the synoptic Gospels because they broadly agree with each other, in distinction from the Fourth Gospel, John's, which has a very different character. In the synoptics Jesus is a profoundly challenging charismatic teacher and a notable healer. He refers to himself as son of man. He teaches in short pithy sayings and commands and in his unforgettable parables of the love of God. He was the final prophet, proclaiming the imminent inbreaking of the kingdom of God: 'there are some standing here who will not taste death before they see the kingdom of God' (Luke 9.27), 'this generation will not pass away until all these things have taken place' (Matt. 24.34; also Mark 16.28). But he made no claim to be divine. In Luke's other book, the Acts of the Apostles, Peter speaks of Jesus as, 'Jesus of Nazareth, a man attested to you by God with deeds of power, wonders, and signs' (2.22). This is in essence the understanding of him in the synoptic Gospels.

In the Fourth Gospel, however, Jesus utters lengthy theological discourses, and these discourses express a later stage of thinking within the Church. Jesus is now divine, pre-existent, and the phrase Son of God has taken on a new meaning. Within Judaism 'son of God' was a very familiar metaphor. The messiah was a son of God in the Jewish sense of someone specially chosen by God for a particular role. Adam was the son of God (Luke 3.38), the angels were sons of God, the ancient kings of Judah were enthroned as sons of God, 'You are my son; today I have begotten you' (Ps. 2.7; 2 Sam. 7.14), Israel as a whole was God's son, indeed any outstandingly pious Jew could be called a son of God. So Jesus was a son of God in the metaphorical sense that was familiar to the Jews of his time, a sense that carried no implication of divinity. But St Paul, within his expansion of the Church beyond the Jewish world, led the elevation of Jesus to a divine status, which is expressed near the end of the century in John's Gospel. Here Jesus is consciously divine, indeed he is God incarnate (1.1, 18; 20.28). It is here that we find the great I am sayings – 'I am the way, and the truth, and the life. No one comes to the Father except through me' (John 14.6), 'The Father and I are one' (John 10.30), 'Whoever has seen me has seen the Father' (John 14.9).

And this, as we all know, is the theology dominating what has come to be called Christianity. It is not the teaching of Jesus, but was gradually created by later members of the Jesus movement and was finally enshrined in the creeds. The Apostles' Creed had nothing to do with the twelve apostles. It is based on what is called the Old Roman Creed, in use around the end of the second century, and was brought into its present form in the early eighth century. The Nicene Creed, which is also used in liturgical worship today, was created in 325 by the Council of Nicaea, in what is today Turkey. I was once at a conference in Turkey and we all made an expedition to visit the ruins of the church at Nicaea where the council had met. One of our number suggested that we all stand and recite the Nicene Creed. Which we did – some said it in Greek, some in Latin, some in English, and a few, including myself, said it in inverted commas!

Why the inverted commas, the quotation marks? Why not affirm it literally? The Nicene Creed speaks of Jesus as 'the only Son of God, eternally begotten of the Father, God from God, Light from Light, true God from true God, begotten, not made, of one Being with the Father'. This is not the human Jesus of history but the divine Christ of faith. And it was reinforced by the official two-natures doctrine of the Council of Chalcedon in 451, creating the insoluble puzzle of how an historical individual could have both the infinite, eternal, perfect, omnipotent, omniscient, omnipresent attributes of God and the finite, mortal, sinful attributes of our humanity, limited in power and in knowledge.

Am I suggesting, then, that we should drop the language of incarnation? No, I'm suggesting that we should understand it in a different way. The idea of incarnation is a powerful metaphorical idea. It means to embody some ideal or conviction in one's life. We all know what is meant when someone says, for example, that Nelson Mandela, after the triumph of the anti-apartheid movement in South Africa, incarnated the spirit of forgiveness and reconciliation. He embodied this in his life and actions. And the metaphor of divine incarnation, according to which Jesus embodied an overwhelming awareness of the goodness and love of God, is intelligible, believable and morally challenging. The official dogma, on the other hand, is neither intelligible, nor believable, nor morally challenging. For if Jesus, as number two in the Trinity living a human life, was sinless and perfect, what sort of a role model is that for us ordinary human beings? We are not God incarnate, we are sinful, frail and imperfect, and we need a human model whom we can follow and by whom we can be challenged. And the human Jesus of Nazareth was just that. We can take him as our lord in the sense of – to use an Eastern word now much in use in the West – our guru, someone whom we try to follow as our role model.

But I would like to add that in my opinion it is a mistake to follow any guru or lord totally, abandoning our God-given reason. Even Jesus was fallible – he was mistaken in expecting the imminent end of the Age. We read in Mark's Gospel that 'Jesus came into Galilee . . . saying, "The time is fulfilled, and the kingdom of God has come near; repent, and believe in the good news"' (Mark 1.14–15). And many prophetic preachers since have proclaimed, Repent, the End is nigh – and they have all been wrong as regards the end being nigh. In Jesus' case other important errors followed from this belief. For if the End was coming soon there was no point in thinking about reordering society to remove injustice, or to make poverty history. Jesus said, 'you always have the poor with you' (Mark 14.7; Matt. 26.11). It is we who have created the social gospel, which is now so rightly central for many of the churches, out of the fact that he identified himself with the poor and the marginalized. But it is historically false to attribute the social gospel to Jesus himself. Again because of what is called his eschatological message, his belief that the end of the Age was soon coming, he was unconcerned for what we today call family values. He called upon his disciples to leave their families and follow him – 'everyone who has left houses or brothers or sisters or father or mother or children or fields, for my name's sake, will receive a hundredfold, and will inherit eternal life' (Matt. 19.29). So there are aspects of his teaching that we rightly leave aside today. And there are other aspects of the New Testament, such as the anti-Semitism of the Fourth Gospel, or St Paul's subordination of women, that we also rightly leave aside today.

So what is left of the Jesus of the New Testament? That's the wrong question. It's not a matter of what is left, but of what is revealed when we remove the barriers of later church doctrines. What is revealed is the heart of Jesus' life and teaching: the challenging moral teaching summarized in the sermon on the mount, preaching an indiscriminate love for all, his vivid parables of the love of God, his powerful criticisms of the ecclesiastical hierarchy, and his identifying with the poor and marginalized, those despised by the establishment, and his treatment of women, welcoming them as disciples, and his healing ministry. And although, as I pointed out a moment ago, he did not himself have a social gospel, because he believed that God was soon to intervene to establish the divine kingdom on earth, there is a social gospel *implicit* in his life. The Jesus of history then, I suggest, minus the impressive but today unbelievable theological structure that the Church has built round him, is rightly our lord, guru, role model. But it's the church-built theological structure that hides him effectively from the 90 per cent.

So I'm suggesting that we see the idea of divine incarnation in Jesus of Nazareth as a metaphorical idea. Jesus embodied, incarnated, to a considerable degree the love that he experienced in the heavenly Father, the heavenly Father of us all. But he was not God's son in the literal sense of having no human father but being miraculously fathered by God the Holy Spirit. The idea of a miraculous birth was widely attributed in the ancient world to great religious figures, including some of the ancient pharaohs and the Buddha and Zoroaster. But the biblical virgin birth story is late, apparently not known to St Paul, who was writing before the Gospels, or to Mark, the author of the first Gospel. It grew up more than two generations after the supposed event, and is pretty clearly mythological. Along, I am afraid, with the whole beautiful Bethlehem Christmas story, created to fulfil supposed Old Testament prophecies (John 7.42). This doesn't mean that we should not continue to celebrate Christmas, but that we should be aware that the story behind it is symbolically rather than literally true.

The doctrine of the incarnation affects in turn the doctrine of the Trinity. This is, in origin, a defensive doctrine to protect the incarnation. For if Jesus was God on earth, and at the same time there was God in heaven, that already gives us a binity, a divine twoness. And when we add the inner sense of God's presence, we have the Trinity: Father, Son and Holy Spirit. But without the starting point of Jesus as God on earth the idea of a divine Trinity does not arise. I think the reason why many faithful Christians cling to it so strongly is that it provides the dimension of mystery that we treasure. But to my mind there is plenty of mystery already. It is a mystery why the perfect God chose to make an imperfect creation. It is a mystery why the omnipotent God allows so much pain and suffering. It is a mystery what happens after death. And we don't need artificially to create new theological mysteries for ourselves.

Another traditionally central doctrine, atonement, also presupposes the literally understood incarnation doctrine. Behind this there is a wealth of imagery – principally Jesus as the Lamb of God who takes away the sins of the world. The main theological theory that sought to understand this presented Jesus as providing in his death a sacrifice to atone for the sins of humanity. In the words of the Anglican prayer book, we pray to God 'who, of thy tender mercy, didst give thy only Son Jesus Christ to suffer death upon the cross for our redemption; who made there, by his one oblation of himself once offered, a full, perfect and sufficient sacrifice, oblation and satisfaction for the sins of the whole world'. Or in the words of a favourite hymn, 'There is a green hill far away, outside a city wall, where the dear Lord was crucified, who died to save us all.' The idea is that God is a loving God but also a just God, and the penalty that his justice demands is paid on our behalf by the agonizing death of Jesus on the cross. But it is only because Jesus was God the Son, the second person of the Holy Trinity, that his death was sufficient to atone for the sins of the world. And so the atonement doctrine does not arise when we have re-understood divine incarnation as a metaphorical idea. The historical probability is that Jesus was executed by the Romans because they, and their Jewish priestly clients, feared that his being hailed as the expected messiah would cause an uprising in a Jerusalem crowded with people there for the Passover.

The other main imagery about the crucifixion is that of Jesus as the victor who defeated sin and death: 'O Christ, thy triumphs now begin o'er captive death and conquered sin.' Death and sin were abolished at Calvary. But of course the question that any ordinary person asks is, *Have* they been abolished? Have not people continued to die, everyone in each generation, since then? And have not people continued to sin as much since as before?

Everything that I have been saying about incarnation, Trinity, and atonement is confirmed by the Lord's Prayer, the Our Father which art in heaven, which is one of the most secure texts in the Gospels. The Lord's Prayer has been well described (for example, by one of the Church Fathers, Tertullian,) as a summary of the gospel. Now in this prayer we are taught to speak directly to God as our Father in heaven. There is no question of a mediator, or of our having to ask through or in the name of Jesus. And we are taught here that God forgives us our wrongdoings when we forgive those who wrong us. There is no question of an atoning sacrifice being necessary. And there is no reference to a divine Trinity. But this summary of Jesus' teaching, when we take it seriously, is extremely challenging and demanding, for we are directly challenged to do God's will now to bring about the divine kingdom of peace and justice and human fellowship here on earth. It is this that is the true work of the Church.

Which brings me to my final question. Is it the task of the Church to convert the whole world to Christianity? There is the missionary commission, 'Go and make disciples of all nations, baptizing them in the name of the Father and of the Son and of the Holy Spirit' (Matt. 28.19). But most New Testament scholars do not think that these are words of the historical Jesus. Nevertheless the assumption that it is God's will that all of humanity will one day become disciples of Christ, although long since tacitly abandoned by most theologians and church leaders, remains embedded in familiar hymns: 'At the Name of Jesus every knee shall bow, every tongue confess him King of glory now.' 'Jesus shall reign where'er the sun does his successive journeys run; his kingdom stretch from shore to shore, till moons shall wax and wane no more.'

I suggest that this Christian supremacism is not only unrealistic but also religiously and theologically mistaken, and should be dropped from our hymn books when they are next revised. More importantly it should be dropped now from our thoughts.

Why is that Christian triumphalism or imperialism theologically mistaken? Consider a very obvious fact – so obvious that it is often not noticed, and hardly ever taken into account by theologians. This is that in the vast majority of cases, probably 98 or 99 per cent, the religion to which anyone adheres (or against which they rebel) depends upon where they are born. When someone is born into a Christian family they are very likely to become a Christian, whether practising or nominal; when into a Muslim family, very likely to become a Muslim; if into a Buddhist family, to become a Buddhist – and so on round the world.

Now given that the large majority of human beings are born and live, and always have lived, outside Christianity, does it make sense to think that it is God's will that 'Jesus shall reign where'er the sun does his successive journeys run'?

So let's ask, Do we mean by salvation going to heaven when we die, or do we also mean a beginning of the transformation of men and women in this life from our natural self-centredness towards a less self-centred outlook and a greater concern for others? If you think, as I do, that salvation is a gradual change, in conscious or unconscious response to the ultimate divine reality, a change which shows itself in our behaviour in relation to our fellow human beings, we can ask, Where do we find this happening? Is it only among Christians, or is it equally among people of all faiths, and indeed of no religious beliefs? I think that so far as we can tell, kindness and unkindness, love and hate, selfishness and unselfishness are spread fairly evenly around the world. There seem to be saints and sinners in more or less equal proportion within each of the great world faiths.

Now is this what you would expect if it is true that in Christ we have a unique knowledge of God through his incarnation on earth in Jesus, a special relationship to God as members of the Body of Christ, taking the divine life into our own lives in the Eucharist, indwelt by the Holy Spirit? If we have these inestimable benefits, which non-Christians lack, should not Christians as a whole be better human beings, morally and spiritually, than non-Christians generally? And yet is this really the case?

From my own limited observations around the world, I don't think so. Of course this can be argued. I would only say that the onus of proof, or of argument, lies on anyone, of any faith, who claims that the adherents of their faith are better persons, morally and spiritually, than the rest of the human race.

So I believe we have radically to rethink our understanding of the place of Christianity in the global religious picture. We have to face the fact that it is one path among others, and then reform our belief system to be compatible with this. This is the big new challenge that theologians and church leaders have yet to face. We have to become consciously what are called religious pluralists.

Finally, this is not going to happen from the top down. Change comes from the grassroots. Already on the ground, in a multi-faith city like Birmingham, a great many Christians are already implicit pluralists. That is to say they don't think that their Muslim or Sikh or Jewish or Hindu or Buddhist or Baha'i neighbour has a lower status than themselves in relation to the ultimate divine reality. They don't think that the souls of these people are in jeopardy. Many of us have friends of other faiths whom we greatly admire. We simply don't believe that they are religiously disadvantaged, even though our official theologies imply that they must be. And in the end reality will inevitably prevail over traditional dogma – at least for all who are not encased in the impenetrable armour of a rigid fundamentalism. It will take a long time, but it will inevitably happen, though quite possibly with a division into two Christianities, one fundamentalist and the other progressive.

Why does all this matter? We only have to look at the state of the world to see why. The Catholic theologian Hans Küng has said that there will never be peace between the nations until there is peace between the religions. And I would add that there will never be genuine peace between the religions until each comes to recognize the equal validity of the others. It will not happen in my lifetime. Whether it will happen within the lifetime of some here, I don't know. But let us all do in our time what we can to bring this about.

7

Literal and Metaphorical Incarnation

Metaphor and Myth

The distinction between the literal and metaphorical uses of language is clear and I want to apply it to Christologies. In particular, I shall look at Chalcedonian-type Christologies, meaning those that assert Jesus' two natures or, in a new contemporary version, two minds, one human and the other divine. I shall try to show that these run into an insuperable difficulty over the freedom of the human nature or mind of Jesus. I shall then argue that a Christology based on the metaphorical character of the concept of divine incarnation can be both logically viable and religiously attractive.

The literal/metaphorical distinction, as I am using it, is very simple. A literal statement uses words in their ordinary standard dictionary sense. Metaphors apply a term's meaning in its ordinary standard context to a different context in which the literal meaning does not apply, the point being to illuminate in some way that second context. For example, 'Knowledge is the mirror of nature.' Knowledge does not literally mirror anything – no physical mirrors are involved – but nevertheless the metaphor expresses vividly a correspondence theory of truth.

There are various categories of literal and metaphorical statements in religious and theological language. There are statements that most of us will agree are metaphorical, such as 'God is our rock', 'The Church is the body of Christ', 'God is the Father of all humanity', and such phrases as 'Holy Mother Church'. There are others that we will all agree are literal, such as 'Jesus lived in the first third of the first century CE', 'Jesus was crucified', 'St Paul died in Rome'. And there are yet others that some of us use literally and others metaphorically – for example, 'This bread is Christ's body', 'This wine is Christ's blood', 'Jesus was the Son of God'. It is the latter kind of christological statement that concerns us here.

Let me dispose at this point of a mistake that some people make when they say that the distinction between literal and metaphorical language should be rejected because *all* our language is metaphorical. This is clearly a mistake because 'metaphorical' only has meaning in distinction from 'non-metaphorical', and if there were no non-metaphorical language it would be meaningless to say of any use of language that it is metaphorical.

Let me now make the connection between metaphor and myth. In the sense in which I shall use 'myth' there can be true as well as false myths. By a true myth I mean a story, description, or statement that is not literally true but that nevertheless expresses and/or tends to evoke an appropriate dispositional attitude to the subject matter of the myth. That is to say, in asserting that a story is mythologically true one is asserting that the attitude that it expresses and/or evokes is appropriate. As a small example, suppose a ten-year-old boy is caught viciously kicking the cat. His angry mother might say, 'The devil's got into him.' Assuming that she does not believe that there are in fact such beings as devils, the statement is metaphorical, transferring meaning from devil discourse to her description of the boy's behaviour. And the connection with metaphor is that a myth is an expanded metaphor. Thus one could describe the behaviour of the boy kicking the cat as devilish. This metaphorical description is expanded into a myth in the brief story that the devil got into him. In due course I shall be suggesting that the metaphor of divine incarnation is expanded into the mythological story of the Son of God coming down from heaven to earth to be born in Bethlehem as the child of a virgin mother and dying on the cross as an atonement for the sins of the world.

One further point: it is sometimes said that there are deep truths that can only be expressed mythologically, and this is particularly likely to be said of religious myths. There is indeed a sense in which myths do communicate something that cannot be otherwise expressed. For myths are expanded metaphors, and metaphors depend on the cloud of associations attached to the literal use, a cloud that is not fixed and definable and in which different elements may resonate with different people. For example, I might speak of the journey of life. This may connect with such notions as movement, change, progress, continual newness. These themes may well be positive for some who like change, adventure, progress; but negative for others who prefer stability, certainty, lack of surprises. The metaphorical statement can activate either set of associations, and probably others as well. And it is this openness of the web of associations that ensures that metaphors can never be fully translated into literal terms. Accordingly myths, as expanded metaphors, lack fixed semantic boundaries and so cannot be definitively replaced by literal statements. In other words, they have a range of possible meanings, each of which, however, taken by itself, can be translated literally, so that there is no untranslatable meaning. But because different people take different meanings from the myth, there can be no one single definitive translation; and it is this fact that gives rise to the idea of some deep mystery hidden within it. But in fact there is no residual mystery. So why use myths? Because as a form of communication a myth is so often much more powerful than a bare literal statement, in spite of the fact that it does not carry any further inexpressible content.

The 'Virgin Birth' of Jesus

Turning now to Christology, I have already mentioned the virgin birth story because it became at some stage part of the Christian myth, though I doubt if many of us today would want the incarnation doctrine to stand or fall by it.

The virgin birth, or more precisely, virginal conception, doctrine is only an issue today for theologically rather conservative Christians. But for their benefit let us pursue it a little. It entails that Jesus had no human father. Such miraculous conception stories were fairly common in the ancient world. There was such a story, for example, about the Buddha and there was also one about Zarathustra in Zoroastrianism. There were ancient Egyptian and also Aztec virgin birth stories. Closer to the New Testament world, the Roman emperor Augustus Caesar, born in 66 BC and, like Jesus, deified after his death, was supposed to have been divinely conceived.[1] Richard Swinburne, whose divided mind theory I shall be discussing presently, says in *The Christian God*[2] that the virgin birth doctrine is secondary and suggests that it would have been better if it had not been enshrined in the creeds. I agree with him, and I applaud his willingness to edit the creeds on the basis of rational considerations, trusting that he will extend the same freedom to others who may want to edit them differently. But although the virgin birth is not, in his view, properly of creedal status, Swinburne says that he is nevertheless 'inclined to believe that the virgin birth did occur'.[3] He holds that the requirements of Jesus' genuine humanity would be 'fulfilled sufficiently by genes being derived from one parent rather than two'.[4] He asks, 'if . . . an individual's genes come only from his mother (parthenogenesis), can that individual still be human? I would have thought', he says, 'that the use of the word "human" by most of us is such as to yield the answer "Yes" to the latter question.'[5] Without making a judgement about that,

I would like to point out another aspect of the matter, available to us today through modern genetics but unknown in the ancient world. The human genetic complement consists of 46 chromosomes, which are the carriers of the genes that determine specific characteristics, 23 chromosomes being provided by each parent. If only the mother's were available, as Swinburne suggests, they would have to be doubled to produce the 46 chromosomes required to produce a viable embryo, and that would then have two X chromosomes and so would be female. So the Virgin Mary's child would be a girl, a result that might well be welcomed by feminist theologians but probably not by most of those who uphold the virgin birth doctrine.

So if we are determined to retain the doctrine we now have to launch on a series of ad hoc stipulations. Having jettisoned reliance on Mary's genes only, we shall have to postulate an additional set of genes that include the Y chromosome necessary for a male child. These chromosomes would have to be miraculously created by God and miraculously inserted into Mary. They would still not be part of the human gene pool, the genetically continuous stream of life constituting the human species. However, since orthodoxy does not countenance the idea of Jesus being genetically half human and half divine, we must now make the further dogmatic stipulation that the 23 divinely created chromosomes are nevertheless to be regarded as authentically human. But can choosing to regard them as part of the human gene pool make them so? Not even God can do the logically impossible. The required stipulation seems to me impermissible.

However, let us for the moment regard it as permissible. What characteristics would they carry? Presumably whatever characteristics God chose. But this provokes further questions. Would the divinely created chromosomes carry perfect characteristics? But does the notion of perfect human characteristics have any meaning? And would they be free from the inherited original sin affirmed by traditional Christian doctrine? If so, would Jesus now really be one of us, a member of the human race, sharing the weaknesses and temptations to which humanity is subject? Or would his genuine humanity be sufficiently ensured by his mother's genetic inheritance? But this was ruled out by another ad hoc stipulation, added later, namely the Immaculate Conception of the Blessed Virgin Mary. By now Jesus' humanity has become highly problematic.

The Chalcedonian Christology

The fact is that some elements of the theological tradition were intro-duced to preserve Jesus' divinity, and others to preserve his humanity; and it does not seem possible to satisfy both concerns. The more we stress his sinless perfection, by-passing the taint of original sin which is said to be at the root of all our problems, the less authentically human he seems. But the more we stress his genuine humanity, subject to the weaknesses and temptations of human flesh, the less he seems to be God. So this brings us back to Chalcedon. Leaving aside its archaic substance language, the central Chalcedonian doctrine is that Jesus was God incarnate, in the trinitarian sense of being the second person of the divine Trinity incarnate, and was also at the same time fully human. That is to say, he had two complete natures, in one of which he was God and in the other a human male.

The basic question that this has always provoked, and which has always been a central problem for Christology, is whether this complex idea is logically coherent. How could a historical individual have at the same time all the essential attributes of God, those attributes without which a being would not be God, and also all the essential attributes of humanity? The essential divine attributes, according to traditional Christian belief, include being infinite and eternal, being the sole creator of everything other than God, and being omnipotent, omniscient, omnipresent and perfectly good. Within Christian theology the essential attributes of humanity are harder to specify, and more open to debate, because they are not listed in any of the traditional dogmas. But surely they must include being a finite creature, and therefore not the infinite creator of everything other than oneself, and not eternal, at any rate into the past, nor omnipotent, omniscient, omnipresent, or untemptable; and also being part of the human species as this has emerged within the process of biological evolution. How, then, can a historical individual be both divinely creator of everything and humanly not creator of every-thing, divinely infinite and humanly finite, divinely omnipresent and humanly located only in a particular part of space, divinely omnipotent and humanly limited in power, divinely omniscient and humanly limited in knowledge, divinely perfect and humanly fallible?

In response to this conundrum some have argued that not all of these human attributes are essential to being human.[6] It has been said, for example, that there could in principle be omnipotent and omniscient humans and even, as the mystery of the virgin birth suggests, that there could be miraculously created humans who have not come to be within the evolving stream of biological life. Indeed, the tradition says that Adam was such. However, fortunately it is not necessary for our present purpose to reach agreement on these abstruse matters. It is enough that a human being is clearly and definitively not the sole creator of everything other than itself, whereas God is.

The Divided-Mind Theory

Various solutions to the problem have been proposed. I am only going to discuss here the one that is most favoured today among many Christian philosophers, namely the two-minds, or divided-mind, theory. This has been most fully presented by Thomas Morris in *The Logic of God Incarnate*[7] and is strongly defended by Richard Swinburne in another version in *The Christian God*, and it is to be found in the writings of several contemporary theologians, including David Brown,[8] Gerald O'Collins,[9] Richard Sturch[10] and a number of others.

In approaching his theory Swinburne invokes Freud's account of a mother whose son has tragically died and who seems to have two partially different belief systems, insisting consciously that her son is alive, and usually acting on that belief, but having also a suppressed awareness that he is dead, and sometimes acting on that. Such a case, says Swinburne, 'helps us to see the logical possibility of an individual for good reason with conscious intention keeping a lesser belief system separate from his main belief system, and simultaneously doing different actions guided by different sets of beliefs of which he is consciously aware'.[11] Building on this, he develops the idea of the divine mind of God the Son internally dividing itself so as to include within it the human mind of Jesus of Nazareth.

Although I don't want to make much of this here, it seems to me that Morris's idea of two complete minds, the human mind of Jesus of Nazareth and the divine mind of God the Son, with the latter enclosing but transcending the former, is more defensible than the idea, based on Freud, of a single mind that is divided within itself. It also seems more faithful to Chalcedon, which insisted on there being two complete natures, not one divided nature. However, I have argued elsewhere that even Morris's stronger version, as it seems to me, fails.[12]

But here I am discussing Swinburne's version. He says,

What in effect the 'divided mind' view is claiming is that the divine and human natures are to some extent separated, and that allows the human nature of Christ to be not a nature as perfect as a human nature could be (e.g. in Heaven), but a nature more like our human nature on Earth, subject to ignorance and disordered desire, yet one connected enough with the divine nature so that Christ does no wrong.[13]

It is this inability of Jesus to do wrong that we need to focus upon. '[A]n incarnate God', says Swinburne, 'could not do wrong . . . The "subjection" of the human will to the divine must then be read only as a subjection which ensured no wrongdoing . . .'[14] He allows that Jesus might sometimes choose to do a lesser good, but insists that he could never do anything that is positively wrong, that is, morally forbidden. Here, in my view, is the Achilles' heel of the theory.

The proposed picture seems to be this. The human mind and will of Jesus, left to himself, might have acted wrongly, both objectively and subjectively. But this could never in fact happen because, if and when the human will chose wrongly, or was in the process of choosing wrongly, the divine mind and will of God the Son would always overrule that choice to ensure that in fact Jesus never actually did wrong, or perhaps even never got to the point of having clearly chosen wrong. Clearly, in this scenario, the divine mind of God the Son is free. But is the human mind of Jesus free? Surely not. He will think that he is free, so long as he is not aware of the divine mind that encloses and controls him, but he is not in fact a genuinely free moral agent. For although he is free to act rightly, he is not free to act wrongly. Curiously, in a footnote criticizing an aspect of Thomas Morris's two-minds theory, Swinburne says, 'If you do not really have such a choice [that is, a choice to act wrongly], then you have the mere illusion of temptation.'[15] This is surely correct; but does it not apply as much to his own theory as Morris's?

The extent to which this matters depends on what the incarnation is for. According to Swinburne, the main reason for the incarnation is to effect atonement for the sins of the world. This is done by '[1] a life of perfect goodness, [2] offered as an atonement, [3] a life showing love for humanity and [4] teaching them on authority important truths otherwise unknowable'.[16] I have inserted the numbers to help us keep track. We can if we wish stipulate, as Swinburne does, that (1) Jesus lived a life of perfect goodness, since on his theory the enfolding mind of God the Son must have ensured this. This can, however, only be an a priori dogma, since we cannot possibly claim to know, as a matter of history, that Jesus always lived a life of perfect goodness. We simply do not have enough information about either his actions or his inner thoughts for this to be a historical judgement. And indeed Swinburne himself acknowledges at one point that 'Even if the evidence suggests that much of the public life of Jesus was perfectly good, how do we know that he did not have secret malicious thoughts?'[17] That he never had any secret malicious or otherwise wrong thoughts can only be a deduction from the Chalcedonian dogma.

But (2), it is highly debatable whether, as a matter of history, Jesus thought of his death as an atonement for human sin. E. P. Sanders, having carefully discussed all the relevant texts, rejects 'the whole line of thought that has Jesus intending to die for others, rather than just accepting his death and trusting that God would redeem the situation and vindicate him'.[18] In that case the atonement doctrine, instead of providing evidence for the incarnation doctrine, is itself another equally a priori dogma. The two hang together within the same dogmatic system, and the system as a whole is a human theory. And the view that it is divinely revealed is simply another human theory.

On the other hand, we can all agree that, as Swinburne says, (3) Jesus showed love for humanity – although this was of course in no way unique to him. But the further idea (4) that Jesus 'taught [humanity] on authority important truths otherwise unknowable' has long been rejected even by conservative New Testament scholars. It is widely agreed that there is nothing in Jesus' teaching about God or about the living of human life that was not already present within Judaism.

So I cannot agree that there is any of what Swinburne calls 'evidence' of divine incarnation. The Chalcedonian two-natures theory has to stand on its own legs without external support. And I suggest that the divided-mind version of it fails because it insists upon the two incompatible conditions, (a) that to be human involves being genuinely free to make right and wrong moral decisions, and (b) that if Jesus had begun to make a morally wrong decision this would have been blocked by the divine mind of God the Son. Under these circumstances the human Jesus could have had the illusion but not the reality of genuine libertarian free will. Swinburne's Jesus thus would not be a fellow human being who faced and overcame our human problems and whom we can take as our ideal of humanity, as many contemporary Christians believe. To put it dramatically, he would be a semi-autonomous puppet whose strings are pulled whenever necessary by God the Son.

The Chalcedonian Fathers believed, as their Definition states, that the two-natures dogma was 'as the Lord Jesus Christ taught us'. But the modern historical study of the New Testament has shown that he taught no such thing. Both the deification of Jesus and the two-natures doctrine were the work of the Church. It is now agreed even among conservative biblical scholars that such Fourth Gospel sayings as 'The Father and I are one' (John 10.30), 'Whoever has seen me has seen the Father' (14.9), and 'No one comes to the Father except through me' (14.6) cannot be attributed to the historical Jesus. They are words put into his mouth sixty to seventy years after Jesus' death, expressing the faith as it had developed toward the end of the first century in the writer's part of the Church. There is general agreement that Jesus, the historical individual, did not claim to be God, or God the Son, second person of a divine Trinity, incarnate.[19]

And so the belief of virtually all Christians down to within not much more than the last hundred and fifty or so years, that Jesus claimed deity, has been abandoned. The fallback position that has emerged is that although Jesus himself did not claim this, nevertheless his deity was implicit in some of his words and deeds. But James Dunn says, 'Just when our questioning reaches the "crunch" issue (Was Jesus conscious of being the divine Son of God?) we find that it is unable to give a clear historical answer.'[20] Jesus' implied deity is a matter of debate, and ultimately of faith, not an assured fact.

The big development, which culminated at Chalcedon in the mid-fifth century, was a gradual process. I have already suggested that no satisfactory literal meaning has been given to the two-natures dogma to which it led. For every meaning that was suggested during the fierce christological controversies preceding and succeeding Chalcedon was rejected by the Church as heretical. Today we do not brand failed theories as heretical, but 1500 years ago the two-minds or divided-mind theory might well have been rejected as heresy by those who insisted on the genuine humanity as well as divinity of Jesus as a morally free human agent. The heresy of which Thomas Morris and Richard Swinburne are guilty is that of falling to the philosopher's temptation to try to spell everything out as an intelligible theory. But the Church has wisely treated the incarnation as a holy mystery, a mystery which we cannot understand but which we accept because it is divinely revealed. This is the position, is it not, of most ordinary believers today?

This assumption that Jesus' combined deity and humanity is a literal truth, but one that is beyond human comprehension, will satisfy many good Christian people. It will not, however, satisfy any who realize that the fully-God-fully-man dogma is a philosophical proposal. It is not a divine revelation but a human creation. And its mysteriousness simply consists in the fact that it is a form of words with no intelligible meaning.

Incarnation as Metaphor

The two-minds, or divided-mind, theory is of course only one attempt to make the traditional two-natures dogma viable today. Alternatives, which however depart further from the two-natures marker, are the family of kenotic theories, and the much vaguer Christ-event theory. I am not going to discuss these here, though I have done so elsewhere.[21] Instead, let me proceed to the radically different conception of divine incarnation as a metaphorical rather than a literal idea.

As a first approach, consider the title Son of God. It is not today a matter of dispute that many figures in the ancient world were referred to as son of God or were otherwise accorded a divine status – some Egyptian Pharaohs, Roman emperors, great philosophers, legendary heroes. Indeed, until the end of the Second World War the Japanese emperors, refusing to enter the modern world, were officially regarded as divinely descended. But it is not easy for us today, when the Christian term 'Son of God' has long been filled with such stupendous meaning as the bearer of an absolute claim, to remember that in the world in which Jesus lived the idea of divinity was much broader and more elastic than it later became in Christian discourse.

It is particularly relevant to remember that the son of God title had long been familiar within Judaism. In Luke's Gospel (3.38) Adam is called the son of God as also, in the Hebrew scriptures, are angelic beings, and Israel as a whole, and also some of the ancient Hebrew kings, who were anointed as son of God – 'You are my son; today I have begotten you' (Ps. 2.7) being probably part of the enthronement ritual. Indeed, any truly pious Jew would be called a son of God. In terms of our modern distinction between the literal and the metaphorical it is clear that all these uses were metaphorical. No one thought that the king was literally, that is physically, God's son. 'Son of' meant in the spirit of, or specially favoured by, or divinely appointed to a special task. And quite likely Jesus, as a notable preacher and healer, was talked about during his lifetime as a son of God in this familiar metaphorical sense. As E. P. Sanders says, 'the first followers of Jesus . . . when they started calling him "Son of God," would have meant . . . a person standing in a special relationship to God, who chose him to accomplish a task of great importance'.[22] But the developed dogma that Jesus was fully God as well as fully man in virtue of having two natures came several centuries later and cannot possibly be attributed to Jesus himself. Jesus as a metaphorical son of God became Christ as the metaphysical God the Son.

The language of incarnation or embodiment or personification works unproblematically when we are speaking of an idea, an ideal, a principle, a value being incarnated in a person or in a work of art. We all know what we mean when we say that 'Great men incarnate the spirit of their age', or 'George Washington incarnated the spirit of American independence', or 'Nelson Mandela incarnates the spirit of the new South Africa', or again that 'The Voortrekker monument at Pretoria embodies the pioneering spirit of the Boers'. These are all cases of something abstract being embodied in something concrete, whether a person or a stone monument. Whether or not we want to call these metaphorical is optional. It could be argued that they are cases of a metaphorical use having developed into a literal use. But when that which is said to be incarnated in a person's life is not an abstraction but a being, the living God, the situation is different. Here a literal understanding of the language is in principle possible, but would have to be given meaning in one or another of the various ways in which theologians have tried to spell it out in the course of Christian history, in terms of two natures, two minds, or of some other metaphysical theory. But when all these have been seen to fail it becomes clear that the incarnation doctrine must instead be understood metaphorically.

How, then, does the metaphor of incarnation apply to Jesus? Jesus lived out – that is, incarnated – the ideal of human life lived in full openness to God; and he lived out – that is, incarnated – the ideal of *agape*, self-giving love; and in so far as he was doing God's will on earth, God was (metaphorically) incarnate in his life. These are all intelligible Christian claims about the significance of Jesus.

But is such a metaphorical understanding of divine incarnation religiously viable? I think it is. For instead of seeing Jesus as God walking the earth, one whom we cannot possibly hope to emulate, we can see him as a fellow human who challenges us in an extraordinarily powerful way. Whenever anyone freely and unselfishly does God's will, in that action and that moment we can say that God becomes in some degree incarnate on earth. In this sense we are all called to incarnate God's love. As the writer of the *Theologia Germanica* says, we are to be to God as one's hand is to oneself. With this theology the Church becomes a servant to humanity, committed to trying to express the divine love in the changing circumstances of our human history. The very practical challenge of Jesus' teaching comes alive as a call to embody his ideals in our own actions.

So, to conclude, I recommend that we abandon Chalcedon and the modern attempts to restate it, and move to a metaphorical conception of incarnation in human life. This is truer to the earliest Jesus tradition, believable in our modern world, more morally challenging to ourselves, and also more open to a recognition of other great religious founders and prophets in an age when it is no longer realistically possible to think of Christianity as the one and only valid way to God.

Notes

1 For further details see, e.g., John Dominic Crossan, *The Birth of Christianity*, San Francisco: HarperSanFrancisco, 1999, pp. 28–9.

2 Richard Swinburne, *The Christian God*, Oxford: Clarendon Press, 1994, p. 235.

3 Swinburne, *Christian God*, p. 235.

4 Swinburne, *Christian God*, p. 196.

5 Swinburne, *Christian God*, p. 29.

6 For example, Thomas Morris says that 'It is not true that an individual must be a contingent being, non-eternal, and non-omnipotent in order to exemplify human nature,' in Ronald Feenstra and Cornelius Plantinga, Jr. (eds), *Trinity, Incarnation, and Atonement*, Notre Dame: University of Notre Dame Press, 1989, pp. 116–17.

7 Thomas V. Morris, *The Logic of God Incarnate*, Ithaca and London: Cornell University Press, 1986.

8 David Brown, *The Divine Trinity*, London: Duckworth; LaSalle, IL: Open Court, 1985.

9 Gerald O'Collins, *Interpreting Jesus*, London: Geoffrey Chapman; Ramsey, NJ: Paulist Press, 1983.

10 Richard Sturch, *The Word and the Christ*, Oxford: Clarendon Press, 1991.

11 Swinburne, *Christian God*, p. 201.

12 John Hick, *Disputed Questions in Theology and the Philosophy of Religion*, London: Macmillan; New Haven: Yale University Press, 1993, ch. 4.

13 Swinburne, *Christian God*, p. 208.

14 Swinburne, *Christian God*, p. 208.

15 Swinburne, *Christian God*, p. 205, n. 14.

16 Swinburne, *Christian God*, p. 221.

17 Swinburne, *Christian God*, p. 221.

18 E. P. Sanders, *Jesus and Judaism*, London: SCM Press, 1985, p. 332.

19 I am not a biblical scholar myself, and so I shall cite three highly respected scholars, choosing English ones because they tend to be more conservative than their American colleagues. These are all people who personally believe wholeheartedly that Jesus was in fact God the Son incarnate, but as honest scholars they freely acknowledge that he did not himself teach this. Charles Moule, who was a great pillar of traditional orthodoxy, says, 'Any case for a "high" Christology that depended on the authenticity of the alleged claims of Jesus about himself, especially in the Fourth Gospel, would indeed be precarious,' in *The Origin of Christology*, Cambridge: Cambridge University Press, 1977. The late Archbishop Michael Ramsey, who was a New Testament professor before becoming a bishop, said bluntly, 'Jesus did not claim deity for himself', in *Jesus and the Living Past*,

Oxford: Oxford University Press, 1980, p. 39. James Dunn concludes from his exhaustive study of Christian origins that 'there was no real evidence in the earliest Jesus tradition of what could fairly be called consciousness of divinity', in *Christology in the Making*, London: SCM Press, 1980. I will add the Dutch Catholic scholar Edward Schillebeeckx, who writes, 'The distinctive relation of Jesus to God was expressed in the primitive Christian churches . . . by use of the honorific title "Son of God" and "the Son." These were Christian identifications of Jesus of Nazareth after his death. Jesus never spoke of himself as "the Son" or "Son of God"; there is no passage in the synoptics pointing in that direction', in *Jesus: An Experiment in Christology*, trans. Hubert Hoskins, London: Collins, 1979, p. 258.

20 Dunn, *Christology in the Making*, p. 29.

21 John Hick, *The Metaphor of God Incarnate*, London: SCM Press; Louisville: Westminster John Knox Press, 1993.

22 E. P. Sanders, *The Historical Figure of Jesus*, London: Penguin, 1993, p. 245.

8

The Resurrection of Jesus

In our usual understanding of the resurrection we tend to amalgamate what the different Gospels say, not noticing the many points at which they disagree. Easter centres on the resurrection message that Jesus was crucified and buried, and on third day rose from the dead. The questions raised by the New Testament scholars focus on what 'rose from the dead' means. There can be no doubt that something of momentous significance happened which we call the resurrection. But what was that event or series of events?

There are two streams of New Testament tradition which we can call the bodily tradition and the visions tradition. The bodily tradition, according to Luke in his Gospel and in Acts, is of an empty tomb and the risen body of Jesus appearing to the disciples from time to time over a period of forty days, and then ascending bodily into heaven. The visions tradition is one of probably several visions of Jesus which gave the disciples a powerful sense of his presence with them and inspired them to remain faithful to him and to witness to his memory and his teachings.

I ought to mention at this point a very radical possibility, and then leave it hanging, so to speak, because I'm not going to take it up – I just don't know what weight it has. But some scholars[1] believe that the whole story of Joseph of Arimathea and his family tomb, and Jesus' burial in it, is a later creation. According to them the dead bodies of crucified criminals were thrown by the Roman soldiers into a limed pit, which dissolves the body quickly and hygienically, and this is the reason why virtually no skeletal remains have been found of the thousands who were crucified outside Jerusalem in the first century. Is this correct? It could be, but frankly I don't know and I'm not going to assume so.

What I would like to do is to ask you to notice the inconsistencies that appear when we compare the different Gospels. Part of the bodily tradition is that Jesus' body was laid in a tomb provided by Joseph of Arimathea. But that is incompatible with another strand of Christian tradition which says that it was not his disciples who buried Jesus but the Jews who had engineered his death. We get this in Acts 13.28–9, reporting a speech by St Paul in which he says, 'Even though they [the Jewish authorities] found no cause for a sentence of death, they asked Pilate to have him killed. When they had carried out everything that was written about him, they [the Jewish authorities] took him down from the tree and laid him in a tomb.' This is different from the Joseph of Arimathea story. Some commentators make the point that Luke is concerned to blame the Jews for Jesus' death. But one puzzle is that Luke's Gospel and the Acts of the Apostles are both believed to have been written by the same person, whom we call Luke. So Luke in Acts differs here from Luke in his Gospel, which has the Joseph of Arimathea story (ch. 23). What are we to make of this? I don't know. But this is the sort of problem that appears when you start to look closely at the texts.

Let us now return to the empty tomb and the bodily resurrection tradition, and focus on the physical aspect. On the one hand, the disciples saw the wounds in the hands and feet of the risen Jesus (Luke), the women at the tomb, meeting Jesus in the garden, 'held on to his feet' (Matthew), and he ate fish with them in Galilee (Luke and John). That indicates something thoroughly bodily, physical. None of this comes, however, in the earlier Mark. But the bodily tradition also holds that the risen Jesus could suddenly materialize in a room without having to come through the door, and could equally suddenly disappear after breaking bread at supper with the two disciples on the Emmaus road. This materializing and dematerializing would also have to apply to his clothes. There is also the strange fact that the resurrected Jesus was several times not at first recognized – in John's Gospel by Mary Magdalene at the tomb, who thought him to be the gardener, and in Luke by the disciples on the Emmaus road, who carried on a long conversation with him without realizing that this was Jesus. And there is also Matthew's puzzling statement that Jesus appeared to the disciples on a mountain in Galilee 'but some doubted', though 'doubted' may possibly be too strong, with something like 'wondered' instead (Matt. 28.17). But either way, there are strange aspects, and what is customarily said is that the risen body was indeed the body that had been placed in the tomb, but somehow transformed or transfigured or transmuted so that it did not now have to obey the ordinary laws of physics. This would account for Jesus suddenly appearing in bodily form in a closed room, but would still not account for some of his disciples not recognizing him. So there are still many puzzles.

Yet another puzzle is: why would the transformed Jesus, if he could pass through walls, and appear and disappear at will, need any help in getting out of the tomb? Why should an angel have to come down and roll away the stone (Matthew)? Would it not have been a much stronger proof of his bodily resurrection if the tomb had remained sealed, and then been officially discovered to be empty when they opened it up? So it seems that the fact that the tomb was already open when the women arrived early on the Sunday morning weakens, if anything, rather than strengthens the traditional story – not only because it seems unnecessary but also because it leaves space for the allegation, which was in fact made at the time (Matt. 28.11–15), that someone had removed the body. These are difficult, possibly unanswerable, questions and I can only leave them with you.

Going back now to the scholarly consensus, another part of it concerns the last chapter of Mark's Gospel, telling of appearances to Mary Magdalene, then to two unnamed disciples, then to the rest and to the eleven as they sat at table, and charging them to preach the gospel throughout the world, saying, 'The one who believes and is baptized will be saved; but the one who does not believe will be condemned'; and finally reporting that Jesus was taken up into heaven to sit at the right hand of God. However, none of this is in the earliest manuscripts, and it is now universally believed to have been a later addition. Because of this many modern versions in English now leave a gap in the print between Mark 16.8 and what follows, the original Gospel having ended at 16.8. This original ending is enigmatic. The two Marys, Magdalene and Jesus' mother, go to the tomb early on the Sunday morning to anoint the body. They find the stone already rolled aside and a young man in a white robe – in Matthew this is an angel and in Luke two angels – who in Mark tells them that Jesus is risen and will appear to Peter and the disciples in Galilee; and then it ends, 'So they went out and fled from the tomb; for terror and amazement had seized them; and they said nothing to anyone, for they were afraid.' So Mark gives us the empty tomb and a promise of appearances to come in Galilee, but no actual appearances, and by implication rules out any appearances in Jerusalem.

Matthew and Luke follow Mark as far as his original ending, but then diverge so much that it is not possible to harmonize them with one another or with John. Luke has no appearances in Galilee. According to him the only appearances are in Jerusalem and on the nearby Emmaus road. These include an appearance to Peter, and then all the disciples together, Jesus suddenly appearing among them, and then they go out to Bethany, and Jesus is carried up into heaven. All this happens in the Jerusalem area on the same day. And the Acts of the Apostles, by the same writer, again restricts the appearances to Jerusalem, instructing the disciples to remain there until they are baptized with the Holy Spirit

– referring to Pentecost. Acts then describes the ascension: 'When he had said this, as they were watching, he was lifted up, and a cloud took him out of their sight' (Acts 1.9). That's Luke.

Matthew on the other hand reports an earthquake and an angel descending to remove the stone from the tomb, and says there were guards at the tomb, presumably Roman soldiers, who trembled and became like dead men. Then the women meet Jesus in the garden and he tells them to tell the disciples to go to Galilee, where he will meet them. There are no more appearances in Jerusalem, contrary to Luke's Gospel. In Matthew the disciples do go to Galilee, where Jesus meets them on a mountain, though as I've already mentioned, Matthew adds 'but some doubted' or 'wondered' (28.17). There Jesus gives them the missionary commission to go and make disciples of all nations. Matthew on the other hand does not have an ascension story.

John, writing later, has extensive appearances in both Jerusalem and Galilee, over a period of forty days, but again no ascension story.

So when we bring the different Gospel narratives together there are mysteries which it is impossible to ignore. Their versions cannot all be right. They represent different traditions. In Mark, the earliest, there is the enigmatic ending and no appearances. Then there is the major contradiction between Matthew and Luke that Matthew has appearances in both Jerusalem and in Galilee spread at least over some days or weeks, traditionally forty days, whereas Luke has appearances only in and around Jerusalem, and all within a matter of hours. There is the puzzle that in Luke and John the first people to see the risen Jesus do not recognize him. And there is the even more mysterious feature of the risen Jesus being able to appear and disappear at will.

There is one other item in Matthew's Gospel which on the one hand supports the bodily resurrection tradition and yet on the other hand raises a question about it. This is Matthew 27.52–3, which tells us that 'many bodies of the saints who had fallen asleep [died] were raised. After his [Jesus'] resurrection they came out of the tombs and entered the holy city [Jerusalem] and appeared to many.' This reminds us that for Jews of that time resurrection *meant* bodily resurrection. So for them it meant that if Jesus was said to have been raised from the dead it must mean that his body came out of the tomb. But on the other hand, it also fits the alternative New Testament tradition of visions only. For if the original proclamation of the disciples was that Jesus had appeared to them, meaning that they had seen visions of him, and if this was enough for them, their proclamation of the risen Lord would almost inevitably as time went on have come to be understood to mean that they had seen his resurrected body, and the Gospels one and two generations after the event would be likely to have taken this form.

Another important point about this story of many of the dead coming out of their graves and walking into Jerusalem and being seen by many is that it shows us what Matthew's readers in the 80s could be expected to accept without question. For in the ancient world physical miracle stories were common and were not received, as they are today, with probing questions. And yet such an event is historically *extremely* improbable. Such an extraordinary event would surely have found its place in the Roman records of the time. But Josephus and Tacitus, who do mention the fact that there was a teacher called Jesus and that he was executed by the Romans, make no mention of stories either about his resurrection or about this mass resurrection of people coming out of their graves and being seen publicly in Jerusalem. But it is hard to see how the Roman authorities in Jerusalem could fail to have been aware of such a startling mass phenomenon, and how it could fail to be recorded as an extraordinary historical event. Imagine a lot of people rising from their tombs in Lodge Hill cemetery here in Birmingham and walking down Bristol Road into the town centre and being seen by many! It would certainly hit the headlines.

Further, the story of the empty tomb, present in all four Gospels, seems to have been a late addition to the tradition. It was not part of the original message that Paul received from the apostles, and does not seem to have been known by Paul. It is not mentioned in any of his letters, and first appears in Mark's Gospel around 70 CE. It seems to many scholars to be a dubious element in the story.

So far we have been talking mainly about the Gospels. But the earliest reference to the resurrection is not in any of them but in Paul, in 1 Corinthians 15.4, dated in the early 50s. This is particularly significant because Paul is also the only person from whom we have a first-hand account of an encounter with the risen Christ – or at least the author of Acts' account of Paul's account. We will come to that in a moment. But in 1 Corinthians Paul reminds his readers of the gospel that he received from the apostles after his conversion in the year 33 or 34 – it being believed today that the crucifixion occurred in the year 30. The message was that

Christ died for our sins in accordance with the scriptures, that he was buried, that he was raised on the third day in accordance with the scriptures, and that he appeared to Cephas [Peter], then to the twelve. Then he appeared to more than five hundred brothers and sisters at one time, most of whom are still alive, though some have died. Then he appeared to James [Jesus' brother], then to all the apostles.

Last of all, Paul adds, as to one untimely born, he appeared to him also. The big question is whether his being raised and appearing means, in this original message, that he was raised bodily, the physical body coming out of the tomb, or whether it consists in Peter and some of the others having visions of him. If we read the much later Gospel stories into Paul's earlier words, as we customarily do, it means a physical resurrection, but if not, it is equally consistent with both the bodily and the visions tradition.

A comment on Paul's reference to the risen Lord appearing to more than five hundred of the brethren at once. We would expect most of any five hundred people to be still alive only two or three years later. So most probably that was not part of the original message that Paul received but something that had become part of the tradition during the nearly twenty years before Paul was writing.

Paul's own account of his encounter with the risen Lord is described first in Acts 9.1–9 and then in his speeches reported in Acts. In Acts 22.6–9 Paul says,

While I was on my way and approaching Damascus, about noon a great light from heaven suddenly shone about me. I fell to the ground and heard a voice saying to me, 'Saul, Saul, why are you persecuting me?' I answered, 'Who are you, Lord?' Then he said to me, 'I am Jesus of Nazareth whom you are persecuting.' Now those who were with me saw the light but did not hear the voice of the one who was speaking to me.

In other words, in this account, it was an inner voice. On the other hand, in the passage in chapter 9 the others hear the voice but see nothing. And later, in Acts 26.13–16, where Paul is speaking to king Agrippa, Paul repeats his story, saying that on his way to Damascus, 'at midday along the road, your Excellency, I saw a light from heaven, brighter than the sun, shining around me and my companions. When we had all fallen to the ground, I heard a voice saying to me in the Hebrew language, "Saul, Saul, why are you persecuting me? It hurts you to kick against the goads."' So here again his companions see the light but do not hear the voice. Here the voice speaks for much longer than in the other account, Jesus going on to commission Paul as his apostle to the gentiles.

Now Paul (according to Luke, the author of Acts) reports this experience as the risen Lord appearing to him. You remember that in his listing of Jesus' appearances he includes this. 'Last of all, as to someone untimely born, he appeared also to me' (1 Cor. 15.8). This was of vital importance to Paul because it was this that made him an apostle. He refers to himself as an apostle in his letters (for example, Gal. 1.1) and says (Gal. 1.16) that God 'was pleased reveal his Son to me'. In 1 Corinthians 9.1 he asks, 'Am I not an apostle? Have I not seen Jesus our Lord?' – using the same Greek verb, *opthe*, for this as for the other apostles' seeing of the Lord. However, the scholars are widely agreed that this word, followed by the dative, is better translated as 'appeared to' or 'was seen by'. In other words, it is compatible with visions rather than a physical presence.

So in this overwhelming experience on the Damascus road there was no physical presence of Jesus, not only because Paul does not speak of one but also because if there had been, those who were with him would also have seen it. Paul saw a bright light, had a vision of Jesus, and heard an inner voice. And it seems very reasonable to treat Paul's experience as our clue to the earlier experience of the first apostles. If so, they had visions of the risen Lord, but no bodily presence was involved.

Indeed the idea that Jesus' resurrection was a physical event would be incompatible, for Paul, with his belief that 'flesh and blood cannot inherit the kingdom of God' (1 Cor. 15.50), and his belief that the resurrection of the faithful will not be in their physical body but a spiritual body. He says, 'It is sown a physical body, it is raised a spiritual body. If there is a physical body, there is also a spiritual body' (1 Cor. 15.44). If this was what Paul believed, he may well have thought that what he saw in his vision was the spiritual body of Jesus.

There is however a possible difficulty in the visions tradition. It is natural that several people at once would see a physical presence, but could they all have the same vision at the same time – all the disciples at once, and the five hundred? It is not uncommon for an individual to have a fleeting vision of a recently dead loved one. (I have had such a vision myself.) But what about collective visions of the dead? It may be relevant that the annals of parapsychology do record a number of cases of collectively perceived apparitions.[2] But the much stronger likelihood is that the stories of all the apostles together, and the five hundred, seeing the risen Jesus simultaneously are later creative developments within the developing tradition. I pointed out earlier that the five hundred cannot have been part of the original message that Paul received from the apostles. So this is another unresolved question.

So we are left with a lot of questions. Whether we opt for the bodily or the visions interpretation of the complex biblical material taken as a whole, we have to accept what are probably insoluble problems.

Finally, what does Easter mean to me? Well, what it means to me has nothing to do with all these unresolved puzzles and conflicting indications in the texts! If nevertheless you ask me, what among all of this incompatible and often conflicting material I feel sure of, I would have to say that I feel sure that there must have been visions of Jesus after his death. I do not feel at all sure that there was a physical body. But my faith in Jesus as Lord does not depend on a balancing of the sort of considerations I have been outlining; and I would not want to have a faith that was precariously balanced on such conflicting considerations. Nor however would I want to have a faith which ignored them. I know of course that many are happy to set all that aside, and affirm a simple straightforward belief that Jesus rose bodily from the grave, and I have no quarrel with them, although I cannot in honesty share their certainty.

So for me Easter is a joyful symbol of a central element of the gospel, God's gift of renewal, of ever new beginnings, of rebirth, of life transcending death. That it comes at spring time when nature is renewing itself is a happy coincidence. But Easter is our Christian symbol of hope, of the ongoing fact of new life, of freedom from the grip of the past, of openness to the future, to new possibilities, ultimately openness to the kingdom of God and an intimation of life beyond death.

Notes

1 For example, Marianne Sawicki, *Seeing the Lord*, Minneapolis: Fortress Press, 1994, p. 180; followed by John Dominic Crossan, *The Birth of Christianity*, New York: HarperCollins, 1988, pp. xxvii, 528, 555.

2 Dr Alan Gauld of Nottingham University says, 'In such cases two or more people simultaneously see what is *prima facie* the same phantasmal figure in the same place . . . [There are] 46 cases in the literature in which second percipients were in a position to see an apparition, 26 were cases of collective percipiency' (Prof. Benjamin Wolman (ed.), *Handbook of Parapsychology*, 1977, p. 602), and William Roll of Duke University reminds us that 'collective hallucinations may be produced by suggestion' (Woolman, *Handbook of Parapsychology*, New York: Van Nostrand Reinhold, p. 398). Applied to the resurrection tradition this would presumably mean that someone, probably Peter, had a vision of Jesus and exclaimed in an awed voice 'Jesus!' or 'Lord!', and the others present then also began to see him. But this is pure speculation.

9

Is the Doctrine of
Atonement a Mistake?

The term 'atonement' is so deeply embedded in Christian discourse that every systematic theologian feels obliged to have a doctrine under this heading. And yet the word is so variously used that some of these doctrines have little in common except the name. In its broad etymological meaning, at-one-ment signifies becoming one with God – not ontologically but in the sense of entering into a right relationship with our Creator, this being the process or state of salvation. But in its narrower sense atonement refers to a specific method of receiving salvation, one presupposing that the barrier to this is sin and guilt. It is in this context that we find the ideas of penalty, atonement, redemption, sacrifice, oblation, propitiation, expiation, satisfaction, substitution, forgiveness, acquittal, ransom, justification, remission of sins, forming a complex of ideas which has long been central to the Western or Latin development of Christianity.

In this narrower sense, Jesus' crucifixion was an act of atoning, or making up for, human sin. On the other hand, in the broader sense in which atonement simply means salvation, or entering into a right relationship with God, Jesus' death may or may not be separated off from his self-giving life as a whole, as having a special significance of its own. As a rough approximation we can say that the broader sense has been more at home in the Eastern or Greek development of Christianity and the narrower in its Western or Latin development.

Let us, for the sake of clarity, restrict the term 'atonement' here to its narrower and more specific meaning. The basic notion is that salvation requires God's forgiveness and that this in turn requires an adequate atonement to satisfy the divine righteousness and/or justice. This atoning act is a transaction, analogous to making a payment to cancel a debt or to remit an impending punishment. In the background there is the idea of the moral order of the universe which requires that sin, as a disruption of that order, be balanced or cancelled either by just punishment

96

of the offender or a substitute, or by some adequate satisfaction in lieu of punishment.

I am going to argue that in this narrower sense the idea of atonement has played itself out; although of course in the broader sense, in which at-one-ment simply means salvation, it is alive and indeed vitally important.

In so arguing I am, I think, reflecting a widespread contemporary perception. Indeed, were it not for its recent revival by some Christian philosophers who, unlike most contemporary theologians, see church doctrine as a set of immutable truths, one could easily think that the notion of atonement, in its narrower sense, had died out among thoughtful Christians. For modern treatments of salvation seldom centre upon Anselm's doctrine of a satisfaction to cancel the insult to God's majesty caused by creaturely disobedience, or the penal-substitutionary idea of an imputed justification won by Christ's having taken upon himself the punishment due for human sin. It is symptomatic of the vanishing role of these ideas that in the 1989 revision of the *Encyclopaedia Britannica*, while there is a brief entry on atonement in the Ready Reference Micropaedia, the more than 100 pages of depth study of Christianity in the Macropaedia include only one reference to the idea that 'the Christian is the one to whom the righteousness of God is ascribed in faith for the sake of the merit of Jesus Christ, which he earned for himself through his expiatory sacrifice on the cross';[1] and the writer immediately adds that 'In the 20th century, however, the schema of justification seems less understandable' because its presuppositions 'are scarcely found any more in religious consciousness'.[2]

As with other traditional doctrines, it is important to try to go back in historical imagination to the original experience out of which it grew. It is evident that the profound and all-absorbing experience of the early post-Easter Christian community was of a living spirit which they identified as the spirit of the risen Jesus, welling up within them, individually and corporately, and drawing them into a new, joyous and exhilarating stream of life, full of positive meaning and free from the besetting fears of the ancient world – of demons, of fate, of sin and of death. This new liberated life, brimming with meaning and hope, was the religious reality that was to be expressed, first in what seem to us today a cluster of bizarre images and later, within medieval Latin Christianity, in various sophisticated theories of a transactional atonement. However, we in the Western churches today, both Catholic and Reformed, may well feel that none of these inherited theories retains any real plausibility and that we should look again at the alternative development within Eastern Christianity of the idea of a gradual transformation of the human by the divine Spirit, called by the Orthodox theologians deification (*theosis*).

These two conceptions do not, of course, entirely exclude each other. Latin theology has also held that the justification won by Jesus' death leads to sanctification, which is the gradual transformation of the sinner into a saint. And Orthodox theology also holds that Jesus' death was somehow crucial in bringing about human 'deification'. And since both traditions use the same stock of biblical images, one can find much the same language somewhere within each. But nevertheless their basic tendencies move in markedly different directions, one guided by a transaction-atonement conception and the other by a transformation conception of salvation.

We shall come back later to the Eastern tradition and its transformational conception, but in the meantime let us look more closely at the transactional model.

Before the division between Eastern and Western Christianity, the earliest attempt to conceptualize the Christian experience of liberation and new life fastened upon the Markan saying attributed to Jesus, that 'the Son of Man came not to be served, but to serve, and to give his life a ransom (*lutron*) for many' (Mark 10.45). The idea of ransom had a poignant meaning in the ancient world, in which a considerable proportion of the population lived in a permanent state of slavery, and free citizens were liable to become enslaved if their tribe, city or nation was defeated in war. Being ransomed, and thus made free, was accordingly a vivid and powerful metaphor, whose force most of us can probably only partially recapture today.

But, making the perennial theological mistake of taking metaphorical language literally, the early Christian writers asked themselves to whom Jesus was, by his death, paying a ransom; and the inevitable answer, in a world plagued by fear of demons, was the devil. In the words of Origen, 'To whom gave he his life "a ransom for many"? It cannot have been to God. Was it not then to the evil one? For he held us until the ransom for us, even the soul of Jesus, was paid to him.'[3] And so for many centuries – indeed virtually until Anselm introduced his satisfaction theory in the eleventh century – it was generally accepted by Christian writers and preachers that the human race had fallen through sin under the jurisdiction and power of the devil and that the cross of Christ was part of a bargain with the devil to ransom us. (We find this same idea in C. S. Lewis's Narnia story.) Within this literature there is also, as a sub-plot, the idea that in this bargain God outwitted the devil, transforming a situation in which he had a just claim over humanity to one in which he put himself in the wrong by taking a greater ransom, namely God the Son, than was due. Thus Gregory of Nyssa proposed that 'in order to secure that the ransom in our behalf might be easily accepted by him who required it, the Deity was hidden under the veil of our nature, that so, as with ravenous fish, the hook of the Deity might be gulped down along with the bait of the flesh.'[4] Augustine even more picturesquely suggested in one of his sermons that 'As our price he [Christ] held out his cross to him like a mouse trap, and as bait set upon it his own blood.'[5] Such imagery is only embarrassing today. But while the ransom theory was never elevated to creedal authority, it was very widely used, occurring in the writing of Irenaeus, Origen, Gregory of Nyssa, Ambrose, Rufinus, Gregory the Great, Augustine and Chrysostom. Nevertheless, it is impossible today to make any sense or use of it. As Anselm later asked, why should we accept that the devil has any valid legal rights over against the infinite Creator?[6] The wonder is that such a notion satisfied some of the best Christian minds for so long. As Grensted says, 'That such a theory could stand for nine hundred years as the ordinary exposition of the fact of the Atonement is in itself a sufficient proof that the need for serious discussion of the doctrine had not as yet been felt.'[7]

When the need for serious discussion did begin to be felt, the theories that were produced began from belief in original sin as an inherited guilt affecting the entire human race and requiring an adequate atonement to expunge it. To attack this idea today is, for most of us, to do battle against a long-extinct monster. Nevertheless, the ecclesiastical reluctance to abandon traditional language is so strong that even today there is point in recalling why we should cease to think and speak in terms of original sin – except as a mythological term for the universal fact of human moral imperfection. For this ancient notion presupposes the wilful fall from grace of the first humans and the genetic inheritance by the whole species, as their descendants, of a sinful and guilty nature. This is something that only doctrinal fundamentalists can believe today. But prior to the Enlightenment of the seventeenth and eighteenth centuries it was a seriously entertained idea. Thus the Council of Trent (1646) pronounced that

If anyone does not confess that the first man Adam, when he had transgressed the command of God in Paradise, straightway lost that holiness and righteousness in which he had been established, and through the offence of this disobedience incurred the wrath and indignation of God, and therefore incurred death . . . [and] if anyone asserts that the disobedience of Adam injured only himself and not his offspring . . . or that . . . only death and the pains of the body were transferred to the whole human race, and not the sin also, which is the death of the soul: let him be anathema . . .[8]

While the Westminster Confession (1647) declared that

Our first parents being seduced by the subtlety and temptation of Satan, sinned in eating the forbidden fruit . . . By this sin they fell from their original righteousness, and communion with God, and so became dead in sin, and wholly defiled in all the faculties and parts of soul and body. They being the root of all mankind, the guilt of this sin was imputed, and the same death in sin and corrupted nature conveyed to all their posterity, descending from them by ordinary generation.[9]

However, today, the idea of an historical human fall resulting in a universal inherited depravity and guilt is totally unbelievable by educated Christians. Instead of the human race being descended from a single specially created pair, we see the species as having evolved out of lower forms of life over an immense period of time. Instead of the earliest humans living in a perfect communion with God, we see them as probably having a primitive animistic outlook. Instead of them living in harmony with nature and one another, we see them as engaged in a struggle to survive in competition with other animals, and with one another, within an often harsh environment. If out of piety towards the traditional language we wish to retain the term 'fall', we can say that the earliest humans were, metaphorically speaking, already 'fallen' in the sense of being morally and religiously imperfect. That is to say, there was a wide gap between their actual condition and the imagined 'original righteousness' or paradisal perfection, so that they can be said to have been *as though* they had fallen from such an ideal state. But since that state never existed, would it not be better to abandon the concept of the fall altogether? If we believe that there never was a human fall from an original paradise, why risk confusing ourselves and others by speaking as if there were?

I take it that our endemic individual and corporate self-centredness, from which the many forms of moral evil flow, is an aspect of our nature as animals engaged in the universal struggle for survival; and that this self-centred propensity exists in tension with a distinctively human capacity for ego-transcendence in response to the felt claim upon us of moral values. In this tension we have a genuine, though limited, freedom and responsibility; and in so far as we are free we are guilty in respect of our wrong choices. There is thus a genuine problem of guilt. I shall return to this presently. But at the moment we are concerned with the ancient notion of original sin.

For it is this that feeds into the traditional conceptions of atonement. In the light of a typical contemporary ethical awareness, the idea of an inherited guilt for being born as the kind of beings that we are is a moral absurdity. We cannot be guilty in the sight of God for having been born, within God's providence, as animals programmed for self-protection and survival in a tough environment. And even if we discount our modern awareness of the continuity between *homo sapiens* and the rest of animal life, the moral principle behind the traditional doctrine is still totally unacceptable. Although evidently believable in the age in which it was propounded, the notion of a universal inherited guilt was losing moral plausibility in the eighteenth century; and at the end of the nineteenth century the forthright humanist critic W. K. Clifford was expressing an already widespread perception when, having in mind the kind of ecclesiastical pronouncement that I quoted earlier, he said that 'to condemn all mankind for the sin of Adam and Eve; to let the innocent suffer for the guilty; to keep anyone alive in torture for ever and ever; these actions are simply magnified copies of what bad men are. No juggling with the "divine justice and mercy" can make them anything else.'[10]

We have already seen in the ransom idea the way in which Christian theology has drawn its soteriological analogies from the structures of contemporary society – in this case the pervasive fact of slavery and the liberating possibility of being ransomed from it. The next model to dominate the Christian imagination was proposed by St Anselm in his *Cur Deus Homo* (completed in its present form in 1098), one of the most influential books of Christian theology ever written. Anselm took over the concept of satisfaction which had long operated in both Church and society. This was the idea that disobedience, whether to God or to one's earthly lord, was a slight upon his honour and dignity, and required for its cancellation some adequate satisfaction in the form of an acceptable penance or gift. In the medieval penitential system a sinner's prescribed act of penance was believed to be accepted by God as a satisfaction restoring the moral balance; and likewise, when one did something to undermine the dignity and authority of one's feudal overlord, one had either to be punished or to give some other sufficient satisfaction to appease the lord's slighted dignity. This notion, reflecting a strongly hierarchical and tightly-knit society, evidently made sense in the cultural climate of medieval Europe.

Against this background Anselm defined sin as 'nothing else than not to render to God his due'.[11] What is due to God is absolute obedience: 'He who does not render this honour which is due to God, robs God of his own and dishonours him; and this is sin . . . So then, everyone who sins ought to pay back the honour of which he has robbed God; and this is the satisfaction which every sinner owes to God' (Part I, ch. 11). Further, 'Even God cannot raise to happiness any being bound at all by the debt of sin, because he ought not to' (Part I, ch. 21). However, it is impossible for humanity to make the required satisfaction; for even if we were perfectly obedient in the future, we would only be giving to God what is already due to him, and a satisfaction requires something extra that was not already due. Further, because God is the lord of the whole universe, the adequate satisfaction for a slight upon the divine honour 'cannot be effected, except the price paid to God for the sin of man be something greater than all the universe besides God' (Part II, ch. 6). And, to add to the difficulty, since it is humanity that has offended God, it must be humanity that makes the restitution. Thus, since the needed satisfaction is one which 'none but God can make and none but man ought to make, it is necessary for the God-man to make it' (Part II, ch. 6). The God-man can give something that was not owing to God, namely his own life: 'For God will not demand this of him as a debt; for, as no sin will be found, he ought not to die' (Part II, ch. 11). Accordingly, Christ's voluntary death on the cross constituted a full satisfaction for the sins of the world. However, in our own more democratic age it is virtually impossible to share Anselm's medieval sense of wrongdoing as a slight upon God's honour which requires a satisfaction to assuage that divine honour and dignity. The entire conception, presupposing as it does a long-since vanished world, now makes no sense to us; and we should, in my view, cease altogether to use it in our theologies and liturgies.

Another emphasis was introduced by the Reformers of the sixteenth century. They made the originally Pauline idea of justification central, understanding it in a legal sense, defined by Melanchthon as follows: 'To justify, in accordance with forensic usage, here signifies to acquit the accused and to pronounce him righteous, but on account of the righteousness of another, namely of Christ, which righteousness of another is communicated to us by faith.'[12] This legal concept of justification, and hence salvation, as being counted innocent in the eyes of God, emerged from the background of an understanding of law that had changed since

Anselm's time. Previously, in the medieval world, law was an expression of the will of the ruler, and transgression was an act of personal disobedience and dishonour for which either punishment or satisfaction was required. But the concept of an objective justice, standing over ruled and ruler alike, had been developing in Europe since the Renaissance. Law was now thought to have its own eternal validity, requiring a punishment for wrongdoing which could not be set aside even by the ruler. It was this principle that the Reformers applied and extended in their doctrine that Christ took our place in bearing the inexorable divine penalty for human sin.

All of us who have been through a fundamentalist phase in our Christian life are familiar with the explanation, derived from the Reformers, that God, being just as well as loving, could not simply forgive even the truly penitent sinner, but in his mercy sent his Son to suffer the inevitable punishment in our stead. In the words of the hymn 'There is a green hill far away':

> He died that we might be forgiven,
> He died to make us good,
> That we might go at last to heaven,
> Saved by his precious blood.
>
> There was no other good enough
> To pay the price of sin;
> He only could unlock the gate
> Of heaven and let us in.

Calvin points out that in order to prompt our imaginations to gratitude the scriptures tell the justified sinner that

> he was estranged from God through sin, is an heir of wrath, subject to the curse of eternal death, excluded from all hope of salvation, beyond every blessing of God, the slave of Satan, captive under the yoke of sin; destined finally for a dreadful destruction; and that at this point Christ interceded as his advocate, took upon himself and suffered the punishment that, from God's righteous judgment, threatened all sinners; that he purges with his blood those evils which had rendered sinners hateful to God; that by this expiation he makes satisfaction and sacrifice duly to God the Father; that as intercessor he appeased God's wrath; that on this foundation rests the peace of God with men; that by this bond his benevolence is maintained toward them.[13]

It is hardly necessary today to criticize this penal-substitutionary conception, so totally implausible has it become to most of us. The idea that guilt can be removed from a wrongdoer by someone else being punished instead is morally grotesque. And if we put it in what might at first sight seem a more favourable light by suggesting that God punished himself, in the person of God the Son, in order to be able justly to forgive human sinners, we are still dealing with the religious absurdity of a moral law which God can and must satisfy by punishing the innocent in place of the guilty. As Anselm pointed out long ago, through the mouth of his interlocutor in *Cur Deus Homo?*, 'it is a strange thing if God so delights in, or requires, the blood of the innocent, that he neither chooses, nor is able, to spare the guilty without the sacrifice of the innocent' (Part I, ch. 10).

However, Richard Swinburne has made an impressive attempt, in his *Responsibility and Atonement*,[14] to retrieve a transactional conception. His understanding of salvation can be summarized as follows:

1 Guilt in relation to God is the great barrier to salvation, that is, to receiving God's gift of eternal life. (This is assumed throughout Swinburne's discussion.)

2 In the case of wrong done by one human being to another, reconciliation requires four things: repentance, apology, whatever reparation (undoing of the harm done) is possible, and penance, that is, some additional act – such as the giving of a costly gift – which is not part of the reparation but is an expression of the reality of one's regret and sorrow at having done the wrong (ch. 5).

3 God is a personal being – though absolutely unique in nature – with whom we exist in the same kind of moral relationship as to our fellow human beings, and the same general conditions for reconciliation apply. (This is assumed throughout Part II, though not explicitly stated.)

4 All wrongdoing to fellow humans is also wrongdoing done to God. For 'Man's dependence on God is so total that he owes it to him to live a good life. Hence when a man fails in any objective or subjective duty of his fellows, he also fails in his duty towards God, his creator' (p. 124).

5 We can repent and apologize to God for our sins, but we cannot on our own offer adequate atonement, that is, reparation and penance. For 'Since what needs atonement to God is human sin, men living second-rate lives when they have been given such great opportunities by their creator, appropriate reparation and penance would be made by a perfect human life' (p. 157).

6 That 'perfect human life' is provided by Christ, who lived without sin and voluntarily endured a death which he openly intended as a sacrifice that we, accepting it from him, can offer to God as atonement for our sins, both individual and corporate. Christ's death is thus 'an offering made available to us men to offer as our reparation and penance'. 'There is no need', Swinburne adds, 'to suppose that life and death [of Christ's] to be the equivalent of what men owe to God (or that plus appropriate penance), however that could be measured. It is simply a costly penance and reparation sufficient for a merciful God to let men off the rest' (p. 154).

7 To be sanctified and thus finally saved is only possible to those who (as well as repenting and apologizing) participate in the Christian worship of God and plead the atoning death of Christ, thereby throwing off their guilt. To be saved we must thus be joined – either in this life or hereafter – to the Christian Church, which is the Body of Christ (p. 173).

I think it must be granted that all this is possible; and indeed those of us who were once fundamentalist Christians, 'washed in the blood of the Lamb', are likely to feel a certain emotional tug towards this set of ideas. The question is not however whether such a schema is logically possible, but whether it is religiously plausible; and to many of us today it is likely to seem highly implausible, even though also with elements of truth within it. I shall comment from this point of view on the seven points listed above.

1   As I pointed out earlier, that the idea of salvation revolved around the issues of guilt and atonement is a central theme of the Latin theological tradition, launched above all by St Augustine. The Greek tradition, on the other hand, stemming from the early Hellenistic Fathers of the Church and preserved within Eastern Orthodoxy, thinks of salvation as deification or (more precisely) transformation. Forgiveness is, of course, an element within this, but does not have the central place that the Latin tradition, followed by Swinburne at this point, gives to it. Swinburne prefers the Greek to the Latin development on a number of issues; but he does not seem to have considered the radical alternative which the Eastern theological trajectory offers. If one sees salvation/liberation as the transformation of human existence from self-centredness to a new orientation centred in the ultimate divine Reality, the transaction theories of salvation then appear as implausible answers to a mistaken question.

2   Swinburne's analysis of guilt and reconciliation between human beings is one of the elements of truth, as it will seem to more liberal Christians, within his total theory.

3   That God is another person, with unique attributes but subject to the same moral requirements as ourselves, and thus with obligations and duties and possibilities of supererogatory deeds; that God's probable procedures can be predicted by means of a human analogy; and that the proper human analogy leads to the belief that God's saving work is confined in its fullness to the Christian strand of history – strikes me as anthropomorphic, parochial and unimaginative to a degree that renders it massively implausible. But I shall say more under point number 5 about Swinburne's transfer of the conditions for reconciliation with a fellow human being to reconciliation with God.

4   That our relationship to fellow human beings involves our relationship to God, so that in all that we do we are also ultimately having to do with God, is from a more liberal point of view another element of truth within Swinburne's theory.

5   When we do wrong the kind of reparation required is that we do what we can to nullify or reverse the consequences of our action. Thus when we contribute – as we do almost all the time – to the common evils of the world, we can do something to counter this by contributing to the common good of the world. When we wrong an individual we can usually do something to recompense the person wronged. And, as Swinburne points out, in such a case it is also appropriate to do something extra, which he calls penance, by offering some additional service or gift to express the reality of our regret and sorrow at having wronged the other person. But the question that has to be asked is whether this fourfold schema – repentance, apology, reparation and penance – can be carried over unchanged into our relationship with God. Swinburne's fundamental error, in my view, is in assuming that it can. Repentance, and apology as an expression of repentance, still apply; the sinner should truly and deeply repent and ask God's forgiveness. But is there also scope, specifically in relation to God, for reparation and the extra that Swinburne calls penance? I suggest that when we have offered reparation-plus-penance to the human beings whom we have injured, there is no further reparation-plus-penance to be made solely for God's benefit. In doing all we can to repair matters with our wronged neighbour we are doing what genuine repentance requires. For God cannot be

benefited, and thus recompensed and atoned to, by any human acts in addition to those that benefit God's creation. In relation to God the truly penitent person, genuinely resolving to do better in the future, can only accept forgiveness as a free gift of grace, undeserved and unearned. It may well be Jesus' life and teaching that prompt someone to do this. But it is not, in my view, appropriate to express that fact by depicting his death as an atoning sacrifice that benefits God and so enables God to forgive humanity.

Swinburne emphasizes that 'One man can help another to make the necessary atonement – can persuade him to repent, help him to formulate the words of apology, and give him the means by which to make reparation and penance' (p. 149). True; and likewise the divine Spirit may prompt us to a true repentance which wants to make reparation to the human individual or community that we have wronged, and to offer any additional service or gift that may be appropriate. But what the Spirit will thus prompt us to do is some act in relation to those human neighbours. It is this that satisfies the principle, which Swinburne rightly stresses, that to take a wrongdoer and his or her wrongdoing seriously entails the need for whatever restitution, and whatever additional gift or service, is appropriate. But the idea that something further, corresponding to this reparation-plus-penance towards our human neighbour, is required by God for himself seems to me groundless. It rests upon a category mistake in which God is treated as another individual within the same moral community as ourselves. For a moral relationship with another person presupposes the possibility of actions that can benefit or injure that other person; but we cannot benefit or injure our Creator over and above our actions in benefiting and injuring our fellow creatures.

Further, even if, despite this, a benefit solely to God were possible and required, Swinburne's unargued assumption that a perfect human life would constitute it is, surely, illogical. A perfect life, fulfilling every 'objective and subjective duty', is already, according to Swinburne, owed by all of us to God, and therefore could not constitute a reparation-plus-penance for not having lived a perfect life in the past. And yet again, even if *per impossibile* it could, how would one single perfect human life, namely that of Jesus, count as all human beings having led perfect lives? Swinburne's answer at this point is that God was free to accept whatever God wished as an atonement for human sin. 'God could', he says, 'have chosen to accept one supererogatory act of an ordinary man as adequate for the sins of the world. Or he could have chosen to accept some angel's act for this purpose' (p. 160). This is a fatal admission, rendering it truly extraordinary that God should require the agonizing death of Jesus. For on Swinburne's view there was no necessity for the cross, such as had been provided in their own way by the satisfaction and penal-substitutionary theories. Swinburne is abandoning the idea of a moral law that could only be satisfied by Jesus' death. For it was, according to him, entirely within God's free choice to establish the conditions for human salvation. But in that case God's insistence on the blood, sweat, pain and anguish involved in the crucifixion of his innocent Son now seems to cast doubt – to say the least – on the moral character of the deity.

6   Swinburne says several times that Jesus openly intended his death as 'an offering to God to make expiation in some way for the sins of men' (p. 122). There is, in fact, no consensus among New Testament scholars as to how Jesus understood his own death. To what extent did he think of it as having religious significance? There is a range of possibilities. A (theologically) minimalist view is expressed by E. P. Sanders. He lists it as 'conceivable'[15] or even 'possible'[16] (in distinction from 'probable', 'highly probable' or 'virtually certain'), that Jesus 'may have given his own death a martyrological significance'.[17] Acknowledging, indeed emphasizing, the historical uncertainties, he notes that

> the idea that a martyr's death is beneficial for others and that his cause will be vindicated is attested in Judaism . . . It is not necessary to assume that Jesus indicated to his followers that they should think in this way. Once he died, it probably seemed entirely natural to attribute benefit to his death and look for vindication.[18]

At the other end of the scale is the older view of Joachim Jeremias, developed in his influential treatment of the Last Supper. He recalls that a lamb was killed at the original Passover and its blood smeared, at Jahweh's command, on the Israelites' doors:

> As a reward for the Israelites' obedience to the commandment to spread blood on their doors, God manifested himself and spared them, 'passing over' their houses. For the sake of the passover blood God revoked the death sentence against Israel; he said: 'I will see the blood of the passover and make atonement for you'. In the same way the people of God of the End time will be redeemed by the merits of the passover blood. Jesus describes his death as this eschatological passover sacrifice: his vicarious death brings into operation the final deliverance, the new covenant of God.[19]

And Jeremias concludes,

> This is therefore what Jesus said at the Last Supper about the mean-
> ing of his death: his death is the vicarious death of the suffering ser-
> vant, which atones for the sins of the 'many', the peoples of the world,
> which ushers in the beginning of the final salvation and which effects
> the new covenant with God.[20]

On Jeremias' interpretation we have to suppose that Jesus, in E. P.
Sanders' words, 'conceived in advance the doctrine of atonement',[21] a
supposition which Sanders regards as historically highly improbable.

> Aspects of Jeremias' view, for example that Jesus identified himself
> with the Suffering Servant of Isaiah, have been disproved, but there
> are general objections to the whole line of thought that has Jesus
> intending to die for others, rather than just accepting his death and
> trusting that God would redeem the situation and vindicate him.[22]

However, let us nevertheless, for the sake of argument, suppose that
Jesus did understand his coming death as a sacrifice to God, analogous
to the original Passover sacrifice, and that he thought of this as required
to inaugurate God's coming kingdom. Such a self-understanding could
only occur within the context of Jesus' apocalyptic expectation, which
was itself a variation on contemporary Jewish restoration eschatology.
But Jesus' expectation, confidently taken up by the early Church, was
not fulfilled, and had faded out of the Christian consciousness before the
end of the first century. The identification of Jesus as the eschatological
prophet inaugurating God's kingdom went with it, being progressively
superseded by his exaltation to a divine status. This in turn made possible the various atonement theories which presuppose his divinity, eventually seeing the cross as (in the words of the Anglican liturgy) 'a full,
perfect, and sufficient sacrifice, oblation, and satisfaction, for the sins of
the whole world'.

However, even conservative New Testament scholarship today does
not suggest that Jesus thought of himself as God, or God the Son, second
person of a divine Trinity, incarnate; and so we cannot reasonably
suppose that he thought of his death in any way that presupposes that.
It is, therefore, much more believable, as a maximal possibility, that
Jesus saw himself as the final prophet precipitating the coming of God's
rule on earth than that he saw himself in anything like the terms later
developed by the Church's subsequent atonement theories.

It is, incidentally, noteworthy that Swinburne departs from the traditional view that the value of Jesus' death was equal to, or exceeded, the evil of human sin, so as to be able to balance it. Swinburne says that 'It is simply a costly penance and reparation sufficient for a merciful God to let men off the rest.'[23] But if a merciful God can properly 'let men off the rest' without a full punishment having been inflicted or full satisfaction exacted, why (as I asked above) may not God freely forgive sinners who come in genuine penitence and a radically changed mind? The traditional atonement theories explained *why* God could not freely forgive penitent sinners. But what was intelligible – whether or not acceptable – on those theories becomes unintelligible, and doubly morally questionable, on Swinburne's view.

7   Swinburne also modifies the traditional exclusivist doctrine that salvation is confined to Christians, so that *extra ecclesiam nulla salus*, by adding that non-Christians may have an opportunity to be converted beyond this life. This epicycle of theory, although departing from established teaching about the finality of death, is the only refuge left for one who is in general a doctrinal fundamentalist but who does not wish to have to defend a manifestly morally repugnant position; and it is a position that other theologians have also taken.

I thus do not find in the least attractive or convincing this attempt to rehabilitate the conception of salvation as being brought about by Jesus' death as an atonement to God for human sin.

The basic fault, as I see it, of the traditional understandings of salvation within the Western development of Christianity is that they have no room for divine forgiveness! For a forgiveness that has to be bought by the bearing of a just punishment, or the giving of an adequate satisfaction, or the offering of a sufficient sacrifice, is not forgiveness at all but merely an acknowledgement that the debt has been paid in full. But in the recorded teaching of Jesus there is, in contrast, genuine divine forgiveness for those who are truly penitent and deeply aware of their own utter unworthiness. In the Lord's Prayer we are taught to address God directly as our heavenly Father and to ask for forgiveness for our sins, expecting to receive this, the only condition being that we in turn forgive one another. There is no suggestion of the need for a mediator through whom to approach God or of an atoning death to enable God to forgive. Again, in the Lukan parable of the prodigal son, the father, when he sees his penitent son returning home, does not say, 'Because I am a just as well as a loving father, I cannot forgive him until someone has been duly punished for his sins', but rather he was filled with compassion; he ran and put his arms around him and kissed him. Then the son said to him, 'Father, I have sinned against heaven and before you; I am no longer worthy to be called your son.' But the father said to his slaves, 'Quickly, bring out a robe – the best one – and put it on him; put a ring on his finger and sandals on his feet. And get the fatted calf and kill it, and let us eat and celebrate; for this son of mine was dead and is alive again; he was lost and is found!' (Luke 15.20–4)

And again, in the Lukan parable of the Pharisee and the publican, the latter 'standing far off, would not even look up to heaven, but was beating his breast and saying, "God, be merciful to me, a sinner!" I tell you, this man went down to his home justified' (Luke 18.13–14).

And yet again, there is the insistence that Jesus came to bring sinners to a penitent acceptance of God's mercy: 'Go and learn what this means, "I desire mercy, not sacrifice." For I have come to call not the righteous but sinners' (Matt. 9.13).

This was fully in accord with contemporary Judaic understanding. E. P. Sanders, in his authoritative work on Jesus' Jewish background, says that 'The forgiveness of repentant sinners is a major motif in virtually all the Jewish material which is still available from the period';[24] and it continues today in this prayer from the service on the Day of Atonement:

O do thou, in thy abounding compassion, have mercy upon us, for thou delightest not in the destruction of the world . . . And it is said, Let the wicked forsake his ways, and the man of iniquity his thoughts; and let him return unto the Lord, and he will have mercy upon him; and to our God for he will abundantly pardon. But thou art a God ready to forgive, gracious and merciful, slow to anger, plenteous in loving kindness, and abounding in goodness; thou delightest in the repentance of the wicked and hast no pleasure in their death . . . turn ye, turn ye from your evil ways; for why will ye die, O house of Israel? And it is said, Have I at all any pleasure in the death of the wicked, saith the Lord God, and not rather that he should return from his way, and live?

For Judaism sees human nature as basically good and yet also with an evil inclination that has continually to be resisted. However, God is aware of our finitude and weakness, and is always ready to forgive the truly penitent. In Islam there is an essentially similar view. God is always spoken of in the Qur'an as *Allah rahman rahim*, God the gracious and merciful. God knows our weakness and forgives those who, in the self-surrender of faith, bow before the compassionate Lord of the universe. Again, in the most widely influential of the Hindu scriptures, the *Bhagavad Gita*, we read,

> Please, God, be patient with me as a father with his son, a friend with his friend, a lover with his beloved.[25]

This sense of divine mercy is indeed found throughout the world's monotheistic faiths, with the Latin Christian belief in the need for an atoning death standing out as the exception. Indeed within modern Protestant thought, outside the continuing fundamentalist stream, there has been a general acceptance of the idea of a free divine forgiveness for those who truly repent. In an attempt to reconcile this with the traditional language about Jesus' death as the instrument of our salvation, various 'moral influence' theories have been proposed in the modern period. Their essence is admirably expressed in the old preachers' story about the tribal chief who urges his people to abandon cannibalism. When his urgings are ineffective he tells them that if they must kill someone, they should go to a certain clearing the next day at dawn and kill the man they find there wrapped in a red blanket. They do so, and on opening the blanket find that they have killed their own beloved chieftain; and they are so struck with remorse that they are at last motivated to give up their cannibalism. Likewise, it is suggested, remorse at having crucified the Son of God can lead to repentance and hence God's forgiveness. Thus the liberal theologian Auguste Sabatier wrote that Jesus' passion and death 'was the most powerful call to repentance that humanity has ever heard, and also the most operative and fruitful in marvelous results. The cross is the expiation of sins only because it is the cause of the repentance to which remission is promised.'[26]

This is no longer a transactional conception of atonement, and indeed is no longer a conception of atonement, in the sense of expiation, at all. It is rather a suggestion about how Jesus' death may have helped to make salvation possible. The limitation of this suggestion is that remorse at having (collectively) killed God the Son can only be felt by that minority of human beings who believe that Jesus of Nazareth was indeed the second person of a divine Trinity. The notion, which the older satisfaction and penal-substitutionary theories made possible, of an atonement offered on behalf of all humanity, is here lost. The moral influence conception of atonement is in fact one of those theological epicycles by which it is sought to abandon an untenable traditional idea – in this case the transaction conception of salvation – while at the same time retaining the traditional language.

We can now move from a critique of the Western/Latin understanding of salvation as hinging upon sin and guilt, and as requiring the atoning sacrifice of Christ, to build upon the work of the Hellenistic Fathers, treating this, however, not as a fully developed theological option but as a movement of thought which can be continued today.

For Christianity is richer and more varied than most Christians, immersed within their own particular strand of it, have commonly been aware. Thus those of us formed by Western Christianity or its missionary extensions are often ignorant of the rather different Eastern development of Christian thought. The Orthodox churches themselves, which are guardians of this tradition, have remained more or less moribund, both theologically and ecclesiastically, for many centuries; and I am not advocating acceptance of their total theological package. But buried in their history there is the groundwork of a profound and attractive alternative to the medieval theology of the Roman church as well as that of the sixteenth-century Reformers and their successors. The difference is between salvation as hinging upon an atoning transaction that enables God to forgive and accept the fallen human race, and salvation as the gradual transformation of human beings, who are already in the 'image' of God, into what the Hellenistic Fathers, on the basis of Genesis 1.26, called the 'likeness' of God. Thus in the eighth century, John of Damascus wrote: 'The expression "according to the image" indicates rationality and freedom, whilst the expression "according to the likeness" indicates assimilation to God through virtue.'[27] This 'assimilation to God' was also frequently called *theosis* (deification). In the words of the seventh-century Byzantine theologian Maximus the Confessor, 'A man who becomes obedient to God in all things hears God saying "I said: you are gods" (John 10.34); he then is God and is called "God" not by nature or by relation but by [divine] decree and grace.'[28] Accordingly, to quote a contemporary Orthodox writer, 'The Christian faith . . . is understood to lead to the transfiguration and "deification" of the entire man; and . . . this "deification" is indeed accessible, as a living experience, even now, and not merely in a future kingdom.'[29] It is this actual human transformation, or 'deification', that constitutes salvation. Thus while on the Latin view to be saved is to be justified, that is, relieved of guilt, by Christ's sacrificial death, on the Orthodox view it is to be in process of salvation by responding to the presence of the divine Spirit and thus undergoing a gradual transformation from natural self-centredness to a radically new centring within the divine life. It should be noted that this Eastern understanding largely coincides with the modern 'liberal' Western approach initiated in the nineteenth century by Friedrich Schleiermacher, who viewed the saving influence of Christ in the context of God's total creative work, so that Christ's 'every activity may be regarded as a continuation of that person-forming divine influence upon human nature'.[30]

In Orthodox thought the deification theme is embedded in a comprehensive theology in which the ideas of incarnation and Trinity are central elements and in which the resurrected Christ plays a vital role in the process of transformation. That role was, however, only described in broad metaphorical terms. Thus Athanasius said that humans 'could not become sons, being by nature creatures, otherwise than by receiving the Spirit of the natural and true Son. Wherefore, that this might be, "The Word became flesh" that He might make man capable of Godhead,'[31] and again, 'He was made man that we might be made God.'[32] But the way in which God becoming human enables humans to become divine was not spelled out. Indeed, it perhaps cannot be intelligibly spelled out other than in terms of the experience, known within all religious traditions, of being influenced and changed by the life and words of a great exemplar. There is perhaps a continuity here with what Adolf Deissmann called St Paul's 'mysticism',[33] with humans undergoing a transformation (*metamorphosis*) in Christ; for we 'are being transformed into [Christ's] image from one degree of glory to another' (2 Cor. 3.18). We are to be transformed from the state of slavery into the state of sonship (Rom. 8.15–17); or again, conformed (*symmorphosis*) to the image of Christ (8.29). 'Do not be conformed to this world,' Paul urges the Christians in Rome, 'but be transformed by the renewing of your minds' (12.2). And, indeed, we may say that to be a Christian is to be one in whose life Jesus is the major, the largest single, influence (often among a variety of influences) for salvific transformation.

Jesus' death has indeed played no small part in this influence. Although the meaning of that death was pictured during most of the first Christian millennium in the crude ransom imagery, and during most of the second millennium in terms of the morally objectionable satisfaction and penal-substitution theories, the cross has continued throughout as the central Christian symbol because it stirs deeper and more complex emotions than are captured by any of these official doctrines. For many people it is a self-evident intuition that an authentic religious leader is willing, if necessary, to be martyred by those who fail to recognize or accept the challenging truths which he or she embodies. It is indeed because true prophets and gurus embody, or live out, or incarnate, their teaching that to reject the message is to reject the messenger; and the most emphatic form of rejection is by inflicting death. To illustrate this from recent history, in the moral and political conflicts of India and the United States in the twentieth century there was a certain tragic appropriateness in the fact that Mahatma Gandhi and Martin Luther King, teaching the universal requirements of love and justice, were assassinated by fanatics motivated by religious and racial prejudice. On the same principle there was a tragic appropriateness in the death of Jesus. He taught the way of life of God's kingdom, and the imminent coming of that kingdom on earth. This was to the ruling Roman power a potential incitement to rise up against it in the name of God, as was to happen in 66–70 CE and again in 135. He also prophesied the destruction of the Jerusalem temple, thus deeply antagonizing its priestly guardians, who collaborated in his arrest and trial. But these historical factors were soon submerged in the Christian consciousness by a religious understanding of the crucifixion. Jesus' acceptance of his death as having some positive meaning inevitably evoked, in the thought-world of his time, the universal language of sacrifice. In the Judaism of Jesus' period, a sacrifice made as a sin-offering to God involved the shedding of blood as a giving of the life essence. However, as a cumulative result of the teaching of Jesus, as well as of Hosea and Amos before him and many others after him, can we not now see that the sacrifice of animal or human blood pointed, in a crude and inadequate way, to the much deeper sacrifice of the ego point of view, so becoming a channel of divine grace on earth? The real meaning of Jesus' death was not that his blood was shed – indeed crucifixion did not involve much bloodshed – but that he gave himself utterly to God in faith and trust. His cross was thus a powerful manifestation and continuing symbol of the divine kingdom in this present world, as a way of life in which one turns the other cheek, forgives one's enemies 'unto seventy times seven', trusts God even in the darkness of pain, horror and tragedy, and is continually raised again to the new life of faith.

Yet even this does not exhaust the felt impact of Jesus' death. For the voluntary death of a holy person has a moral power that reverberates beyond any words that we frame to express it. Even on a lower level, when someone knowingly gives his or her life for the sake of another – say, in a rescue from fire or avalanche or bomb or an oncoming train or car, or in some other way – something has happened that is awe-inspiring and, in an indefinable way, enriching and enhancing to the human community. And so it was, in a much greater way, with the death of Jesus. This is no doubt why the mythological pictures of a ransom paid to the devil, or of a sacrifice to appease the divine honour or justice, were able to last so long; for since we cannot fully articulate the impression made upon us by the crucifixion of one who was so close to God, no ecclesiastical language about it has been ruled out as too strange or extravagant.

Nevertheless, we have to insist that these ecclesiastical theories are all misleading. It is misleading to think that there is a devil with legitimate rights over against God. It is misleading to think of the heavenly Father on the model of a feudal lord or a stern cosmic moralist. And it is misleading to see an acceptance of the Christian mythology of the cross as the only way to salvation for all human beings. Let the voluntary sacrifice of a holy life continue to challenge and inspire us in a way that transcends words. But let us not reduce its meaning to any culture-bound theological theory.

To summarize and conclude: Jesus' death was of a piece with his life, expressing a total integrity in his self-giving to God; and his cross continues to inspire and challenge us on a level which in no way depends upon atonement theories developed by the Church. Those theories have no doubt helped people in the past to rationalize the immense impact upon them of the cross of Christ, and they did so in ways that cohered with the plausibility structures of their time. But our own intellectual world is so different, both within the Church and outside it, that those traditional atonement theories no longer perform any useful function.

Notes

1 *Encyclopaedia Britannica*, 1989, vol. 16, p. 285.

2 *Encyclopaedia Britannica*, vol. 16, p. 285.

3 Origen, *In Matt.*, xvi.8, quoted by L. W. Grensted, *A Short History of the Doctrine of the Atonement*, Manchester: Manchester University Press, 1962, p. 38.

4 Gregory of Nyssa, The Great Catechism, chapter 24, in *Nicene and Post-Nicene Fathers*, Series II, vol. 5, p. 494. Cf. Rufinus, *Comm. in Symb. Ap.*, 16.

5 Augustine, Sermon 130, quoted by Grensted, *A Short History*, p. 44.

6 Anselm, *Cur Deus Homo*, Part I, chapter 7.

7 Grensted, *A Short History*, p. 33. What Gustav Aulen called the 'classic' theory of atonement, according to which Christ was victor over the devil, seems to me to be a variation on the ransom model rather than an alternative theory. 'Its central theme', says Aulen, 'is the idea of the Atonement as a Divine conflict and victory; Christ – Christus Victor – fights against and triumphs over the evil powers of the world, the "tyrants" under which mankind is in bondage and suffering' (*Christus Victor*, trans. A. G. Herbert, London: SPCK, 1953, p. 20.

8 *Denzinger*, 788f.

9 Westminster Confession, ch. 6.

10 W. K. Clifford, *Lectures and Essays*, vol. 1, London: Macmillan, 1901, p. 221.

11 Anselm, *Cur Deus Homo?*, chapter 11, trans. J. G. Vose, in S. N. Deane, *St. Anselm: Basic Writings*, Lasalle, IL: Open Court, 1962, p. 202.

12 Melanchthon, *Apol. Conf. Aug.*, p. 125, quoted by Grensted, *A Short History*, p. 193.

13 Calvin, *Institutes of the Christian Religion*, Book II, chapter 16, para. 2, trans. Ford Lewis Battles, Library of Christian Classics, 20, London: SCM Press; Philadelphia: Westminster Press, 1961, p. 505.

14 Richard Swinburne, *Responsibility and Atonement*, Oxford: Clarendon Press, 1989.

15 E. P. Sanders, *Jesus and Judaism*, London: SCM Press, 1985, p. 326.

16 Sanders, *Jesus and Judaism*, p. 332.

17 Sanders, *Jesus and Judaism*, p. 326.

18 Sanders, *Jesus and Judaism*, pp. 324–5.

19 Joachim Jeremias, *The Eucharistic Words of Jesus*, 1965; trans. Norman Perrin, London: SCM Press, 1966, p. 226.

20 Jeremias, *Eucharistic Words*, p. 231.

21 Sanders, *Jesus and Judaism*, p. 332.

22 Sanders, *Jesus and Judaism*, p. 332.

23 Swinburne, *Responsibility and Atonement*, p. 154.

24 Sanders, *Jesus and Judaism*, p. 18.

25 *Bhagavad Gita*, trans. Kees Bolle, Berkeley: University of California Press, 1979, p. 141.

26 Auguste Sabatier, *The Doctrine of the Atonement*, 1901; trans. Victor Leuliette, London: Williams & Norgate; New York: G. P. Putnam's Sons, 1904, p. 127.

27 John of Damascus, *On the Orthodox Faith*, II.12.

28 Maximus the Confessor, *Ambigua*, cited by John Meyendorff, *Byzantine Theology*, New York: Fordham University Press, 1987, p. 164.

29 Meyendorff, *Byzantine Theology*, p. 125.

30 Friedrich Schleiermacher, *The Christian Faith*, para. 100, trans. H. R. Mackintosh and J. S. Stewart, Edinburgh: T. & T. Clark, 1956, p. 427.

31 Athanasius, *Discourses Against the Arians*, Discourse II, ch. 21, para. 59, trans. in *Nicene and Post-Nicene Fathers*, Series II, vol. 4, p. 380.

32 Athanasius, *On the Incarnation of the Word of God*, para. 54, in *Nicene and Post-Nicene Fathers*, Series II, vol. 4, p. 65.

33 Adolf Deissmann, *The Religion of Jesus and the Faith of Paul*, trans. William E. Wilson, 2nd edn, London: Hodder & Stoughton, 1926, pp. 193f.

10

Christianity and Islam

(A lecture delivered to the Institute for Interreligious Dialogue
in Tehran in 2005)

I should like to say first how pleased I am to be here in Tehran and to
have the opportunity to meet Muslim scholars and to try to contribute
something to the ongoing dialogue between our two faiths.

First let me indicate my own position within Christianity, which is as
internally varied as is the Islamic world. I am an ordained minister of the
United Reformed Church, which is a small part of the section of
Christianity that split away from the Roman Catholic church in the
sixteenth century, and within this I belong to the reforming end of the
spectrum of positions. It is from this point of view that I am speaking. I
am not however an official representative of that church, but am here
entirely in my own personal capacity.

Islam and Christianity are both based on revelation, both religions of
the Book, meaning the holy Qur'an, revealed through the Prophet
Muhammad (peace be upon him), and the holy Bible, revealed through
a number of different writers – which according to one Islamic view are
both, together with other holy scriptures, expressions of the heavenly
Hidden Book or Preserved Book referred to several times in the Qur'an.

The traditional Muslim belief, as I understand it, is that the Qur'an
was revealed to the Prophet over a period of some twenty years through
the angel Gabriel; and that the Torah and the New Testament are likewise from God but that the texts have become corrupted at the various
points at which they differ from the Qur'an. In the case of the New
Testament a prominent example of the distortion claim is the biblical
account of Jesus' death on the cross.

From a modern Christian point of view the situation is more complex
than this. First, it is often said by Christian theologians that our revelation is contained, not in a book, but in the person of Jesus (peace be
upon him). However, we only know about Jesus through the New
Testament, particularly the four Gospels. For many centuries, until
within about the last 150 years, it was almost universally assumed by

Christians that these are contemporary and historically reliable accounts of Jesus' life and teachings. But the modern historical study of the New Testament has led to the generally agreed conclusion that the earliest Gospel, that of Mark, was written around 70 CE, about forty years after the time of Jesus; that Matthew and Luke were written in the 80s, using Mark as their main source together with a possible, but disputed, second common source called Q, and other separate sources of their own; and that the Gospel of John was written around the end of the century, some sixty or seventy years after Jesus' time. None of them was written by an eyewitness to Jesus' life, but they relay stories and sayings handed down, and inevitably elaborated in the retelling, within the early Christian community, the different writers moulding their material in distinctively different ways according to their own interests and points of view. The result is that there is today endlessly inconclusive discussion and disagreement about whether this or that saying and action attributed to Jesus in the Gospels is or is not historically authentic.

So from the point of view of modern Christian scholarship the New Testament does indeed contain doubtful sayings attributed to Jesus and doubtful stories about him, not however because the original text was infallible and later became corrupted, but because of the nature of the Gospels as having been written two or three generations after the event by different writers over a period of about thirty years, and in an age when the modern concept of biographical accuracy was unknown. This is a result of the historical study of the Gospels, and I suppose the equivalent use in Islam of an historical method to discriminate between more and less reliable material is in the careful sorting out of the hadiths. But the basic difference between Islam and Christianity in this area is that, while both the Bible and the Qur'an are sacred scriptures, within Christianity there is space for discussion and variety of opinion as to the accuracy of the narrative and teachings, whereas within Islam there is no uncertainty about the sayings and narratives, but space for discussion and variety of opinion in their interpretation.

However, for many centuries, as I said, Christians generally assumed that, as the famous evangelical preacher Billy Graham once put it, 'The Bible is a book written by God through sixty secretaries.' And there is still a numerous and strong body of Christians who adhere to that view, mainly in Africa and in the southern part of the United States of America. But among Christian scholars there has come to be an increasing recognition of the human contribution to the formation of the scriptures. The four Gospels, and also the letters of Paul and the other New

Testament documents, reflect the cultural and political situations within which they were written, the religious ideas and practices of the Judaism of the time, the presupposed worldview of first-century CE Mediterranean culture, and the individual concerns of the writers and of their own local Christian communities. This, I would suggest, is to be expected. For any divine revelation to humanity, if it is to be intelligible to us human beings, must come through human minds and must be expressed in a human language and in terms of the conceptual world embodied in that language, all of which are the products of a particular culture in a particular part of the earth at a particular point in human history. This does not mean that the process is not genuinely revelatory, but that revelation is necessarily mediated through human beings in all their specific historical particularity.

Further, in the Bible there are two very different and incompatible conceptions of God and of God's will for humanity. The Torah tells us that when the Israelites came out of Egypt to occupy the land of Canaan, and were fighting the existing tribe of Amorites, 'the Lord threw down huge stones from heaven on them . . . there were more who died because of the hailstones than the Israelites killed with the sword' (Josh. 10.11), and then that God made the sun stand still for a whole day so they could have more time to slay the Amorites (10.15); and later, when they were fighting the tribe of Amalek, God commanded the Israelites, 'Now go and attack Amalek, and utterly destroy all that they have; do not spare them, but kill both man and woman, child and infant, ox and sheep, camel and donkey' (1 Sam. 15.3). This is a picture of a violent tribal warrior god. But there are other, later books of the Hebrew scriptures in which a quite different understanding of God is expressed, as the universal Lord who is gracious and merciful to all and not only to the Israelites. In the words of one of the psalms, 'as the heavens are high above the earth, so great is his steadfast love towards those who fear him; as far as the east is from the west, so far he removes our transgressions from us' (Ps. 103.11–12).

In line with this latter Jewish conception of God, in the teaching of Jesus God is a God of love and mercy, and we should emulate these virtues on earth. He taught,

> You have heard that it was said, 'You shall love your neighbour and hate your enemy.' But I say to you, Love your enemies and pray for those who persecute you, so that you may be children of your Father in heaven; for he makes his sun rise on the evil and on the good, and sends rain on the righteous and on the unrighteous' (Matt. 5.43–5).

Again, later in the New Testament we read, 'God is love . . . those who do not love a brother or sister whom they have seen, cannot love God whom they have not seen' (1 John 4.16, 20). The result of this wide variety within the Bible is that in using it we all inevitably select, either consciously or unconsciously. Some Jews and some Christians appeal to the violent and vengeful conception, and others, the greatest number today, to the very different conception of God as Love.

Now I would suggest that the general principle of human mediation must apply to the formation of the Qur'an. This is in a particular human language, Arabic; it has as its religious background the Prophet's decisive break with the existing Arabian polytheism; it reflects the life-story of the Prophet himself, the history of the new Muslim community in Mecca, the Hijra, the community's battles against those who were trying to destroy the new faith, their later return in triumph to Mecca, the social life of the new community, and all this against the background of the basic cultural ethos of Arabia at that time.

There is in one respect, however, a significant difference between the Qur'an and the Christian Gospels. In the Arabia into which the Prophet was born the whole commercial and political structure of Mecca was bound up with the existing polytheism. The ruling merchant aristocracy depended upon their control of the sacred place, the Kaaba, with the lucrative pilgrimages and trade that it attracted. In this situation the revelations to the Prophet inevitably had political and economic implications that profoundly threatened the existing system. Because the message that he brought required radical social reform, it was strongly and sometimes violently resisted by the Meccan ruling class, to the point at which the then small Muslim community had to leave – hence the Hijra to Medina. Here they set up an Islamic state, for the governance of which the Qur'an contains a good deal of social teaching about such matters as the observance of treaties, trade and commerce, lending and borrowing, marriage and divorce, punishment for crimes, the rules for a just war and the conduct of war, and other matters.

In contrast to this, the Gospels contain no social teaching in the sense of rules and laws for the governance of society. For Jesus had no political power or responsibility. He lived in an occupied country under foreign rule, that of Rome. And he seems to have expected the end of the present Age to come quite soon, and the return of the messiah, within the lifetime of his hearers: 'there are some standing here who will not taste death before they see the Son of Man coming in his kingdom' (Matt. 16.28; Luke 9.27); 'this generation will not pass away until all these things have taken place' (Matt. 24.34). The existing society would then be swept away and God's rule established on earth. The early Church, as reflected in the letters of Paul, continued in this belief, which however we see gradually fading over the decades as the End failed to come and the Christian community had to come to terms with life in a continuing and increasingly hostile environment. But in Jesus' teaching the supposed imminent end of the Age meant that it was not within his horizon of concerns to formulate laws for an independently organized national state. Principles of social justice and peace are certainly implicit in his basic moral teaching, available for the future, and many of the churches today are trying to apply them to society, but in Jesus' own teaching they remained implicit. It was only four centuries later, after Christianity had become the religion of the Roman empire, with church and state being now virtually one, that Christian bishops and abbots became political authorities taking part in the governance of society. It was only then that the Church began to develop its equivalents of the social teaching of the Qur'an.

An important question that arises for both religions is whether the social norms and practices of Christianity in the Roman empire and medieval Europe, and of Islam in its first decades after the Hijra, are divinely intended for all time, or were specifically for those historical situations. In the case of Christianity, some of the laws and social norms developed in the Roman empire and since are now regarded as relevant and valid today while many others are not. Many have been left behind in the past because they presupposed a culture and a state of human knowledge which have been superseded. For many centuries the churches persecuted and murdered Jews, and there was a time when Jews lived much more safely under Islamic rule. Again, for many centuries Christians believed in witchcraft, and thousands of women identified as witches were persecuted and many killed. This latter would count as murder today. At one time people who questioned any of the established doctrines of the Church were labelled heretics and many were burned or hanged. This would also count as murder today. For two and a half centuries, until the abolition movement beginning in the late eighteenth century, British and American society, supported in this by the churches, accepted slavery as divinely ordained. Again, more recently, for many years the Christian churches of the dominant Dutch Reformed tradition defended apartheid, the virtual slavery of the majority black population in South Africa, on biblical grounds. All these practices were incompatible with the basic moral teaching of Jesus about valuing others as you value yourself and about reflecting the divine love and forgiveness in our dealings with others.

And so within Christianity today, except, as I must add, within much of the very large highly conservative wing, we distinguish between on the one hand Jesus' own ethical principles, and on the other hand the fallible and changing rules adopted by different Christian societies in different places and at different times. And I would pose the question whether the same basic distinction may be in order within Islam. This would be in accordance with those Muslim scholars who distinguish between the basic religious truths revealed in the early Meccan suras, which are eternally valid and relevant, and the later development of social legislation for the Muslim community in Medina and in the second Meccan period in a cultural, political and historical situation which no longer exists today. It would also be in accord with the development of our human understanding of what justice and fairness mean. For I understand that many contemporary Muslim thinkers, condemning the practice of slavery in the past within Muslim societies, now maintain that this was specific to a particular epoch and that its abolition, which was not then possible, has since become timely. The eternal validity versus the continuous adaptability of past social practices is, I know, a controversial question within Islam, but my impression is that an element of the shariah such as the stoning to death of someone taken in adultery (not found in the Qur'an itself) is on the statute books in Iran but, I understand, not in fact practised. The cutting off of a thief's hand does have a basis in the Qur'an (5.38). This is practised in Saudi Arabia, and is on the statute books in some other Islamic countries, including Iran, even though today, I understand, very rarely carried out. It was a pre-Islamic practice that was accepted at the time of the Prophet, but it derives from a time and a society in which there were no prison systems such as exist today, in which graded punishments are possible by means of longer and shorter prison sentences. I imagine that in due course, as legal systems evolve, such extremely harsh practices will be left behind.

At any rate, it seems to me as a non-Muslim who has nevertheless made some amateur study of the Qur'an, that its most powerful and pervasive message is of Allah's unfathomable grace and mercy. As you know, every sura except one (no. 9) invokes the name of Allah *rahman rahim*, gracious and merciful, and there are throughout numerous statements such as that 'If you follow the path shown by God, He will give you a standard, and overlook your sins, and forgive you. God is abounding in benevolence' (8.28), and injunctions such as 'Repel evil with good. Then you will find your erstwhile enemy like a close, affectionate friend' (41.34), or 'Those who are helpless, men, women, and children . . . who do not know the way, may well hope for the mercy of

God, and God is full of mercy and grace' (4.98), or 'Beg your Lord to forgive you and turn to Him. Indeed [He] is compassionate and forgiving' (11.90), Allah is 'all-forgiving and merciful' (2.54), with very numerous other verses of the same kind. Allah is as infinite in mercy as in power. Should not this fundamental message of Allah's grace and mercy then be reflected in the norms and laws of Muslim societies?

There is, I should add, the same message within Christianity of the limitless love of God, and the same failure to mirror this at many points in the behaviour of Christian countries throughout history. There is today nothing Christian about the treatment of prisoners in the Abu Graib prison in Baghdad or in the American prison at Guantanamo Bay or in American support, strongly encouraged by President George W. Bush's huge fundamentalist constituency in the United States, for the Israeli treatment of the Palestinians. And yet many such things, within both faiths, have been defended on biblical or on qur'anic grounds. In my opinion we all need to be open to new ethical insights as the state of human society develops.

'Fundamentalism' is used sometimes to describe a state of mind, sometimes a way of understanding sacred scriptures, and very often the conjunction of both. As a state of mind it is dogmatic, intolerant, constantly seeking to impose itself on others, and readily inclined to verbal and sometimes physical violence. This mentality can be found within every one of the great world religions, and also, I would add, in purely secular societies. For in this sense, there can be fundamentalist atheists. And as a way of understanding Scripture, fundamentalism is uncritically literalistic, taking no account of the human circumstances within which revelation occurs, and always selecting some scriptural verses as authoritative while ignoring others that conflict with them. We are familiar within Christianity with the term 'Christian fundamentalist', meaning those who are fundamentalists in both senses, and I personally prefer the equivalent term 'Muslim fundamentalist', when it applies, rather than the term 'Islamist' which is today widely used in the West. Within Christianity we don't call our fundamentalists 'Christianists' or 'Christianityists'. And likewise I would prefer to speak of Muslim fundamentalists than of Islamists because 'Islamist', applied to violent extremists justifying their activity by a selective use of the Qur'an, suggests that they represent authentic Islam. I can understand how it is that oppressed peoples, whether in Palestine or elsewhere, faced with the overwhelming firepower of tanks and helicopter gunships, resort to the desperate forms of resistance available to them, including using themselves as weapons in suicide bombing, first practised by the Japanese kamakazi pilots in the Second World War, and also more recently by some of the Tamil Tigers in Sri Lanka. But when this ceases to be a form of warfare and becomes a form of terrorism, targeting innocent men, women and children, I cannot see that it can ever be morally and religiously justified. The son of a friend of mine was killed in the Bali bombing in 2002, which has been attributed to 'Islamist' extremists. He and his friends were completely innocent non-political civilian tourists. And to kill them, as part of a general opposition to the West, was to my mind beyond justification. I would say the same of the indiscriminate shelling and bombing of cities in which great numbers of civilian men, women and children are being killed by the armies and air forces of Christian nations.

Let me now turn to theological questions. First, concerning Jesus. The official Christian doctrine, finally established at the Council of Chalcedon in 451 CE, is that Jesus Christ was both God and man, having two complete natures, one divine and the other human. This doctrine involved the further doctrine of the Trinity, with Jesus as God the Son, the second person of a divine Trinity, incarnate. This has been the orthodox Christian belief ever since, with those in the past, and indeed today within the Catholic Church, who have questioned it often being persecuted as heretics. In recent decades, however, in the light of the modern historical study of the New Testament and Christian origins, there has been a good deal of new thinking and re-understanding. It is now widely agreed among New Testament scholars that Jesus himself, the historical individual, did not think of himself as divine and did not teach anything like the later doctrine of the incarnation. The New Testament sayings in which Jesus seems to claim divinity, such as 'He who has seen me has seen the Father', 'I and the Father are one', 'I am the way, the truth, and the life; no one comes to the Father but by me', are all in the Fourth Gospel, the Gospel of John, and it is widely agreed that they cannot responsibly be attributed to the historical Jesus, but are words put into his mouth by a Christian writer around the end of the first century, 60 to 70 years after Jesus' time, and expressing the developing faith of the Church at that time.

There is no reason why you should be familiar with the names of contemporary Christian biblical scholars, but let me very briefly quote just a few. The ones I shall quote are all personally firm believers in the orthodox doctrine of the incarnation; but nevertheless they do not believe that Jesus himself taught it. Referring to the Fourth Gospel sayings which I have just cited, the then doyen of conservative New Testament scholars in Britain, the late Professor Charles Moule of

Cambridge University, wrote, 'Any case for a "high" Christology [that is, one affirming Jesus' divinity] that depended on the authenticity of the alleged claims of Jesus about himself, especially in the Fourth Gospel, would indeed be precarious'.[1] Then a former Archbishop of Canterbury, Michael Ramsey, who was also a distinguished New Testament scholar, wrote quite bluntly, 'Jesus did not claim deity for himself.'[2] And one of the leading generally conservative British New Testament scholars today, Professor James Dunn of Durham University, says that 'there was no real evidence in the earliest Jesus tradition of what could fairly be called a consciousness of divinity'.[3] Indeed in the earliest Gospel, that of Mark, Jesus is reported as saying, 'Why do you call me good? No one is good but God alone' (Mark 10.18).

I come now to the term 'Son of God'. Again, modern historical scholarship has thrown important light. We now know that the term 'son of God' was a familiar metaphor within Judaism. Israel as a whole was called God's son, Adam was called God's son, the angels were called sons of God, the ancient Hebrew kings were enthroned as sons of God and we have in the Old Testament the enthronement formula: 'You are my son; today I have begotten you' (Ps. 2.7); and indeed any outstandingly pious Jew could be called a son of God, meaning someone who was close to God, doing God's will, perhaps with a special mission from God. Within Judaism this was quite obviously a metaphor. Jesus himself used it in this way when he said that we are to forgive our enemies 'so that you may be sons of your father who is in heaven' (Matt. 5.45). Again, in the prayer that he taught, we address God as 'Our Father who is in heaven', for in this metaphorical sense we can all speak of God as our Father. But what happened in the period between Jesus' lifetime and the full development of the trinitarian doctrine is that the metaphorical son of God was transformed in Christian thinking into the metaphysical God the Son, second person of a divine Trinity. It is this development that is questioned by a number of Christian thinkers today.

Within the very early Church a division soon began between the original Jewish Christianity based in Jerusalem, which continued for a while as a new movement within Judaism, seeing Jesus as a human being with a special divine calling, and on the other hand the Pauline development which took the Jesus movement far beyond Judaism into the Hellenistic world and exalted Jesus to a divine status. From then on the dominant Christian theology was done in Hellenistic terms. But the great Christian historian Adolf von Harnack, followed by others, has argued that the Judaic Jesus movement lingered on further east, into

Syria and possibly to the borders of Arabia, its ideas being known even more widely, and that their picture of Jesus as a great prophet of God may well have been known in Arabia in the time of the prophet of Islam. This is uncertain, and a matter of debate among the historians, but the understanding of Jesus within Jewish Christianity was very similar to the picture of him in the Qur'an. So much so that some have speculated that the Prophet's own knowledge about Jesus may have come from this source.

My own understanding of Jesus as a human being rather than as God incarnate (or as the second person of a divine Trinity incarnate) differs from the Qur'anic understanding of him only at two points. One is the doctrine of the virginal conception of Jesus by Mary. We read in the Qur'an 'She [Mary] said: "How can I have a son, O Lord, when no man has touched me?" He [an angel] said: "That is how He decrees a thing, He says 'Be', and it is"' (2.47). This is similar to the story in Matthew's Gospel, 'When his mother Mary had been engaged to Joseph, but before they lived together, she was found to be with child from the Holy Spirit' (Matt. 1.18), and again in Luke's Gospel (Luke 1.25). However, in the New Testament as a whole the story has a very slender basis, occurring only in these two relatively late Gospels, 80 or more years after the event, and seems to be unknown to all the other, mostly earlier, New Testament writers, including Paul. For this reason, together with the fact that miraculous birth stories tended to gather around great figures in the ancient world – for example, the Buddha, Zoroaster, and various figures in Greek and Roman religion – many New Testament scholars today doubt its historicity. Following them I myself do not affirm the virginal conception of Jesus.

The other point at which I differ from the qur'anic account of Jesus is in his crucifixion. As you know, this account says that 'they neither killed nor crucified him, though it so appeared to them' (4.157, or 155 on a different arrangement of the text). And the reason for this, I presume, is the idea that so great a servant and messenger of God could not be killed by human hands. If I may enter into a non-polemical discussion about this, I would point out that in the Qur'an we read (3.144), 'Muhammad is only a messenger; and many a messenger has gone before him. So what if he dies or is killed! Will you turn your back and go away in haste?' Could not this same principle be applied to Jesus? Historically it is very difficult to dispute the qur'anic verse since presumably it would not be possible for observers at the time to tell the difference between Jesus being crucified and his only appearing to be crucified – unless what is suggested is that someone else was crucified in his place. But any historical evidence that there is, both in the New Testament and also in non-Christian Roman references (Josephus and Tacitus), indicates that he was indeed executed by the Romans – who were very efficient executioners. For more orthodox Christians, who believe that Jesus' death was necessary as an atonement for human sin, and that his resurrection demonstrated his divinity, this is a vital issue. But because, together with many other Christian scholars today, I do not myself believe that Jesus' resurrection was a bodily event, or that his death was a necessary atonement for human sin, whether he died on the cross is not a vital theological issue, although as a matter of historical evidence I believe that in fact he did die.

I do not however reject the idea of divine incarnation in all its possible meanings. The sense in which I use it is its metaphorical meaning. In English we often use the word 'incarnate' as a metaphor. We might say, for example, that Winston Churchill incarnated the British will to resist Hitler in 1940 – meaning that he embodied it, that it was expressed in him in an exemplary way. In this metaphorical sense, whenever a human being carries out God's will in the world we can say that in that action God's will becomes incarnate, or embodied, on earth. I know that the word 'incarnation' is alien to Muslim discourse, but I would suggest to you that the concept of God's will being embodied in human actions is familiar. For Islamic discourse includes such metaphors as 'Soul of Allah', referring to Jesus, and 'the Blood of Allah', referring to the third Shiite Imam; and in the Qur'an itself there is the metaphorical term 'the Hand of Allah'. Some Christians today, although a minority within the theological community, use the term 'incarnation' in this same metaphorical way. Indeed one of my own books is called *The Metaphor of God Incarnate*.

There is another important theological difference between Islam and orthodox Christianity. This is the Jewish-Christian doctrine of the primal fall of humanity, resulting in 'original sin' from which, according to traditional Christian teaching, redemption is needed by the blood of Christ, versus the Islamic belief that we are weak and fallible creatures, needing God's forgiveness, which comes purely by God's grace. However, not all Christians today affirm original sin and the need for a vicarious atonement. I myself, along with many others, and following the early Christian thinker Irenaeus rather than the later Augustine, take the view that humanity was created as a weak and immature creature capable of growing through our experience of life in this world towards the beings ultimately intended by God.

So, finally, for I have already spoken for long enough, there are forms both of Islam and of Christianity that are incompatible. And there are also forms of Islam and of Christianity that are different but not incompatible. They are such that they can exist side by side in peace and in mutual enrichment. My own work as a Christian theologian has been within the reforming movement in contemporary Christianity. As within Islam, this is at present a minority position, strongly opposed both by the Vatican in Rome and by Protestant (that is, non-Catholic) evangelicals and fundamentalists. But I believe in the long-term power of thought to bring about change. I believe that in time mainstream Christianity will come to see itself, not as the one and only true faith, but as one among a plurality of true faiths, Judaism and Islam being others, even though there will probably always be a continuing fundamentalist element in the Church which rejects this position. And I venture to hope that an equivalent long-term development is also gradually taking place within Islam.

Notes

1 C. F. D. Moule, *The Origin of Christology*, Cambridge: Cambridge University Press, 1977, p. 136.

2 Michael Ramsey, *Jesus and the Living Past*, Oxford: Oxford University Press, 1980, p. 39.

3 J. D. G. Dunn, *Christology in the Making*, London: SCM Press, 1980, p. 60.

11

Apartheid Observed (1980)

Prologue: On Durban Beach

After three months in South Africa, and a foray into Botswana, I am sitting on the beautiful holiday beach at Durban, trying (with the aid of 90 pages of diary) to sort out a multitude of impressions. Much of the paradox of South Africa is visible from where I sit. A line of big ships moving towards the harbour is a sign of South Africa's buoyant and expanding economy. The golden sand, the gorgeous sunshine, the hundreds of happy holiday makers, the dozens of surfboard enthusiasts riding in on an endless succession of foaming breakers, are a picture of South Africa, the white man's paradise. For everyone here, including myself, enjoying this glorious scene is white. The other 85 per cent of the population of the country are represented by the Indian waiters from the carry-out cafés, the black women employed to hire out deckchairs and sunbeds, and the black men in overalls who clean the beach and pick up the rubbish. Notices say 'Under Section 37 of the Durban beach by-laws this bathing area is reserved for the sole use of members of the white race group'; some of the nearby toilets do and others do not have Whites (or Europeans) Only signs.

The black woman from whom I hired my sunbed probably lives in the black township of Qua Mashu. We (my wife and I) were inside Qua Mashu on another visit to Durban a few weeks ago. It consists of a vast depressing sprawl of small houses and huts, some miles outside white Durban, from which the buses begin at 4.30 a.m. to bring the workers into town. I remember the scores of women carrying cans and buckets of water from a communal tap.

On the plane down from Johannesburg this morning I sat next to an elderly white man just back from a holiday in Europe. He said he was glad to be back and would not want to live anywhere other than South Africa. Meat was incredibly expensive in England, and it was impossible to afford servants there. Here you can have one living in a hut in your back yard for very little. I said that perhaps this arrangement is more costly than it seems but that the cost is borne by the black servants and their families. 'Yes,' he replied, 'but they're still just savages, you know.'

I have only had a short time to form an impression of a country, and I do not pretend that my conclusions are other than impressionistic. The time has been spent mostly in Pietermaritzburg, Johannesburg, Cape Town, Durban and Kimberley. We have made a deliberate effort to break out of the exclusively white society in which a visitor's time would otherwise be spent, and have been able to visit five black as well as five white universities and colleges; to go into five black townships (usually taken there by an inhabitant of the township or by local white clergy); to see one of the notorious Resettlement Camps, and two of the 'black spots' from which the people are to be moved because their area has been declared white; to talk with a number of both white and black people who know a great deal about the South African situation; as well as listening to a variety of taxi drivers, fellow travellers by train and air, colleagues, and people who wanted to talk to visiting English people. Although our visit has been so brief, and we have been able to see so relatively little, it is nevertheless astonishing to realize that we have in fact seen more of the conditions under which the black majority live than the average white citizen of the country. This is not because it is too difficult (although it is sometimes not easy) to enter the black townships and to make contact with their inhabitants, but because most white South Africans do not want to know at first hand how the population they are exploiting lives.

I am in South Africa at the invitation of one of the universities. Most of the academic staff we have met are in principle, and some in practice (and occasionally at real cost to themselves), opposed to apartheid. Within the department of which I have been a temporary member we met with nothing but warmth and genuine hospitality from both colleagues and students, and have in fact made a number of new friends with whom we shall always want to remain in contact. I accepted the university's invitation so that we could see the South African situation for ourselves, and I made it clear that I would speak freely about what I saw. Much of what I have seen has, in fact, profoundly shocked me.

For South Africa consists of a relatively affluent white minority of 4.5 million exploiting a black (that is, black, coloured and Asian) majority of nearly 26 million, depriving them by law of the freedom to live and work where they wish and of a vote with which to change their situation peacefully, denying them any but miserably inadequate educational opportunities, and trying to keep them as a race of 'hewers of wood and drawers of water'. The system is now manifestly beginning to break down; and the question is whether the abolition of apartheid and the achievement of black majority rule will come about by negotiation, to the accompaniment of only relatively low-level violence, in time to avoid a holocaust which will destroy the economy of the country for black as well as white. And the question for us in Britain is whether there is anything that we can do to influence the movement of events towards the relatively more peaceful options.

Some of the Complexities

From outside South Africa one has, or at any rate I had, the impression of a solid white block confronting a solid black block. But the situation is in fact much more complex and varied than this. The whites consist of two populations, the Afrikaans-speaking (generally of Dutch descent) and the English-speaking (generally of British descent). The Afrikaaners are the more numerous and more cohesive group, and rule the country through the National Party, which has been continuously in power since 1948, during which time it has introduced the apartheid legislation, legalizing and perpetuating an already existing situation. The English-speaking population contains many critics of apartheid. In liberal circles, including many within the English-speaking universities, one can almost take a theoretical rejection of apartheid for granted.

Much of the English-language press is outspokenly opposed to the government and its policies. But on the other hand, the great majority of English-speaking South Africans are living happily enough on the proceeds of apartheid – the deprived social status, low wages, education for servitude and appalling living conditions of the black workers, including their own servants. The dirty work of imposing apartheid has been done by the Afrikaaners, who therefore bear the blame, but the English South Africans seem ready enough to share its benefits as members of the white master race. As one young black said to us, with the simplicity that asserts an undeniable moral truth, 'Yes, the English whites say they're against apartheid; but if the white kids had stood with us at Sharpeville the police would not have shot us.' (The memory of Sharpeville is still alive. We met a young black married woman who was a girl of ten in Sharpeville at the time and vividly remembers being soaked in the blood of someone, standing next to her, who was shot.)

But it is true that it is the Afrikaaners who created legal apartheid, and that if there is to be any voluntary dismantling of it, it is the Afrikaaners who must take the lead. It is easy for us in Britain to forget that the Afrikaaners (then known as the Boers) were themselves once an oppressed group – oppressed by the British – and that they showed superb qualities of heroism and dogged determination in their own struggle for independence. They, if anyone, ought to be able to understand the aspirations of the blacks for freedom and dignity and equal opportunities. And there are significant stirrings of thought and conscience within Afrikaanerdom. We met some of the Afrikaaner intellectuals who have made a break with the entrenched traditional attitudes, and have in consequence been ostracized and attacked by their own community. That community is indeed 'the white tribe of Africa', bound together by a common historical memory and mythology, and with a common loyalty enforced by its own mafia, the Broederbond, so that to break away from the tribe must be a profoundly traumatic and costly move. One Afrikaaner scholar who questioned some of the accepted Boer mythology was recently tarred and feathered at a public meeting – a reminder to the world that Afrikaanerdom has a very long way to go before its central mass will accept any fundamental change. I think he would be an optimist indeed who can see the development of the Afrikaaner attitude moving fast enough by its own inner mobility to avoid a violent black revolution.

The black majority is also divided along many lines. According to the 1980 census figures there are 15.9 million blacks, plus those in the 'independent' states of Transkei, Bophuthatswana and Venda (amounting to about 6.7 million); 2.5 million coloureds (that is, of mixed descent, mostly in the Cape); and 795,000 Asians (mainly in Natal). Among the blacks there is the difference between the rural population in the so-called 'homelands', and the urban population in the black townships near the white cities. The 'homelands' (the three 'independent' states, plus six 'self-governing territories') were created by the apartheid legislation to deprive blacks of South African citizenship. They are generally pockets of rural poverty with many of their productive workers absent, serving the white-owned industries in the cities. In the case of some, the 'homeland' is the place where they were born and are content to live. But much larger numbers have no interest in residing in or being citizens of an artificial state instituted to make them foreigners in the land in which they live and work.

There are also the differences between the ethnic groups, such as the Zulus, the Xosas, the Vendas and the Tswanas, these differences being roughly equivalent to the differences between the English, Scottish, Welsh and Irish.

How do the 85 per cent Live?

It is the urban blacks whom the white person, including the white visitor, normally meets. These are the millions of unskilled and relatively unskilled industrial workers, as well as those who do all the menial jobs in the towns and cities and act as servants in homes, hotels and offices. In the late afternoon they pour towards the buses and trains that take them out to their black townships. Only two groups are allowed to live in the white city. One consists of women domestic workers living in servants' quarters separate from but within the grounds of a white residence. We occupied a flat consisting of half a large bungalow, with another white family living in the other half. Separate from the house was a garage, with two small rooms built onto the back. In each there lived a middle-aged black 'maid', one working next door and the other elsewhere. Unlike our own house, these two small rooms had no electricity and were lit by candles and oil lamps. They had no running water and used a tap in the yard. There was one outside toilet, of the hole in the ground variety, for the pair.

In 1976 Africa Enterprise conducted a survey among churchgoers in Natal which produced the following facts on domestic workers and their employers:

Live-in maids are expected on average to work an 8- or 9-hour day, five days of the week. On the remaining two days they are regarded as partly on duty, and work between 4 and 5 hours; 7 per cent of those questioned expected their worker to be fully on duty seven days a week. While 65 per cent of employers are prepared to pay medical expenses, 8 per cent actually deduct wages when the domestic is off sick. Only 14 per cent of employers subscribed to a pension plan or savings account in the name of their employee.

In 1980 the average starting wages for female domestic workers in Pietermaritzburg were:

live-in   R35 a month
live out   R50 per month (this includes bus fare, which can amount
           to as much as R20 per month).

There are roughly two rands to the pound sterling. The minimum living wage for a black family of two adults and four children in Pietermaritzburg is estimated at about R175 a month; and in a number of cases the woman is the main or the only bread-winner in the family. Although legally the 'maid' cannot have her husband living with her in the servants' quarters, we heard of a number of cases in which the husband did in fact live there, the white employer turning a blind eye. It is not however possible for the children to live with them – these have to be left with a granny or with another family in the 'homeland' or black township.

The other group of blacks living in a white city are the men in the vast workers' hostels. I visited one of these in Johannesburg, housing 4,000 men, with hundreds of rooms in tiers round several courtyards, four or six men in a room in which the beds almost filled the floor space. The hostel is for men only – their families, whom they support with payments from their wages, being hundreds of miles away in one of the 'homelands'. There is no privacy in the hostel, and there are no recreations except for the numerous 'bottlestores' in the street outside and, doubtless, brothels somewhere in the neighbourhood. Nothing could be less conducive to family life than a labour system which requires these hostels for separated men. Indeed it is one of the most inhuman aspects of apartheid society that it undermines family life for so many.

Millions of blacks live in the black township outside the white cities and towns. At the entrance there may be a notice like this:

GALESHEWE BANTU RESIDENTIAL AREA Kimberley Municipality. It is an offence in terms of Sec. 9 of Act 25 of 1945 and the Municipal Regulations to enter this area without permission which is obtainable at the Admin. Office Galeshewe.

The black townships vary, both internally and from one to another, in the quality of housing and in the amenities provided. The houses are either endless rows of identical small bungalow 'council houses', or else are built by their inhabitants and vary from tin or mud shanties to the occasional well-built brick house with enclosed garden and TV mast. In some townships there is electricity, in others not. (Soweto, outside Johannesburg, a vast black city of over a million people, is about to begin a programme of electrification.) In some, water is laid on to a point outside each house, in others only to communal taps. (It was announced while we were in Pietermaritzburg that in the nearby black area of Sweetwater no one has to walk more than two kilometres for water!) Some have outside flush toilets, others only toilet seats over a hole in the ground.

In some the houses are crowded together, while others are unplanned sprawls. Most of the internal roads lack hard surfaces, and there is little or no street lighting. The general appearance invariably reflects poverty

and deprivation. In these crowded communities, with high unemploy-
ment and large pockets of desperate need, there is inevitably a high
crime rate and it is dangerous to go out after dark – especially on pay
day. In Soweto, for example, there were 368 murders in the year from 1
July 1977 to 30 June 1978. The main police station in Soweto is an
armed fortress.

These black townships are usually some miles from the cities containing the factories and other places of work. Consequently the black
worker has to get up extremely early, often between 4 and 5 a.m., to
travel by crowded bus to his place of work. Leaving home before dawn
and getting home after dark, he can see little of his family. If both
parents are working the children have to fend for themselves, or be
looked after by neighbours, throughout the daylight hours. Once again,
the strain put upon the traditionally close-knit African family is one of
the chief moral evils of apartheid.

Another hazard of life for a black family is to have the area in which
they live declared white, so that they are then in a 'black spot' and are
scheduled for compulsory removal to a resettlement camp. We visited
two such 'black spots', viable farm communities now anxiously await-
ing deportation. Whatever the size of the family, they are usually moved
into identical small lots containing a small metal toilet and a metal hut
or tent, which is on loan until they build their own house. One can imagine the anguish of being expelled from ancestral lands, removed from a
spacious farm to a small metal hut, and forced to seek work in a distant
factory. The South African Council of Churches, in collaboration with
the (Anglican) Church of the Province of South Africa, has produced a
slide show on the resettlement camps, with taped commentary, called
'The Promised Land', which is also now being shown in Britain.

About 2 million people have been moved under the government's
various resettlement schemes and about another million are scheduled
to be moved.

The broad picture, then, is of a deprived, poverty-stricken black
population supporting by their labour a small affluent white ruling
class. The labouring population are virtually slaves, in that they have no
voice in the ordering of their own lives. It is true that there are other
countries, including other African countries, in which there is even
greater poverty. But what is unique to South Africa is that the poverty is
assigned by law on the basis of colour, the black community having
been kept by a deliberate policy of educational deprivation from rising
above it. South Africa has in fact immense natural resources, and could
become much wealthier still if it developed its human resources. There

could then be a higher standard of living for all, instead of special privileges restricted to those with a white skin.

Education for Servitude

The amounts per head spent by South Africa on the education of its children are:

Whites	R640 (R724 including capital expenditure)
Asians	R297 (R357 including capital expenditure)
Coloureds	R197 (R225 including capital expenditure)
Blacks	R68 (R71 including capital expenditure)

What does this last figure signify in practice? It means that even the most basic primary education is not compulsory for black children; that there are not nearly enough black teachers, and that many have very inferior training; that classes are much too big for genuine educational activity – classes of 60, 70, 80 and more are common; that the parents (who are generally extremely anxious to obtain education for their children) have to pay for the school books as well as paying a tuition fee. We visited several schools in different black townships, and talked to teachers as well as seeing classes in action. One will serve as an example.

It is a primary school with 1,500 pupils, presided over by an able and dedicated black head who is however battling against impossible educational odds. The head has no secretarial help, and the school has no janitor, the children themselves doing all the cleaning and maintenance. Each teacher has a class of 100 children, and a much-too-small hut as a classroom. In each class 50 children come for the first part of the day, joined by the other 50 for the second part (so that she is then teaching 100 children at once), while for the third part of the day the first 50 depart and the second 50 enjoy the relative luxury of being part of a class of only 50. The children sit two or three at a desk, or stand or sit on the floor. Many cannot afford the textbooks, and share or do without; others cannot afford exercise books. All equipment, such as chalk, has to be bought from a fund created by parents' contributions. The parents also contribute to a building fund, which the government will match rand for rand, so that one day there may be a proper school building. Because the parents generally have to leave home by 5 or 6 a.m. or earlier, they give their children breakfast before they leave, and the next meal when they get back at night. Until recently there were many cases of children fainting or being unable to work for lack of food during the day; but now a white church charity provides milk and a slice of bread for each child at midday.

In another township I noted the amounts paid by parents. In the lower primary school: R15–20 per annum for tuition and for the payment of additional teachers beyond those provided by the government; R3–6 per annum for exercise books; R8 per annum for textbooks. In the higher primary school: R25–30 for tuition and additional teachers; R5–7 for exercise books; R10–15 for textbooks. (Quazulu, with a black population of 2.9 million, has 15,000 teachers, of whom 3,000 are 'extras' paid by the parents themselves.)

Despite the heroic work of many of the teachers, all this amounts to a deprivation of education for black children, imposed by an allocation of state funds which does not permit genuine education. There is of course no way of changing this overnight; nor did it come about overnight – it is the result of decades of the deliberate withholding of education from the black population, beyond the low level required for servitude. It is true that many new schools are now being built all over the country. But this does little more than keep pace with the growing black population, whose rate of increase during the last decade was 31 per cent.

Because education is fundamental to the fulfilment of the human potential, as well as to economic and political advancement, the deliberate withholding of education from South Africa's black children, in comparison with the white children (on whose education between 9 and 10 times as much is spent per head), can only be described as a major crime against humanity.

The South African Police State

I am not going to mention any names in this report, much as I should like to thank a number of both black and white people who enabled us to see a good deal of what we wanted to see and to meet many of those whom we wanted to meet. But although neither we nor any of those who helped us did anything illegal, to name them could nevertheless be dangerous for some of them. For South Africa is, from the point of view of anyone actively opposed to the existing system, a very effective police state. Dissidents, who reject the apartheid ideology, have to be careful about what they say on the phone; and several people whom we met know that their letters are opened before being delivered. In one case, for example, a parent posts regular letters at the same time to a son and a daughter living in the same town, but one of them is always delivered three days late.

People whom the government regards as a threat to its ideology, even though they have broken no laws, are placed under a banning order: usually they may not meet with more than one other person at a time, and nothing that they say can be reported. (I met with two of the 150 or so persons, mostly black, who are banned at the present time.) Others, invariably black, receive much tougher treatment: they are arrested and 'taken out of circulation' for a period of days, weeks or months, and then released, having never been charged or brought before any court. There is no *habeas corpus* (the right to be brought before a court) and the police can imprison and re-imprison without having to bring a charge. I met a young coloured man who had just been released after five days in solitary confinement, without any reading matter. Eleven of his friends were still being detained. We met another man, an ordained minister, who was imprisoned for five months before being released, without any charge having been brought. At any given time there are a considerable number of people under detention without trial at the will of officials who are not answerable to a court.

But the situation is more serious than detention without trial. Many blacks have lost their lives while in police custody – Steve Biko's case being only the best-known. In a church in a black township, where I attended the service one Sunday, there is a plaque commemorating a man aged 27 who died in 1977, 'falling' from the sixth floor of the police headquarters.

Perhaps the most morally corrupting aspect of the South African police state is the network of informers who spy on actual and potential dissidents. Many of these informers are black. They may be actuated by different motives: money, or some hold which the police have over them. It must indeed be an almost irresistible temptation for a black person, desperately poor and vulnerable, and with a family to support, to gain police favour and some extra money by reporting on his neighbours. Once, when we were standing with our hosts outside a house in a black township, a black man drove by in a car, and we were told that he was a known informer and that shortly the police would call round to ask who the white visitors had been. We were told in a black school of a child who was recently found with a concealed tape recorder in a history lesson – history being a sensitive subject in which the government-prescribed textbook teaches a biased view of black history, so that black teachers are tempted to correct it in class.

What is so corrupting about the system of informers is that it breeds suspicion of one's neighbours. We were told of a recent incident in which a teacher's house had been burned down by pupils in a black township. The teacher and his family were taken into the house of some friends until they could find a new place to live. The hosts were then told by two normally reliable sources that the teacher was an informer, whom the pupils had identified as such. When they taxed the teacher with this he vehemently denied it and solemnly swore that he had never informed. It was impossible to be certain of the truth in such a case, and the infection of suspicion and resentment inevitably remained. Thus the existence of police informers corrupts and poisons human relationships in the black community.

Of course, from the point of view of the average white citizen South Africa is not a police state. Those who benefit from the apartheid system of life which the police are protecting overlook or tolerate police violence, arbitrary arrests on political grounds, spying on dissidents, bannings and censorship (James Michener's new novel, *The Covenant*, which is about South Africa, has just been banned) although they are not slow to condemn similar practices in other police states, particularly Soviet Russia.

The South African police state is motivated by fear – fear of the large and increasing black majority. But in the government propaganda the enemy is invariably identified as communist subversion. According to the official publicity, a 'total assault' upon South Africa is taking place, seeking to undermine this haven of democracy and Christian civilization. Indeed the propaganda to which the people of South Africa are subjected often reaches paranoid levels, reminiscent of Nazi Germany.

The Churches

The largest and most united church in the country is the Dutch Reformed Church (DRC), which supplies the Afrikaaner community with a religious validation of apartheid. The DRC theologians do not of course defend any harshnesses or excesses that may occur in the course of implementing 'the separate development of the races' – they either deny that they occur, or treat them as mistakes which are separable from the concept of apartheid as such. And of course the bare idea of different ethnic groups living in different places – the Chinese in China and the Finns in Finland – does not, as such, imply any injustice. But anyone who is not blinded by self-interest can see that in the actual circumstances of South Africa apartheid and injustice are inseparable. The industries of South Africa's great cities cannot function without their black labour force; and to deprive millions of workers of South African citizenship, forcing them to live in special black townships with markedly inferior amenities, or to live in vast 'bachelor' hostels separated from their families, is manifestly unjust.

The alternative would be to allow all workers to live and vote in the areas where they work, with a common and equal system of public services, including education, and without any racial restrictions on whom anyone may marry or associate with, and with free trades unions, freedom of expression, and equality before the law. This would remove the injustice of apartheid; but it would do so in the only way that is possible, namely by removing the whole apartheid apparatus. One therefore has to conclude that the Dutch Reformed Church's theological defence of apartheid is a classic case of the use of religion to justify selfish and acquisitive human attitudes and vested interests. If there is a 'sin against the Holy Spirit', this is surely it. Despite all the undoubted piety and personal moral probity which it nourishes, in the weightier matters of justice and mercy and social righteousness the DRC condemns itself as a supreme example of Christian hypocrisy.

The churches of the English-speaking community are, in most of their top and some of their local leadership, committed to oppose apartheid; but the leadership has all-too-little support from the ordinary lay members. There is a fear of 'getting involved in politics'; and the small minority who seek to apply the Christian ethic to the society around them are often regarded with suspicion as 'liberalists' (a peculiarly South African term of abuse), or even as communist-inspired agitators and part of the 'total assault' on the country. One escape route from political involvement, taken particularly within the Anglican Church, is into personal pietism of the charismatic variety.

The chief Christian voice against apartheid is that of the South African Council of Churches (which does not include the DRC), under its present General Secretary, Desmond Tutu. He is a brave and dedicated Christian bishop, with magnetic qualities of leadership, whom the government would no doubt ban if it could without thereby contradicting its own new widely publicized policy of conciliation and co-operation.

Much the greatest number of Christians in South Africa belong, of course, to the black churches. Here I can only offer a tentative impression. The new generation which has been making itself felt in the school boycotts is clearly important for the future; but the black churches do not seem generally to be providing either a forum for their ideas or a support for their actions. This is in surprising contrast to the role of the black churches during the civil rights movement in the southern states of the USA. Such paralysing caution is due to fear of the very real power and brutality of the South African police state. But the resulting picture is an unhappy one for the future of the churches. How will they stand on the day of liberation, which will also inevitably be a day of judgement? I was in a black township, attending a church service, where the secondary school students were boycotting the schools in protest against inferior black education, and it was noticeable that there was practically no one in church between the ages of about 15 and 30. Apparently those taking part in the boycott were accustomed to meet on their own, and were not in contact with the churches.

The radical black students with whom I met on another occasion had an ambivalent attitude to the churches. The black consciousness leader Steve Biko had pointed out 'the logic of placing missionaries in the forefront of the colonization process'.[1] Basically, they regarded the churches as part of the colonial and postcolonial history of the white man's oppression. But at the same time they were aware of individual clergy who were on their side in the liberation struggle. (Steve Biko's memory is alive and powerful. I attended a moving meeting on the third anniversary of his death, at which several hundred young black men and women rededicated themselves to the cause for which he died, ending by standing to sing, with the clenched-fist salute, the national anthem of the yet-to-be-free South Africa.)

And so the overall picture of the churches in their relationship to the central problem of South Africa today is not good. The electorate which has supported apartheid since 1948 is predominantly Christian and churchgoing. The biggest white church directly supports apartheid; the other white churches have a leadership opposed to apartheid but a membership largely acquiescing in it; and the black churches are generally afraid to engage in political activity.

The Next Ten Years

Almost every informed person whom I consulted in South Africa believes that within ten years, despite the country's great economic and military power, it will have a black government; though there were different views as to how this will come about.

Externally, the protecting wall of white-dominated states surrounding South Africa has fallen, with new black governments in Botswana, Angola, Mozambique and Zimbabwe and, soon, in Namibia. In particular, the transformation of Rhodesia into Zimbabwe has profoundly impressed both blacks and whites throughout South Africa.

Internally, the development of South Africa's immense economic resources is becoming increasingly incompatible with the maintenance of the majority of the population at a social and economic level at which they are only capable of unskilled work in labour-intensive industries. For South Africa's industries are beginning to move into the phase in which more and more skilled workers will be needed – far more than the small white population can provide. There is a growing need for more highly educated workers than the present Bantu educational system can produce. Thus the insistent black demand for educational parity is beginning to coincide with white industry's need for better educated workers. But education inevitably fuels the general demand for political and economic rights. A better educated population is more politically conscious and more open to new ideas and wider information. There is thus an inbuilt logic in the situation which points in only one direction – towards the political liberation of the blacks and eventual majority rule.

Indeed the sweet smell of freedom from white oppression has already wafted over the borders from the north and changed the psychological situation. The black workers whom a white person encounters as gardeners, street sweepers, garage attendants, shop assistants, maids, and so on, seem mostly to have been brainwashed into servility. They call a white *baas* (boss); and when they meet whites on a town street they generally move to one side. But the new generation is resisting this brainwashing. Many of the young blacks in their teens and twenties have a noticeably different bearing. The students at a coloured school in Cape Town recently burnt their Afrikaans dictionaries in protest against its definition of *baas* as white man, and *meit* (maid) as black or coloured woman. Instead of averting their faces they look a white man in the eye; and instead of getting out of the way they hold their place. They are asserting their existence as fellow human beings, who have been denied their rights and who will never be satisfied until they obtain them. It is this new generation that has in recent months been making itself felt by boycotting black schools and universities in protest against the quality of education available to the black population.

Another and probably even more important new force which is begin-ning to assert itself is trades-unionism. The black trades unions are mostly unofficial and still in their organizational infancy. In August 1980 there was a strike of some 10,000 Johannesburg municipal workers, seeking better pay and conditions. The strike was defeated by arresting the strikers' leader while he was with his lawyers in the court building, about to seek an injunction against the employers; and surrounding the workers' compound with armed police and giving each man the choice of going back to work immediately or being dismissed and sent back on a waiting bus to his 'homeland'. Even faced with loss of job, and deportation from the urban job market, about a thousand still refused to submit, and were loaded into the waiting buses. While this incident showed the ruthless power of the police state, it also showed that the servility of the black worker can be dropped like a false mask. It is inevitable that the black trades unions will continue to grow in strength and become a major factor in the liberation struggle. For the whole industry of South Africa, as well as the basic services of the white cities, are dependent upon black labour and are dangerously vulnerable to strike action.

It seems certain, then, that there will be increasingly militant black trades union demands for higher wages and better working conditions; increasingly strong agitation from the young for educational parity, and all that flows from it; and increasing guerilla activity not only on the borders but also in the urban areas. As in Rhodesia, it will become harder for the country to flourish. Industrial profits will suffer and the business community will be pressing the government to achieve peace. There will be more and more casualties among the young white conscripts on the borders, and the electorate will be increasingly uneasy. On the other hand there may well at some stage be a white backlash and perhaps an intensification of police repression.

Responding to the incoming tide of change the government of Mr P. W. Botha has begun to promise far-reaching concessions and reforms. Presumably they hope to preside over a carefully controlled development which will move fast enough to keep the revolutionary pressure below explosion point, and yet slowly enough for the reluctant acquiescence of their stubbornly backward-looking Afrikaaner constituency. But how far does a white Afrikaaner government contemplate going? Will it enter into genuine negotiations to share the political and economic goods of the country with the black majority, or will it make only secondary concessions and be prepared to fight to the death for white minority rule? For it is clear that there can never henceforth be peace, or therefore stable prosperity, in South Africa until the blacks are acknowledged as full citizens of the country, with equal rights in every sphere; and this can only mean eventual black majority rule.

But subject to this inevitable outcome there could be considerable room for negotiation. For example, there may well be much to be said,

in multi-racial South Africa, for some kind of proportional representation in Parliament, rather than the 'winner takes all' system that we
have in Britain. Proportional representation favours minorities and
could permit significant white, coloured and Asian representation in a
one-man-one-vote Parliament. Black majority rule would inevitably
mean immense changes for South Africa's white population, but if it
comes about by negotiation rather than by revolution they could still
have a good future in a country which they will no longer dominate.

A foreigner is surprised by the degree of patience and goodwill shown
by the South African blacks. Africans seem to be capable of a human
relationship even with their enemies. Certainly as a visitor in houses,
schools, colleges, and a hospital in various black townships I never felt
resentment against myself as a white man – though I was conscious of
smouldering looks from groups of youths in Soweto and of an almost
palpable wall of suspicion when first encountering black students. But it
does not yet seem too late for a peaceful change to black majority rule,
if the white minority is willing to relinquish power.

However, what is not too late today will become too late tomorrow
or the day after tomorrow. And it has to be said that there are at present
no signs of white willingness to relinquish power. There are conciliatory
speeches from the Prime Minister and other members of the government, from which the outside world might think that apartheid is in
process of being dismantled. But in fact even the 'petty apartheid' of
whites-only toilets and hotels and bars is still largely intact. (At the
beginning of 1979 there were only 58 hotels with 'international status',
that is, allowed to rent accommodation to blacks, out of 1,450 hotels in
the country.) More importantly, the arrest without trial and the banning
of political dissidents continues unabated; compulsory removals of
black communities from areas newly declared white continue; the
grossly inferior educational system for black children, the grinding
poverty, the separation of workers from their families, the deprivation
of citizenship, all proceed as in the past. More importantly still, there is
no meaningful dialogue through which major developments could be
negotiated rather than imposed.

The newly formed President's Council, which is supposed to work
out a plan for constitutional change, includes no black members; and its
coloured and Asian members are not representative of those communities but are individual nominees chosen by the government. (No doubt
there will soon be black nominees also, appointed by the government.)
And South Africa's black political leaders are still mostly in prison or
in exile. This lack of consultation is perhaps the most fundamental

grievance of the black community. For they are not interested in improved conditions of slavery; they intend to be citizens in their own land, with all the rights of citizenship. But, unhappily, more than thirty years of National Party rule have developed a climate of racism in the white electorate and have forged bonds of colour prejudice which now narrowly restrict the government's options. In such a situation the prospects for a peaceful transition to majority rule cannot be good. The possibility of violent black revolution, involving bloodshed on a gigantic scale, is very real. This is certainly a time for other countries to exert every possible pressure to add to the reasons for voluntary change.

What Can We Do in Britain?

What can we in Britain do to help? Not much. But we must support every form of international pressure upon the white ruling minority in South Africa to move rapidly towards full citizenship for blacks, with all that this implies. Nothing less than this can earn recognition for South Africa as a part of the civilized world. No minor improvements in the living conditions of blacks can ever be a substitute for the basic rights of citizenship.

To begin with a relatively small matter, the sports boycott should be continued and applied more consistently. South African government propaganda would lead one to think that apartheid in sport is a thing of the past. But in fact multi-racial sport exists at present only to a minuscule extent. Until apartheid is abolished in sport, no rugby, cricket or other teams from South Africa, even with token black players added, should be received in Britain, and no British teams should be sent there. To insist that apartheid is incompatible with the true spirit of sport can only help those in South Africa who are trying to move their country out of the apartheid era.

But the main form of pressure available is through British investment in South African firms and in international companies operating in South Africa. Most black leaders would probably wish the world to disinvest from South Africa, in spite of the fact that this would cause hardship to the black population, because disinvestment would hasten the end of the present white minority regime. But the vested interests are probably too great for this to happen. What however we can and must do is to press for certain basic conditions to be attached to all future British investment in South Africa.

1 The workers must be allowed to live with their families near their work.
2 Free trades unions must be permitted.
3 There must be equal pay for equal work between black and white.
4 A significant part of the firm's profits must be put into black education.

The first of these conditions would cause South African industry to demand and obtain the repeal of the group areas and pass laws, which prescribe where people may live, under which 203,347 people were arrested last year.

Whereas in the past many British businessmen have felt that they could best protect their South African investments by supporting the white minority government, they should realize that the time has now come when it is in their interest to press that government as hard as they can towards the granting of full civil rights to the black population. The alternative will almost certainly be a level of violence in which their investments must suffer massive damage. For it is clear that the transition to majority rule is going to be preceded by some degree of violence – and the greater the resistance to change, the greater the violence. The lesson of Zimbabwe, starkly evident to all in southern Africa, is that without the prolonged guerilla activity of the 'terrorists'/'freedom fighters' the white minority regime would never have given way.

There is already guerilla activity along South Africa's borders, and this will undoubtedly become more extensive and presumably more effective. I do not, as a lifelong pacifist, advocate this development; but I have to acknowledge its virtual inevitability. And only the white electorate in South Africa can decide whether the country is to descend into a state of spreading war in defence of white minority rule, with all the profound disruption to industry, commerce and ordinary life that this must entail, or whether it will avoid this by radical constitutional change brought about through negotiation. But the inevitability of change, whether accompanied by greater or by lesser levels of violence, is now so clear that, whether from respect for the rights of the black majority or from self-regarding economic motives, we in Britain should give unequivocal support for United Nations sanctions against the white minority government of South Africa and, so far as the churches are concerned, support for the World Council of Churches' Programme to Combat Racism.

But it is not only in the long-term economic interests of Britain to press the white minority in South Africa to enfranchise the black majority. It is also, and has long been, a moral imperative. It is ethically intolerable for one human group to treat another as the whites treat the blacks in South Africa – as an inferior breed destined to be their servants and labourers. And religiously it is disgraceful that a white population which regards itself as a bastion of Christian civilization should systematically and ruthlessly exploit its black neighbours, depriving them of educational opportunities and of citizenship in their own country. Indeed in its deliberate disregard for basic human rights South Africa stands out today as one of the most conspicuously unchristian sections of the community of mankind.

But, finally, Britain should also implement more effectively the rights of its own black and brown citizens; for the struggle for human rights is ultimately indivisible.

Appendix

The 1980 South African Census

Blacks in the Republic of South Africa	15.9 million
(Blacks in the 'independent' states of Transkei, Bophuthatswana and Venda)	6.7 million
Whites	4.5 million
Coloured	2.5 million
Asians	795,000
Total	30.4 million
White proportion	14.8 per cent

(This chapter was published as a pamphlet by AFFOR (All Faiths for One Race) in Birmingham, and was banned in South Africa as soon as copies arrived there.

Ten years after this report, in 1990, Nelson Mandela was released from prison on Robben Island, and in 1994 became the first democratically elected President of South Africa.)

Note

1 Basil Moore (ed.), *Black Theology: The South African Voice*, London: Hurst, 1973, p. 44. The book is banned in South Africa.

12

Is there a Global Ethic?

That there is a global ethic, at least in the area of human rights, was agreed by the General Assembly of the United Nations in 1948 in its Declaration of Universal Human Rights. The term used was universal human rights, not a universal ethic, but presumably universal human rights constitutes at least an element within a global ethic. The term global ethic was introduced a generation ago by the German Catholic theologian Hans Küng – a theologian who has long been at odds with the Vatican because of his rejection of the idea of papal infallibility and his participation in inter-religious dialogue beyond mere gestures of good will. He meant an ethic which is common to the different civilizations, cultures and religions of the world. This connects with the Preamble to the United Nations Declaration, which says, 'Disregard and contempt for human rights have resulted in barbarous acts which have outraged the conscience of mankind.' I shall return to that phrase 'the conscience of mankind' later.

The Global Ethic Foundation, inspired by Hans Küng, held major international conferences in Germany, addressed by Tony Blair, and in Chicago addressed by Kofi Annan, whose speeches can be read on the internet, and the Foundation has produced a draft of a Declaration of a Global Ethic, which I shall come to later.

Is there any universal, or near universal, human ethic? We have to distinguish various levels of moral principles. All of the long-lived cultures have thus far been religiously based. Within the world religions, at the most general level, there is the universality of what in Christianity is called the Golden Rule. In either its positive form, Treat others as you would wish them to treat you, or its negative form, Do not treat others as you would not wish them to treat you, it occurs in the teachings of all the great religions. Starting in India, in the Hindu *Mahabharata*, 'One should never do that to another which one would regard as injurious if done to one's own self. This, in brief, is the rule of Righteousness.' In the Jain *Kritanga* sutra we are told that one should go about 'treating all creatures in the world as he would himself be treated'. In the Buddhist scriptures there are many sayings such as this: 'As a mother cares for her son, all her days, so towards all living things a man's mind should be all-embracing' (*Sutta Nipata*); and for Buddhism the key virtues are *karuna*, compassion, and *metta*, usually translated as loving-kindness. Moving to China, Confucius taught, 'Do not do to others what you would not like yourself', and in a Taoist scripture (*Tai Shang*) we read that the good man will 'regard [others'] gains as if they were his own, and their losses in the same way'. In ancient Persia (including today's Iran) a Zoroastrian scripture declares, 'That nature only is good when it shall not do to another whatever is not good for its own self.' Jesus taught, 'Do to others as you would have them do to you' (Luke 6.31). In the Jewish *Talmud*, 'What is hateful to yourself do not do to your fellow man. That is the whole of the Torah.' And in the Hadith of Islam we read the Prophet Muhammad's words, 'No man is a true believer unless he desires for his brother that which he desires for himself.' So this general principle of benevolence is enshrined in the teachings that have shaped all civilizations since the axial age around the mid-first millennium BCE.

The Golden Rule seems to rest on a basic human moral sense which is presupposed by all ethical theories. This is presumably the 'conscience of mankind' referred to in the preamble to the United Nations' Declaration of Universal Human Rights. The moral philosophers from Kant to Mill to Rawls to today, whether appealing to duties or to calculation of consequences or to virtues or to human nature, are all trying to spell out the logical structure of an insight or feeling that is already there and is shared by us all. One cannot prove such a fundamental principle. It is too basic to be derived from prior premises, but the whole of our moral discourse hinges upon it. The Confucian teacher Mencius in the fourth and third centuries BCE expressed this basic insight:

> I say that every man has a heart that pities others, for the heart of every man is moved by fear or horror, tenderness and mercy, if he sees a child about to fall into a well. And this is not because he wishes to make friends with the child's father and mother or to win praise from his countryfolk and friends, nor because the child's cries hurt him. This shows that no man . . . is without a heart for right and wrong.[1]

There are in fact some who lack this heart, who are gratuitously cruel and who take pleasure in causing pain and distress, and they usually end up in prison or in an institution for the insane. Either such psychopaths have always lacked the capacity for consideration of others, or they have been so circumstanced from birth that this capacity has never been developed, my guess being the latter.

We are talking so far about the most general moral principle, which I shall call the principle of benevolence, a principle that seems to be virtually universally recognized and accepted in theory. But when we look at the world around us both locally and globally it is very evident that the Golden Rule is, in Hamlet's phrase, more honoured in the breach than the observance. At least, this is true on the large scale of national policies. Locally, among ourselves and our neighbours and friends, there is a good deal of mutual kindness and consideration, though we are also well aware of the all-too-familiar social and psychological conditions which run counter to the Golden Rule, selfishness, greed, lust, envy, and so on.

Is it also the case that seriously held beliefs have interpreted the basic principle in their own way so as in effect to nullify it? I presume that Hitler and the Nazi leadership and a part of the then German population sincerely believed that the Jews were responsible for most of Europe's problems and were an evil that ought to be exterminated. For centuries white people believed that black people were a lower, more primitive species, and that it was accordingly morally permissible to exploit and enslave them. This has remained true in our own lifetimes. I was for a while in South Africa during the apartheid era, with Desmond Tutu and others who were opposing apartheid, and there were then theologians of the largest Christian church, the Dutch Reformed, who seriously defended apartheid on biblical grounds. They sincerely believed that it was God's will that the white man should rule and black Africans serve. In Britain today presumably the neo-fascist British National Party leaders and their supporters sincerely believe that the native white population has a higher priority on all social issues than black and brown immigrants and their descendants.

I said that *presumably* all these people are sincere in their various racist beliefs. In fact I am inclined to think that, paradoxically, the most sincere have also been the most evil, the Nazis. But in South Africa I thought at the time and still think that most whites who benefited from apartheid were wilfully deceiving themselves. The Bible can be used selectively, as by the Dutch Reformed Church, to justify almost anything. And I think that most of those who support the BNP are supporting what they think is in their own private interests, reinforced by an irrational racism.

However, it remains true that there does seem to be a universal moral sense, however often this is overridden by individual and group interests.

Richard Dawkins, in his widely read book *The God Delusion*,[2] speaks of 'our feelings of morality, decency, empathy and pity . . . the wrenching compassion we feel when we see an orphaned child weeping, an old widow in despair from loneliness, or an animal whimpering in pain' and 'the powerful urge to send an anonymous gift of money or clothes to tsunami victims on the other side of the world whom we shall never meet' (p. 215); and he has his own biological explanation of this. He lists four Darwinian sources of morality. One depends on what he calls 'the selfish gene'. He says that 'a gene that programs individual organisms to favour their genetic kin is statistically likely to benefit copies of itself. Such a gene frequency can increase in the gene pool to the point where kin altruism becomes the norm' (p. 216). Hence, he thinks, derives parents' care for their children, both in humans and other animals. This care is undoubtedly the case. But whether an individual 'selfish gene' wants to benefit itself by making unconscious statistical calculations about how best to do this seems to me to be suspiciously like an anthropomorphic fairy tale. And indeed how does it benefit an individual gene that there exist many copies or near copies of itself? The second Darwinian source of morality, according to Dawkins, is reciprocal altruism: 'You scratch my back and I'll scratch yours.' This occurs not only within but between species. 'The bee needs nectar and the flower needs pollinating. Flowers can't fly so they pay bees, in the currency of nectar, for the hire of their wings' (pp. 216–17). This is the basis of all barter, and ultimately of the invention of money.

So, according to Dawkins, 'kinship and reciprocation' are 'the twin pillars of altruism in a Darwinian world' (p. 218). Secondary sources are reputation, including a reputation for kindness and generosity, which may motivate altruistic behaviour; and as another secondary source, generosity as 'an advertisement of dominance or superiority' (p. 218). Dawkins points out that in the early days of humanity our ancestors lived in small villages or roving bands. In these circumstances many of your group would be relatives, and others would be people you met frequently. If relatives, kin altruism would operate. If non-kin but familiar acquaintances, the principle of reciprocity would operate. And in a small group there would be ample scope for the motivations of reputation and superiority-advertisement. All this, he thinks, evolved in us a general rule of thumb: be nice to people you have to do with. 'What natural selection favours', he says, 'is rules of thumb, which work in practice to promote the genes that built them' (p. 220). And today, when so many live in towns and cities, this rule of thumb continues to operate as the Golden Rule long after the original conditions which produced it have ended. The Golden Rule is thus a by-product or, as Dawkins says, a misfiring of an originally biologically useful rule of thumb. Birds have a rule of thumb to feed the young in their nest. 'Could it be', Dawkins asks, 'that our Good Samaritan urges are misfirings, analogous to a reed warbler's parental instinct when it works itself to the bone for a young cuckoo?' 'An even closer analogy', he adds, 'is the human urge to adopt a child' (pp. 220–1).

To summarize Dawkins's theory, the moral sense embodied in the Golden Rule is a left-over by-product of a biologically useful rule of thumb developed in the earliest period when life was lived in small closed communities. As another example of a biological by-product he points out that sexual lust continues when there is no prospect or intention to conceive; and he says, 'There is no reason why the same should not be true of the lust to be generous and compassionate, if this is the misfired consequence of ancestral village life' (p. 222). 'Both', he says, 'are misfirings, Darwinian mistakes: blessed, precious mistakes' (p. 221). So he values morality highly, while giving a purely naturalistic account of it. But do we have a *lust* to be generous and compassionate that is any way comparable in its immediacy and intensity with sexual lust? This seems to me a rhetorical exaggeration.

Is Dawkins's theory acceptable? It is highly speculative, and is not a scientific hypothesis since it is not capable of empirical verification or falsification. But is it nevertheless a plausible speculation? Not very, I think. It is of course true that we are social animals and that the early humans lived in small groups in which kinship and reciprocity would be important factors. But that this situation should have bred into our genes the rule of thumb, 'Be nice to everyone you meet', and that this has been inherited in our genes today, does not seem to me very plausible. The earliest anatomically modern humans, *homo sapiens sapiens*, appear in Africa in the fossil records approximately 200,000 years ago, though the datings differ between 130,000 and 250,000 years. In evolutionary time this is the blink of an eye. In small enclosed groups, like the varieties that Darwin observed on isolated Galapagos islands in the Pacific, evolution can be relatively rapid. But a species-wide development, in the case of a species spread throughout the world, takes millions, not thousands of years. Is it credible that 'the powerful urge to send an anonymous gift of money or clothes to tsunami victims on the other side of the world whom we shall never meet', or our feelings when we see 'an animal whimpering in pain', to quote two of Dawkins's own examples of altruism, are expressions of the rule of thumb developed in small enclosed societies, 'Be nice to everyone you meet'? This seems to me highly implausible. These examples – and many others – conform to none of the four sources of morality that he recognizes, kinship, reciprocity, reputation and assertion of superiority. On the contrary, it seems that we have an innate sense of sympathy or empathy with others, 'the conscience of mankind', which is formalized in the Golden Rule.

Where does this innate sense come from?

Let me now offer a tentative suggestion about the origin of altruism. The Golden Rule, as a consciously held principle, came about in the axial period, usually dated as between about 800 and 200 BCE. It was in this period that remarkable individuals appeared across the world, standing out from their societies and proclaiming momentous new insights. In China there were Confucius, Mencius, Lao-Tzu (or the anonymous author of the *Tao Te Ching*) and Mo-Tze. In India there were Gautama the Buddha, Mahavira the founder of the Jain tradition, the writers of the Upanishads and later of the *Bhagavad Gita*. In Palestine there were the great Hebrew prophets – Amos, Hosea, Jeremiah, the Isaiahs, Ezekiel. And in Greece there were Pythagoras, Socrates, Plato, Aristotle. It used to be thought that Zoroaster also lived in this period, but he is now thought to have lived much earlier, around 1200 BCE. But if we see Christianity as presupposing Judaism, and Islam as presupposing both Judaism and Christianity, then all the 'great world religions' have either their origins or their roots in the axial age.

Pre-axial peoples generally lived in small village communities in which the members thought of themselves as cells in the social organism, rather than as fully autonomous individuals. But during the axial period cities developed, specialized production and exchange of goods, and the development of writing, and in the relatively peaceful environments of large empires the dawning sense of individual personality emerged from the communal consciousness of the tribe, spreading beyond kings, emperors and high priests to ordinary people. This meant that whereas previously the gods were the gods of particular places or groups, the great axial sages and prophets could speak to the individual with a message that was potentially of universal significance, not confined to any one particular area or community. And it was in this new situation that the Golden Rule was taught within each of the emerging traditions.

So whereas kinship and reciprocity may well have been the basis of village and small group morality in the long pre-axial era, my suggestion is that the more universal principle of the Golden Rule came with the new religious insights of the axial age. We would not respond to the needs of tsunami victims, or victims of extreme poverty in Africa, or of oppression and torture, thousands of miles away, on the basis of kinship or reciprocity, but we do respond on the basis of the open ended sympathy and empathy taught for the first time in the axial age by the great prophets and sages and formalized in the Golden Rule. Where did they get it from? From a religious point of view, they had an enhanced awareness of an ultimate transcendent reality, some being conscious of this as personal and some as beyond the distinction between the personal and the impersonal. This enhanced awareness of the Transcendent carried with it a moral imperative. We probably see the logic of this most clearly in Buddhism, where liberation (or in Western terms salvation) is liberation *from* the self-centred ego, which is the source of all selfishness and unhappiness, and liberation *for* an impartial concern for all, self and other. And ego-transcendence is also central to each of the other world faiths.

But from a naturalistic, or non-religious, point of view, how did this universal sense come about? Not, I have suggested, from human biology, which does not change sufficiently through the short period of human existence. How then? That is a question for naturalistic thinkers to answer.

But however it came about, it remains a fact that the Golden Rule is universally acknowledged, in principle though by no means also in practice. But it is a very general principle. It is when we try to spell out its implications in specific circumstances that the problems arise. Here we have to distinguish between two levels of specificity, between what we can call intermediate principles and specific rules. An example of an intermediate principle might be 'Order society in such a way as to treat everyone fairly', while an example of a specific rule might be 'To treat everyone fairly requires one-person-one-vote democracy.'

The Global Ethic Foundation has published a Declaration to which people of all cultures and religions are invited to subscribe. This is a very long document, and I shall use instead a shorter version proposed by one of the leading figures in this movement, Professor Leonard Swidler of Philadelphia. He offers nine what he calls Middle Principles. I will mention them all but comment only on some.

The first concerns legal rights and responsibilities: 'Because all human beings have an inherent equal dignity, all should be treated equally before the law and provided with its equal protection.' The only comment I would make here is possibly only a niggle, namely that much depends on what the law is. Some laws contain discrimination within them. For example, there was recently a proposed law in the USA to allow illegal immigrants who have lived and worked in the country for five years to apply for citizenship, discriminating between these and those others settled there for less than five years. There is thus discrimination between the two groups. But the law makers could argue that all the immigrants are being treated equally according to the law, and that the law was justified as being in the interests of the USA. It is the law, not people's treatment in accordance with it, that is discriminatory. The question that this formulation of the first Middle Principle leaves unanswered is: How should we distinguish between justifiable and unjustifiable discriminatory laws?

The second Middle Principle is that, 'because humans are thinking, and therefore essentially free-deciding beings, all have the right to freedom of thought, speech, conscience and religion or belief'. And there is the rider, 'At the same time, all humans should exercise [this right] in ways that will respect themselves and all others and strive to produce maximum benefits, broadly understood, for both themselves and their fellow human beings.' Again, the general principle seems right, but it does not help us to decide particular cases, such as the Danish cartoons showing the Prophet Muhammad with a bomb in his turban, associating him with today's suicide bombers. My own personal view is that the Danish cartoons were misleading and irresponsible – because for Islam suicide is a sin, and also because Muhammad forbade attacks on non-combatants and on enemy property, and misleading in a way that stirred up hatred and prejudice against Muslims. Others may judge differently. But either way, the Middle Principle itself does not help us at this point. So much depends on the particular circumstances.

The third Middle Principle is that, 'Because humans are thinking beings with the ability to perceive reality and express it, all individuals and communities have both the right and the responsibility, as far as possible, to learn the truth and express it honestly.' Once again, this seems right, but leaves unanswered the difficult questions. In some areas the principle seems uncontroversial: in the public arena, the truth concerning straightforward matters of fact – Did Iraq have weapons of mass destruction? What are the UK immigration figures? and so on. But in the private arena of family and neighbourhood life, is it always best to tell the truth – for example, to spread the knowledge of some scandal or misbehaviour? But there is certainly an important message here for the press and other media. If they always tried to 'learn the truth and express it honestly', without headline exaggerations, without spin and bias, society would undoubtedly be in a better state. But when we come to matters about which there is no agreement, and is never likely to be, such as questions concerning religion and ideology, this Middle Principle does not help us.

The fourth Middle Principle is that, 'Because human beings are free-deciding beings, all adults have the right to a voice, direct or indirect, in all decisions that affect them, including a meaningful participation in choosing their leaders and holding them accountable, as well as access to all leadership positions for which their talents qualify them' – in short the claim is that democracy is inherent in a global ethic. Personally, I agree with this. But I wonder whether it is as self-evident as we in our culture think. There are some very important things that democracy does not do well. Because rulers are elected for a limited period they generally do not tackle long-term problems that require presently unpopular decisions. The obvious example is global warming. If our government, and other European governments, and the US government, were drastically to curtail air travel for pleasure, tax heavily the use of private cars for pleasure or convenience, and any unnecessary use of electricity and gas, they would lose the next election. On the other hand, an enlightened despot, Plato's philosopher king, could do such things. But the problem here, of course, is the impossible one of ensuring that the despot is genuinely enlightened. Because this is impossible, democracy still seems the least bad system. But this is a pragmatic judgement rather than a moral principle.

The fifth Middle Principle is that, 'Because women and men are inherently equal and all men and all women have an equal right to the full development of all their talents as well as freedom to marry, with equal rights for all women and men in dissolving marriage or living outside marriage.' I note that nothing is said here, or elsewhere, about homosexual relationships, or civil partnerships.

The sixth Middle Principle is that, 'Because humans are free, bodily and social in nature, all individual humans and communities have the right to own property of various sorts.' The phrase 'property of various sorts' is very vague. Does it include industries, owned by an individual or small group? To newspapers and other media owned by individuals, like Berlusconi or Murdoch? If so, it is debatable. But the principle itself does not help us here.

The seventh Principle is that, 'All humans should normally have both meaningful work and recreative leisure.' By way of comment, there is at present a lot of work that is necessary but that is not otherwise meaningful, but is dull, repetitive and uninteresting. Is it possible for everyone everywhere to have what they regard as meaningful work? How many today have such work? Leisure is easier to legislate for. A case could be made for saying that the less meaningful the work, the greater the leisure time that should be available. But the Principle itself does not help us to settle such questions.

The eighth Principle is that, 'Because peace as both the absence of violence and the presence of justice for all humans is the necessary condition for the complete development of the full humanity of all humans, all should strive to further the growth of peace on all levels.' And the proviso which the document adds is that 'violence is to be vigorously avoided, being resorted to only when its absence would cause a greater evil'. But questions will always arise at the time about which is the greater evil. It may be only in hindsight that we can be sure.

And the ninth and last Principle is that we should all respect the ecosphere on which we depend. This, I imagine, is something to which everyone everywhere will subscribe in theory. But we all violate it in practice. And the Principle does not help us to determine what specific measures are practicable in a property-owning democracy.

Now a general comment on these principles taken as a whole. We are all conscious today that our world has become a virtual communicational unity, that its nations and regions are increasingly economically interdependent, and that war is insanely destructive. The survival and flourishing of the human family requires at this point in history the articulation of at least a basic ethical outlook, and if possible a set of ethical principles, on which all the major streams of human culture concur and which can be used to influence their behaviour. We need to uncover and cultivate the ground of human unity beneath the multiplicity of nations, cultures, social systems, religions and ideologies among which and between which conflicts occur.

Since the European Enlightenment culminating in the eighteenth century the West has been increasingly suffused with an individualistic, democratic, liberal, science-oriented, historically minded outlook, an ethos that can comprehensively be called modernity. During this period the West has also been basically Christian, or today largely post-Christian. Indeed Christianity, as a cultural influence, is identified in the minds of many Christians, particularly when they make comparisons with other religions, with these liberal ideals of modernity. From an historical point of view this is incorrect. For what has happened is that secular modernity has transformed the outlook of the Christian world, at least in the West, rather than that Christianity has out of its own distinctive religious resources introduced these modern liberal values into Western culture. During much the greater part of its history Christianity has been neither democratic, nor liberal, nor science-oriented, nor historically minded. These Intermediate Principles clearly come out of contemporary Western post-Enlightenment culture. Anyone reading them can readily identify their provenance, reflecting as it does the concerns and presuppositions of modernity.

Now most of us, as ourselves products of modern Western culture, are likely to be in favour of these Intermediate Principles, though perhaps improved in certain details. And we would like them, or something like them, to become a truly global ethic. For this reason it is important to note the contrast between Enlightenment and pre-Enlightenment culture. Both, as we have seen, are linked in the West with a Christian, including post-Christian, mindset. But there is no prospect whatever of modern Christianity becoming the global religion, displacing Islam, Judaism, Hinduism, Sikhism, Buddhism . . . But perhaps there is a prospect of the Enlightenment values, which Christianity has largely adopted, becoming globally accepted. For it may well be that some of the same influences are at work throughout our increasingly unified world, transforming other cultures and religions in ways parallel to that in which they have transformed Christianity – or rather, much of Christianity, for there is still, and is likely to continue to be, a large fundamentalist block which remains pre-Enlightenment.

But on the other hand this may prove to be only partially the case. Some, but not all, of the influences that have formed the Western version of modernity are affecting the other cultures. But there may well be yet other influences upon them that have not affected the West, but in due course will. There are Chinese and African and Indian and other ways of thinking and feeling that perhaps the West needs to assimilate. For example, there is the African concept of *ubuntu* in the Nguni group of languages or *botho* in the Sotho languages. As Desmond Tutu explains it,

> It is to say 'My humanity is caught up, is inextricably bound up, in yours'. We belong in a bundle of life. We say, A person is a person through other persons . . . A person with *ubuntu* . . . has a proper self-assurance that comes from knowing that he or she belongs in a greater whole and is diminished when others are humiliated or diminished, when others are tortured or oppressed, or treated as if they were less than they are.[3]

This outlook, which is not based on duties and obligations, is not only concerned with the relations between individuals, but had huge political significance because it lay behind Nelson Mandela's policy of reconciliation rather than revenge, and was expressed in the Truth and Reconciliation Commission when apartheid had ended. This *ubuntu* outlook might introduce another distinctive element into the idea of a global, that is a human, ethic. Again, the same outlook lay behind Mahatma Gandhi's principle of non-violence. He accepted the traditional Hindu belief that the *atman*, or soul, in each of us is ultimately one. To injure someone else is to injure part of oneself. 'To be true to such religion,' he said, 'one has to lose oneself in continuous and continuing service of all life.' Again, this had huge political significance because it lay behind his ultimately successful non-violent campaign for Indian independence. And there may be distinctive Chinese and other ways of thinking that should likewise contribute to a genuinely global ethic. The different ways of being human that are the great civilizations and cultures of the earth may in some respects take different forms within a global modernity, thus affecting any future global ethic.

So my conclusion is that a global ethic remains to be uncovered, and that to do this requires worldwide consultation going beyond the present Western versions.

Notes

1 Mencius, *The World's Wisdom*, ed. Philip Novak, New York: Harper-SanFrancisco, 1944, p. 135.

2 Richard Dawkins, *The God Delusion*, London: Bantam Press, 2006.

3 Desmond Tutu, *No Future Without Forgiveness*, New York and London: Doubleday, 1999, p. 31.

13

Mahatma Gandhi's Significance for Today

Many of us will have seen Richard Attenborough's film life of Gandhi at some time since it was first screened as long ago now as 1982. It was inevitably selective and inevitably it simplified and cut corners, and it was probably unfair to Jinnah, the creator of Pakistan, but nevertheless it was, I would say, taken as a whole, a faithful portrait of Gandhi. I'm going to presuppose a basic knowledge of the course of Gandhi's life, which everyone who has seen the film, and also many others, will have. In making it Attenborough relied largely on Louis Fischer's *Life of Mahatma Gandhi*.[1] Fischer knew Gandhi personally, living for a while in his ashram, observing his way of life, eating with him, having long daily conversations with him, observing his followers, listening to his interviews with streams of visitors. Both before and since Fischer there have been a great number of other biographies and studies, including such full-length biographies as *The Life and Death of Mahatma Gandhi* by Robert Payne (1969), *Rediscovering Gandhi* by Yogesh Chadha (1997) and *Gandhi's Passion* by Stanley Wolpert (2001). According to one recent writer, there are about 5,000 books of what he calls 'Gandhiana'. But possibly the most comprehensive, balanced and reliable critical biography is *Gandhi: Prisoner of Hope*, by Judith Brown (1989), based on a number of years of a professional historian's research. Then there are also the more specialized studies by Erik Erikson, *Gandhi's Truth* (1969), Raghavan Iyer's *The Moral and Political Thought of Mahatma Gandhi* (1978), and Margaret Chatterjee's *Gandhi's Jewish Friends* (1992), *Gandhi and the Challenge of Religious Diversity* (2005) and *Gandhi's Diagnostic Approach Rethought* (2007).

But others have thought very differently of Gandhi. For example, Winston Churchill, in his famous protest against Gandhi's presence at the independence negotiations, said:

It is alarming and also nauseating to see Mr. Gandhi, a seditious Middle Temple lawyer, now posing as a fakir of a type well known in the East, striding half-naked up the steps of the viceregal palace, while he is still organising and conducting a defiant campaign of civil disobedience, to parley on equal terms with the representative of the King-Emperor.[2]

On the other hand Churchill's contemporary and friend, Jan Smuts of South Africa, who at one time would have largely agreed with Churchill about this, later came to think differently. Smuts is recorded as having said to Churchill: '[Gandhi] is a man of God. You and I are mundane people.'[3]

A couple of books have also appeared which take a critical view of Gandhi. These are not books primarily about Gandhi himself but about the last days of the *raj*. Patrick French, using British government documents on the transfer of power, depicts Gandhi as a charlatan. He speaks of 'The plaster Mahatma encapsulated in Richard Attenborough's 1982 film',[4] and says that, 'Far from being a wise and balanced saint, Gandhi was an emotionally troubled social activist and a ruthlessly sharp political negotiator.'[5] Another writer, Lawrence James, speaks of 'the facade of the simple prophet-cum-saviour'.[6] So there is a school of thought, I think a small one, which sees Gandhi as a crafty politician, a ruthless manipulator posing as a religious leader and presenting a façade of spirituality. We are now entering the phase, which always comes at some point after the death of a great man or woman, when a new generation of writers, needing something new to say on the subject, are tempted to look for a way of attacking the accepted view by starting a debunking trend. Indeed, there were always some among Gandhi's opponents who denounced him as a charlatan.

But there can be no doubt that the myth-making tendency of the human mind has long affected the public image of Gandhi. Some Western enthusiasts have uncritically glorified his memory, filtering out his human weaknesses; and the popular picture of him among devotees in India has attained mythic proportions, so that he is regarded by many as a divine *avatar* or incarnation. But to enable us to see through those clouds of adoration, there have until comparatively recently been some who knew Gandhi; and over thirty years ago, when I was in India for the first time, I was able to meet a number of people who had known Gandhi, had vivid memories of him, and in most cases had been deeply influenced by him. But apart from personal testimonies, Gandhi's is probably the most minutely documented life that has ever been lived.

His own writings, including letters and notes, speeches, interviews, newspaper articles, pamphlets and books fill 93 volumes of *The Collected Works of Mahatma Gandhi* published by the government of India. Hundreds of people who knew him have published books and articles about him. And so the available historical materials do enable us to form a reasonably accurate and rounded picture of a life that was lived so comparatively recently and so publicly and that has been recorded so fully and from so many different angles.

Speaking of the clouds of adoration, there is a little anecdote about Gandhi in Birmingham while he was in Britain in 1931. He stayed, as you might expect, in Woodbrooke, the Quaker Study Centre in Selly Oak. Next week a lady who was an enthusiastic admirer of Gandhi stayed overnight at Woodbrooke and was told that she would be in the guest room in which Gandhi had slept the previous week. She was delighted at the prospect of being able to say that she had slept in a bed in which the Mahatma had slept. However, when she went to her room she found that there were two beds. So, resourcefully, she set her alarm clock for the middle of the night, and when it went off she moved from one bed to the other. At breakfast next morning she asked as casually as she could, 'By the way, which bed did Gandhi sleep in?', and was told, 'Oh, Gandhiji always slept on the floor!'

But Gandhi himself would have nothing to do with his own idealization. He rejected the title of Mahatma (great soul). He said, 'I myself do not feel like a saint in any shape or form.'[7] But the ordinary village people of India began spontaneously to see Gandhi as a mahatma, and as the title became universally used, he had to put up with it. But neither he nor his friends used it. In the earlier days his followers called him *Bhai* (brother), and as he grew older *Bapu* (father), and referred to him as Gandhiji – the *ji* being a common mark of respect. He was acutely, sometimes painfully, conscious of his own faults. He blamed himself for many misjudgements and mistakes, including the major one that he called his 'Himalayan blunder' – his call to the people to practise a mass non-violent revolt before they were ready for it. So Gandhi was not ashamed to change his mind.

Indeed one of the things about Gandhi that I want to stress is that while he had basic convictions which never wavered, within this rock-like consistency of conviction his approach to life was always one of openness to new experiences and new insights, willing to admit mistakes, always ready to grow into a different and fuller understanding. To quote Judith Brown,

He saw himself as always waiting for inner guidance, to which he tried to open himself by prayer, a disciplined life, and increasing detachment not only from possessions but also from excessive care about the results of his earthly actions. He claimed to be perpetually experimenting with satyagraha [spiritual-force or Truth-force], examining [its] possibilities as new situations arose. He was, right to the end, supremely a pilgrim spirit.[8]

And, 'His profound spiritual vision of life as a pilgrimage generated in him a mental and emotional agility which responded to change as an opportunity to be welcomed rather than resisted with fear.'[9] He did of course experience times of deep sorrow and despair, particularly at the partition of India in 1947, which he had tried so hard to avoid, with its terrible aftermath of violence. Nevertheless, Gandhi was basically an optimist to the end of his life, a believer in the power of good ultimately to overcome evil. Margaret Chatterjee says,

All who were close to Gandhi have testified to his irresistible sense of fun, his bubbling spirits which seemed to well up from an inner spring in face of adversity. Those who knew him say that he was nearly always genial and friendly, often laughing, often poking gentle fun both at himself and at his friends.[10]

Gandhi was indeed a living paradox, both extraordinarily attractive and yet powerfully dominating, and in admiring him we ought to be aware of both sides of his character. His moral insights were so strong and uncompromising that he imposed them upon his followers by the sheer force of conviction. This force arose above all from the fact that Gandhi lived what he taught. He never taught an insight or made a moral demand that he had not lived out in his own life. Once, when asked by a foreign visitor what his message was, he replied 'My life is my message.'[11] This is why he was so challenging a person to encounter. People were confronted not just by an idea which laid a claim upon them but by a living incarnation of that idea. Indeed such was Gandhi's overwhelming charisma that he could in effect be a dictator within his immediate circle. And beyond his inner circle he was capable of clever manoeuvring to get his way within the Congress movement. For example, in 1938–9 Subhas Chandra Bose was elected, against Gandhi's wishes, as Congress President. Bose believed in achieving freedom by violence, and was later to lead the Indian National Army, composed of prisoners of war held by the Japanese, in their advance through

Southeast Asia, aiming at the conquest of the British in India. Gandhi rejected Bose's outlook and in 1939 engineered his downfall as Congress President. It was this kind of political manoeuvring that led to Gandhi's being regarded by some as sly and devious – in the words of a recent English critic, Patrick French, 'a ruthlessly sharp political negotiator'.[12] Some, probably thinking of saintliness as inherently incompatible with politics, see Gandhi's considerable political skill as nullifying his reputation for saintliness. But why should not a saint be highly competent in practical affairs? It is clear that Gandhi was politically formidable, combining appeal to reason and evidence with an instinct for the symbolic actions that would rally the Indian masses behind him. But what to some was sly cunning was to others Gandhi's ability so often to outwit those – whether the British rulers or rival Indian leaders – who were trying to outwit him.

Indeed one reason, I would suggest, why Gandhi is so significant today is that he was the first great example of a typically modern phenomenon, the political saint. I use the word 'saint' for want of a better, but by a saint or mahatma I do not mean a perfect human being, because then there would be no saints, but someone whom we spontaneously feel to be much closer to God, or the ultimate reality, than the rest of us. Before the rise of democracy such individuals generally had no political power or, therefore, responsibility, and saintliness typically took the form either of acts of individual charity or of a life of secluded prayer and contemplation. But since Gandhi – and many of them are directly influenced by him – we have seen Vinoba Bhave, Ghaffar Khan, Kushdeva Singh in India, Martin Luther King in the United States, Oscar Romero in San Salvador, Thich Nhat Hahn in Thailand, Aung San Suu Kyi in Burma, Nelson Mandela and Desmond Tutu in South Africa, as well as very numerous lesser figures in many places. For each one of whom we have all heard there are probably a hundred who are only known locally. Dedication to needy and suffering humanity has now become the main arena in which spiritual greatness is expressed.

But returning to Gandhi, he was undoubtedly sometimes a difficult person with whom to deal. Perhaps most importantly, Gandhi's family sometimes found him hard to live with. As his demanding ideals made him hardest on himself, they made him next hardest on his sons, and the oldest of them broke down under the burden of being the Mahatma's son, becoming estranged from him and going to pieces in middle age. And Gandhi inherited the traditional Indian understanding of the wifely role: he said, 'A Hindu husband regards himself as lord and master of his wife who must ever dance attendance on him,'[13] and during the early years of their marriage his wife, Kasturbai, had a good deal to put up with. But I have already stressed that Gandhi was able to learn and change, and he later said, 'Her determined submission to my will on the one hand and her quiet submission to the suffering my stupidity involved on the other, ultimately made me ashamed of myself and cured me of my stupidity in thinking that I was born to rule over her; and in the end she became my teacher in non-violence.'[14] And they became, for the greater part of their long marriage, a model of mutual devotion. There was incidentally, in *The Sunday Times*, 25 October 1998, an article about the personal failures of great individuals, which included a sentence about Gandhi, 'Mahatma Gandhi forced his wife to clean out latrines as a punishment for her materialism.' This is a wanton distortion to fit Gandhi into the writer's thesis. Gandhi insisted that everyone in the ashram, including himself and his wife and family, should do their share of the dirty chores of the community. But this was not in any sense a punishment; it was the practical democracy of the ashram.

Concerning Gandhi's sexuality, which always fascinates Western writers, the one thing that they know about Gandhi, even if they know very little else, is the vow of sexual abstinence that he made when he devoted himself to community leadership, and his deliberate testing of this vow for a while in old age by sleeping under the same blanket with young women disciples. He believed that his power as a spiritual and political leader depended on his inner soul-power, which in turn depended on absolute faithfulness to his vows. As he prepared to confront the crisis of Hindu–Muslim strife in Bengal immediately after Independence he felt that he had to be victorious in testing this most demanding of vows. However, given the inevitability of hostile publicity, we must count it as one of his blunders, and he was persuaded to end the experiment. But – and this is the other side of the story – the inner spiritual force which Gandhi maintained in this way was real and powerful. To quote a recent historian,

That more lives were not lost in Bengal owed much to the pervasive influence of Mahatma Gandhi, who had moved to Calcutta before Independence Day. There he had taken up residence in one of the city's many poor districts, living among the Untouchables and the dispossessed and threatening to fast to death should violence break out. Miraculously, there was no repetition of the mass murders that had disfigured Calcutta a year earlier and the whole province of Bengal remained reasonably calm.[15]

One of the Viceroy's staff said that 'Hardened press correspondents report that they have seen nothing comparable with this demonstration of mass influence. Mountbatten's estimate is that he has achieved by moral persuasion what four Divisions would have been hard pressed to have accomplished by force.'[16] But Gandhi's quite extraordinary moral and spiritual power and magnetism arose from an absolute inner integrity, which included faithfulness in keeping his vows. If he had failed in this his spirit would have been broken within him, and his power to influence the masses lost. This may be largely incomprehensible to the Western mind; and yet it made sense at the time to Gandhi, and it enabled him to work what has been called the miracle of Calcutta.

Now a word about Gandhi as a Hindu. What is sadly lacking in the contemporary critics whom I have mentioned is that, as secular scholars, they have no sense of the religious dimension of such a person as Gandhi. They see him only as a politician. But everything that Gandhi said shows that he was primarily a seeker after God, Truth, the Ultimate, and a politician because this led him into the service of his fellows and so into conflict with any form of injustice. For him there was in practice no division between religion and politics, for true religion expresses itself politically, and the only way to achieve lasting political change is through the inner transformation of masses of individuals, beginning with oneself. He once said, 'Man's ultimate aim is the realization of God, and all his activities, social, political, religious, have to be guided by the ultimate aim of the vision of God. The immediate service of all human beings becomes a necessary part of the endeavor simply because the only way to find God is to see Him in His creation and to be one with it. This can only be done by service to all.'[17] And there was ultimately no distinction, for Gandhi, between one's own salvation and that of others.

It is sometimes said that Gandhi was more a Christian than a Hindu, because his moral teaching was so similar to that of Jesus in the Sermon on the Mount. Some Christians have assumed that Gandhi must have received the ideal of love of enemy from the teaching of Jesus. However, this is not the case. He first met Christians, and first encountered the New Testament, when he went to London as a young man to study law. But long before that he had been brought up on such Hindu sayings as, 'If a man gives you a drink of water and you give him a drink in return, that is nothing. Real beauty consists in doing good against evil,'[18] and 'The truly noble know all men as one, and return with gladness good for evil done,' which, as he says in his *Autobiography* (chapter 10), became his guiding principle. As a Hindu his great object was to attain to union with the ultimate reality which he called God or Truth. But one of Gandhi's special insights was that this quest can take the form of the service of truth in its more immediate and relative forms – truthfulness in thought and speech, truthfulness in dealing with one's opponents, truthfulness in presenting a case, truthfulness in every aspect of life. Another form of this insight was that the deluded state in which humanity normally lives, in Hindu terms *maya*, illusion, takes social, political and economic forms. Moral delusion is institutionalized in the structures of society. This was brought home to Gandhi in South Africa when he was thrown off the train at Pietermaritzburg because as a non-white barrister he was travelling in a first-class compartment. It dawned on him that racism was a spiritual delusion embodied in an entrenched social system. As Rex Ambler says,

> The great illusion, the social maya, as we may call it, is that human beings are fundamentally different from one another, and that some are inherently superior to others and are, thereby, entitled to dominate them . . . His life's work was largely devoted to the exposure of that illusion and the realization of the hidden Truth of human oneness.[19]

In Gandhi's ashrams the day began and ended with prayer, readings (mainly from the *Bhagavad Gita*), hymns (including some Christian hymns), and often a short talk by Gandhi. But worship for him also took the form of spinning, or sweeping the floor, or cleaning the latrines, or nursing the sick, or attacking some specific injustice, or planning some aspect of the campaign for independence. There was, for him, no separation between religion and daily life.

Although a devoted Hindu, Gandhi was a radical reformer, strongly opposed to many aspects of traditional Hindu culture, such as animal sacrifices in the temples, child marriages, and untouchability. 'Untouchability', he said, 'is a soul-destroying sin. Caste is a social evil.'[20] For while he generally acknowledged the traditional caste division of labour he did not see it as religiously based, and he increasingly criticized its harmful aspects. Indeed in his ashrams he overturned them. Here people of all castes, colours, nationalities and religions ate and worked together, everyone, including Gandhi and his family, joining equally in the manual labour traditionally allocated to the *Shudras* (the lowest caste), and such dirty jobs as latrine cleaning traditionally done only by the outcastes. He regarded untouchability as a 'useless and wicked superstition',[21] and was revolted by its defence in terms of the doctrine of karma. In his eyes there was no difference between a Brahmin and an outcaste; and he defended marriages between people of different castes. He refused to wear the sacred thread of a caste Hindu because, 'If the *Shudras* may not wear it, I argued, what right have the other *varnas* [castes] to do so?'[22] And while he supported the traditional Hindu reverence for the cow, he said, 'Cow protection, in my opinion, includes cattle-breeding, improvement of the stock, humane treatment of bullocks, formation of model dairies, etc.'[23] In short, Gandhi's moral insights had far greater authority for him than established traditions, and in his maturity he had no hesitation in sweeping away long-accepted ideas and practices that he regarded as harmful excrescences on the body of Hinduism.

Gandhi did however cleave to certain basic Hindu beliefs which were the source of his practical intuitions.

Two closely related Hindu beliefs are that in the depths of our being we are all one, and that in the depths of each of us there is a divine element. 'The chief value of Hinduism', Gandhi said, 'lies in holding the actual belief that *all* life (not only human beings, but all sentient beings) are one, i.e. all life coming from the One universal source, call it God, or Allah, or Parameshwara.'[24] Accordingly, 'To be true to such religion one has to lose oneself in continuous and continuing service of all life.'[25] The unity of life means that no one can be totally alien and irredeemably an enemy, and that 'one's true self-interest consists in the good of all'. Again,

> All living creatures are of the same substance as all drops of water in the ocean are the same in substance. I believe that all of us, individual souls, living in this ocean of spirit, are the same with one another with the closest bond among ourselves. A drop that separates soon dries up and any soul that believes itself separate from others is likewise destroyed.[26]

This means in practice that in situations of conflict there is something in the opponent that can be appealed to – not only a common humanity but, in the famous Quaker phrase (and Gandhi felt great affinity with the Quakers), 'that of God in every person'. 'I have a glimpse of God', he said, 'even in my opponents.'[27] And closely connected with this is the principle of *ahimsa*, non-killing, and more generally non-violence. This is an ancient Hindu, but more particularly Jain, principle. It obviously coheres with the belief that all life is ultimately one and that there is a divine element in every person. It means in practice that in the midst of injustice the right way to deal with oppressors – whether the South African government in its treatment of the 'coolies' or the British *raj* dominating and exploiting the people of India – is not violent revolt but an appeal to the best within them by rational argument and by deliberate and open disobedience to unjust laws even when this involves suffering, violence and imprisonment. Willingness to suffer for the sake of justice, appealing as it does to the common humanity of both oppressor and oppressed, is the moral power for which Gandhi coined the word *satyagraha*, the power of Truth, Reality. He believed that a policy of non-aggression in the face of aggression, of calm reason in response to blind emotion, of appeal to basic fairness and justice, together with a readiness to suffer for this, are more productive in the long run than meeting violence with violence. He was convinced that there is always something in the other, however deeply buried, that will eventually, given enough time, respond. For,

> Non-violence is the law of our species as violence is the law of the brute. The spirit lies dormant in the brute and he knows no law but that of physical might. The dignity of man requires obedience to a higher law – to the strength of the spirit.[28]

But in order for this to happen the *satyagrahi* must have the courage to face the oppressor without fear. Without such courage, which Gandhi was able to evoke in many of his followers, genuine non-violent action is impossible. 'Non-violence', he said, 'is a weapon of the strong. With the weak it might easily be hypocrisy.'[29] A *satyagrahi* can be non-violent precisely because he does not fear the oppressor. 'Fear and love', Gandhi said, 'are contradictory terms . . . My daily experience, as of those who are working with me, is that every problem would lend itself to solution if we are determined to make the law of truth and non-violence the law of life.'[30]

However, Gandhi was not opposed to the use of force in all circumstances. He accepted that violence was necessary in restraining violent criminals; and he said, 'I would support the formation of a militia under *swaraj* [self-rule].'[31] 'In life,' he said, 'it is impossible to eschew violence completely. The question is, where is one to draw the line?'[32] But in general, he insisted, 'non-violence is infinitely superior to violence'.[33]

In the colonial India in which Gandhi most notably applied his principles he had to carry the masses with him. And so a great deal of his time was spent in 'consciousness raising' by public speaking, often to great crowds throughout the country, by a constant stream of newspaper and journal articles, and by interviews with individuals and groups from both India and abroad. He knew that the ideal of total non-violence, which involves loving one's enemy, was not going to be attained by the masses in any foreseeable future. He said that,

> for me the law of complete Love is the law of my being . . . But I am *not* preaching this final law through the Congress or the Khalifat organisation. I know my own limitations only too well. I know that any such attempt is foredoomed to failure.[34]

But although perfect non-violence was an ideal rather than a present reality, something approaching it, namely non-violent non-cooperation with the foreign ruler, was possible and would eventually bring about the nation's freedom. He said, 'I know that to 90 per cent of Indians, non-violence means [civil disobedience] and nothing else.'[35] Again,

> What the Congress and the Khalifat organisations have accepted is but a fragment of the implications of that law [of non-violence]. [But] Given true workers, the limited measure of its application can be realised in respect of vast masses of people within a short time.[36]

And he was able to convince a critical mass of his fellow countrymen that 100,000 Englishmen could only rule 300 million Indians so long as the Indians weakly submitted to their rule. If they had the courage to withdraw their co-operation, and deliberately disobey unjust laws – such as the salt tax – the British *raj* would be helpless and the imperial rulers would see that their position was both morally and politically untenable. Although in 1930 there were 29,000 Congress activists in jail, the government could not imprison millions; and although there might be further outbursts of violence, like the terrible Amritsar massacre in 1919, the world would react against this and in the end the imperial power would be defeated and would have to depart. And in the end this is what happened. After the 1939–45 war the Labour government of Clement Attlee came to power in Britain and made the momentous decision to grant full Indian independence. It was evident that the demand and expectation for this were growing to the point at which only brute force could check it, and this in an India in which the whole administrative machinery had been gravely weakened during the war, and when the British soldiers now wanted to go home and were certainly not willing to become agents of imperialist oppression. In 1946 the then Viceroy, General Sir Archibald Wavell, reported to

London that 'Our time in India is limited and our power to control events almost gone.'[37]

And so, at this late stage, Independence had become virtually inevitable. In that immediate situation it was the result, not of Gandhi and the Congress, but of the collapse of British power. But on a longer view this end-game was only made possible by the progressive achievements of the independence movement during the previous thirty years. It was Gandhi and his colleagues who had made Indians proud of their culture and confident of their capacity for self-rule, and who had built up the finally irresistible expectation and demand for independence.

Throughout the long struggle it was Gandhi who provided the inspiration, the moral authority and the immense unifying symbolic power. But in the detailed negotiations during the final phase it was mainly Jahwarhalal Nehru and Vallabhbhai Patel who moulded the settlement on the Congress side – Nehru the brilliant, sophisticated, charismatic disciple of Gandhi, chosen by him as Congress President at this critical juncture, and Patel the shrewd, tough, forceful political operator. And so the *raj* ended as Gandhi had always said it would, with the British voluntarily handing over power and leaving in friendship – despite the strong opposition at home by old-style imperialists led by Winston Churchill. Instead of going in bitterness and enmity, the British went with great pomp and ceremony, leaving a free India which has continued to this day to be a member of the British Commonwealth of Nations. It seems very unlikely that history would have taken this course but for Gandhi's influence over the previous thirty years – somewhat as, more recently, it seems very unlikely that apartheid in South Africa would have ended so peacefully but for the personal influence of Nelson Mandela.

We can now try to formulate the main lessons of Gandhi's life and thought for ourselves today. Gandhi himself believed that his basic message would only have its main impact many years after his own death. It is a mistake, and one which secular historians are very prone to make, to think of him only in the context of the movement for Indian independence, inseparable though his memory is from that. He did not see political independence as such as his great aim, but rather a profound transformation of Indian society. True *swaraj* meant freedom from greed, ignorance, prejudice; and most of Gandhi's time was spent in trying to educate and elevate the masses, dealing with basic questions of cleanliness, sanitation and diet, combating disease, and fostering mutual help and true community. As Judith Brown writes,

He visualised a total renewal of society from its roots upwards, so that it would grow into a true nation, characterised by harmony and sympathy instead of strife and suspicion, in which castes, communities, and both sexes would be equal, complementary and interdependent.[38]

Thus Gandhi's vision went much further than the immediate political aims that he shared with his colleagues in the Indian National Congress. What elements of his long-term project are relevant today?

First is the Gandhian approach to conflict resolution, based on a belief in the fundamental nature of the human person. Not however of human nature as it has generally manifested itself throughout history, but of its further potentialities, which can be evoked by good will, self-giving love, and a sacrificial willingness to suffer for the good of all. As Lamont Hempel puts it, 'Gandhi's crowning achievement may have been his ability to inspire *homo humanus* out of *homo sapiens*.'[39] But this was only in a number of individuals, not in society as a whole. Individuals continue to be inspired by Gandhi's teaching and example. But neither India nor any other state has based its policies consistently on Gandhian principles. It is particularly tragic that his own country has failed to live up to his ideals. The rise of the Hindu supremacist movement – which was already responsible for Gandhi's assassination – has intensified communal tensions, including the destruction of the Ayodia mosque in 1992. All this would make Gandhi weep. Unregenerate human nature has triumphed once again over what Gandhi called Truth – as it has over the teachings of enlightened religious leaders in every century.

Nevertheless, the attempt to inspire humans to rise to true humanity must never cease. It involves an unwavering commitment to fairness, truthfulness, open and honest dealing, willingness to see the other's point of view, readiness to compromise, readiness even to suffer. In the familiar but in practice disregarded words of Jesus, it requires us to love our enemies. Such a response refuses to enter the downward spiral of mutual recrimination, hatred and violence. The lesson of history is not that this has been tried and failed, but that the failure has been in not trying it.

But *ahimsa* as practical politics is a long-term strategy. It took time and patience and ceaseless effort and example to evoke the limited realization that non-violent action in India, even simply as a tactic, is more effective than violent revolt. It is thus pointless to ask how Gandhi would have fared in, for example, Nazi Germany. He would no doubt have been quickly eliminated. The more useful question is what would have happened if a German like him had been at work there during the previous twenty years.

Another implication of Gandhi's thought concerns ecology and the preservation of the earth and the life on it. Here Gandhi anticipated the widespread Green movement of today. To quote James Gould,

> Gandhi has emphasised opposite values to those of the consumer society: the reduction of individual wants, the return to direct production of foodstuffs and clothing, and self-sufficiency rather than growing dependency. As the limits of growth and the inherent scarcity of resources broke upon the world in the 1960's, the Gandhian idea of restraint suddenly made sense.[40]

E. F. Schumacher, author of the influential *Small Is Beautiful*, regarded Gandhi as the great pioneer in insisting that the rampant growth of capitalist industrialism is incompatible with a sustainable world ecosystem. Schumacher said,

> Gandhi had always known, and rich countries are now reluctantly beginning to realise, that their affluence was based on stripping the world. The USA with 5.6% of the world population was consuming up to 40% of the world's resources, most of them non-renewable. Such a life-style could not spread to the whole of mankind. In fact, the truth is now dawning that the world could not really afford the USA, let alone the USA plus Europe plus Japan [and today we must add China], and other highly industrialised countries. Enough is now known about the basic facts of spaceship Earth to realise that its first class passengers were making demands which could not be sustained very much longer without destroying the spaceship.[41]

Gandhi saw this in terms of his native India, which was then still a developing country in which people in the hundreds of thousands of villages lived in extreme poverty. And so instead of building up modern industries with labour saving machinery in the cities, drawing the villagers into the urban slums, he urged basic employment for all. He wanted 'production by the masses rather than mass production'. Every policy should be judged by its effects on the multitude of ordinary citizens. For example, cottage industries, such as spinning, required very little capital equipment and should be encouraged and supported throughout the vast rural areas. That is what Gandhi saw as the need at that time. Had he lived a generation later he would no doubt have accepted industrialization, but would have worked to humanize it and to undo the great gap between the rich and the poor.

In the matter of aid to impoverished countries Gandhi was at least a generation ahead of his time. In 1929 he wrote,

> The grinding poverty and starvation with which our country is afflicted is such that it drives more and more men every year into the ranks of the beggars, whose desperate struggle for bread renders them insensible to all feelings of decency and self-respect. And our philanthropists, instead of providing work for them and insisting on their working for bread, give them alms.[42]

But that aid should be given in such a way as to free the recipients to help themselves is now an accepted principle in international aid circles.

Gandhi's 'feminism' – though that is not a term that he used – is also of interest today in shifting the focus from the transformation of women to the transformation of men. In the Indian context his concern for the position of women in society was ahead of his time. He was impressed when in England by the courage and dedication of the suffragettes, although he did not approve of their occasional resort to violence. And when women responded to his call in South Africa and India, showing themselves as willing as the men to face violent police action and jail, Gandhi saw that they had a unique contribution to make. He was quick to see that women could become the 'leader in the *Satyagraha* which does not require the learning that books give but does require the stout heart that comes from suffering and faith'.[43] Further, because for Gandhi true liberation always went much further than political independence, to the humane transformation of society, he 'believed that by taking part in the nationalist struggle, women of India could break out of their long imposed seclusion'.[44] His conception of the kind of gender revolution that is needed was novel in his time. For the wholehearted adoption of non-violence can be seen as making for a gentler and less aggressive masculinity. Sushila Gidwani puts the point challengingly in this way: 'Indian feminism aims at changing men to become qualitatively more feminine while modern feminism aims at changing women to become qualitatively more masculine.'[45]

And finally, another aspect of Gandhi's thought which is relevant today. This is not novel in the East but is highly controversial within Christianity, though much less so today in many circles than in Gandhi's time. This is his understanding of the relation between the great world faiths. 'The time is now passed', he said, 'when the followers of one religion can stand and say, ours is the only true religion and all others are false.'[46] In his youth Gandhi lived within a very ecumenical community. He was particularly influenced by a Jain, Raychandbhai, who introduced him to the idea of the many-sidedness of reality (*anekantavada*), so that many different views may all be valid. And this includes religious views. Gandhi shared the ancient Hindu assumption that 'Religions are different roads converging at the same point. What does it matter that we take different roads so long as we reach the same goal?' He regarded it as pointless, because impossible, to grade the great world faiths in relation to each other.

> No one faith is perfect. All faiths are equally dear to their respective votaries. What is wanted, therefore, is a living friendly contact among the followers of the great religions of the world and not a clash among them in the fruitless attempt on the part of each community to show the superiority of its own faith over the rest. Hindus, Muslims, Christians, Parsis, Jews are convenient labels. But when we tear them down, I do not know which is which. We are all children of the same God.[47]

However, his 'doctrine of the Equality of Religions', as it has been called, did not move towards a single global religion, but enjoins us all to become better expressions of our own faith, being enriched in the process by influences from other faiths.

These, then, are ways in which Gandhi's thinking was ahead of his own time and is alive today in our time. And underlying all this, as an available source of inspiration for each new generation, is Gandhi's indomitable faith in the possibility of a radically better human future if only we will learn to trust the power of non-violent openness to others and to the deeper humanity, and indeed divinity, within us all. To most people this seems impossible. But Gandhiji's great legacy is that his life has definitively shown that, given true dedication, it *is* possible in the world as it is.

Notes

1 Louis Fischer, *The Life of Mahatma Gandhi*, New York: Harper & Row, 1950.

2 Fischer, *Life of Mahatma Gandhi*, p. 177.

3 Yogesh Chadra, *Rediscovering Gandhi*, London: Century, 1997, p. 382.

4 Patrick French, *Liberty or Death: India's Journey to Independence and Divison*, 1997, London: HarperCollins, p. 17.

5 French, *Liberty or Death*, p. 17.

6 Lawrence James, *Raj: The Making and Unmaking of British India*, London: Little, Brown, & Co., 1997, p. 524.

7 *Young India*, 20 January 1927.

8 Judith M. Brown, *Gandhi: Prisoner of Hope*, New Haven: Yale University Press, 1989, p. 80.

9 Brown, *Gandhi*, pp. 312–13.

10 Margaret Chatterjee, *Gandhi's Religious Thought*, London: Macmillan, 1983, p. 108.

11 Brown, *Gandhi*, p. 80.

12 French, *Liberty or Death*, p. 17.

13 *The Selected Works of Mahatma Gandhi*, Ahmedabad: Navajivan, 1968, vol. 1, p. 275.

14 Quoted by Ranjit Kumar Roy, in Antony Copley and George Paxton (eds), *Gandhi and the Contemporary World*, Chennai: Indo-British Historical Society, 1997, p. 225.

15 Trevor Royle, *The Last Days of the Raj*, London: Joseph, 1989, pp. 195–6.

16 Brown, *Gandhi*, p. 379.

17 *Harijan*, 29 August 1936.

18 Chatterjee, *Gandhi's Religious Thought*, p. 50.

19 John Hick and Lamont Hempel (eds), *Gandhi's Significance for Today*, London: Macmillan, 1989, p. 93.

20 *Selected Works*, vol. 5, p. 444.

21 Brown, *Gandhi*, p. 58.

22 *Selected Works*, vol. 2, pp. 586–7.

23 *Selected Works*, vol. 3, p. 636.

24 Rhaghavan Iyer (ed.), *The Moral and Political Writings of Mahatma Gandhi*, vol. 3, Oxford: Oxford University Press, 1973, p. 315.

25 Iyer, *Moral and Political Writings*, vol. 1, p. 461.

26 *Indian Opinion*, 29 April 1914.

27 Iyer, *Moral and Political Writings*, vol. 1, p. 438.

28 Iyer, *Moral and Political Writings*, vol. 2, p. 299.

29 Iyer, *Moral and Political Writings*, vol. 1, p. 294.

30 Iyer, *Moral and Political Writings*, vol. 1, p. 294.

31 Iyer, *Moral and Political Writings*, vol. 2, p. 298.

32 Iyer, *Moral and Political Writings*, vol. 2, p. 298.

33 Iyer, *Moral and Political Writings*, vol. 2, p. 363.

34 *Young India*, 9 March 1922.

35 Lamont Hempel, in Hick and Hempel, *Gandhi's Significance*, p. 5.

36 *Young India*, 9 March 1922.

37 French, *Liberty or Death*, p. 245.

38 Brown, *Gandhi*, p. 13.

39 Hempel, in Hick and Hempel, *Gandhi's Significance*, p. 5.

40 James Gould, in Hick and Hempel, *Gandhi's Significance*, p. 12.

41 Quoted in Copley and Paxton, *Gandhi and the Contemporary World*, p. 141.

42 *Selected Works*, vol. 2, p. 647.

43 Ranjit Kumar Roy in Copley and Paxton, *Gandhi and the Contemporary World*, p. 224.

44 Surur Hoda in Copley and Paxton, *Gandhi and the Contemporary World*, p. 141.

45 Sushila Giwani, in Hick and Hempel, *Gandhi's Significance*, p. 233.

46 *Indian Opinion*, 26 August 1905.

47 *Harijan*, 18 April 1936.

14

The Second Form of the Ontological Argument

This 'second form' has been independently formulated, on the basis of Anselm's *Proslogion* III, by two American philosophers, Charles Hartshorne and Norman Malcolm. The main contention of this critique will be that two importantly different concepts of necessary being are involved in the Malcolm-Hartshorne proof, and that the proof is vitiated by a shift in mid-course from one of these concepts to the other. These two concepts of 'necessary being' or 'necessary existence' employ the quite distinct notions of logical necessity and ontological or factual necessity.

Logical Necessity

Consider first the notion of logical necessity, and its use in relation to the question of divine existence. In contemporary philosophical literature to say that a given proposition is logically true, or logically necessary, or analytic, is generally intended to signify that it is true by virtue of the meanings of the terms which compose it. Applying this usage in theology, to say that God has (logically) necessary being, or that his existence is (logically) necessary, would be to say that the meaning of 'God' is such that the proposition 'God exists' is a logical, analytic or a priori truth; or again that the proposition 'God does not exist' is a self-contradiction, a statement of such a kind that it is logically impossible for it to be true. But it is an implication of this contemporary empiricist view of logical necessity as analytic that an existential proposition (that is, a value of the propositional function 'x exists') cannot be logically necessary. On this view, the correct analysis of 'a exists' is simply to make an assertion. Such an analysis implies that existence cannot properly be included among defining properties of a – except of course in the trivial sense that only existing entities can be instances of anything. Thus

179

within the thought-world of modern empiricism the notion of logically necessary existence is not admissible, and cannot be employed as the foundation of a valid theistic argument.

This fact was used by J. N. Findlay in his once much discussed article 'Can God's Existence Be Disproved?'[1] as the foundation of a strict disproof of divine existence. Findlay puts the ontological argument into reverse by contending that the concept of a deity whose existence is logically necessary, so far from guaranteeing the existence of an entity corresponding to it, is such as to guarantee that nothing corresponds to it.

Findlay defines the concept of God as that of the adequate object of religious attitudes, a religious attitude being described as one according to which we tend 'to abase ourselves before some object, to defer to it wholly, to devote ourselves to it with unquestioning enthusiasm, to bend the knee before it, whether literally or metaphorically'. Such an attitude is rationally adopted only by one who believes that the object to which he thus relates himself as a worshipper has certain very remarkable characteristics. First, it must be conceived as being infinitely superior to ourselves in value or worth. (Accordingly, Findlay refers to this object in personal terms as 'he' rather than as 'it'.) Second, he must be conceived as being unique: God must not be one of a class of beings of the same kind, but must stand in an asymmetrical relationship to all other objects as the source of whatever value they may have. Third, says Findlay, the adequate object of religious attitudes must be conceived as not merely happening to exist, but as existing necessarily; if he merely happened to exist, he would not be worthy of the full and unqualified attitude of worship. And fourth, this being must be conceived as not merely happening to possess his various characteristics, but as possessing them in some necessary manner. For our present purpose we may conflate these two necessities, necessary existence and the necessary possession of properties, and treat them as one. It should be borne in mind throughout that in Findlay's argument 'necessary' means 'logically necessary'.

It is the last two in his list of requirements that provide the ground for Findlay's ontological disproof of theism:

For if God is to satisfy religious claims and needs, he must be a being in every way inescapable, one whose existence and whose possession of certain excellencies we cannot possibly conceive away. And modern views make it self-evidently absurd (if they don't make it ungrammatical) to speak of such a Being and attribute existence to him.[2]

For no propositions of the form 'x exists' can be analytically true. Hence, Findlay argues, the concept of an adequate object of religious attitudes, involving as it does the notion of a necessarily existent being who possesses his characteristic in a necessary manner, is a self-contradictory concept. We can know a priori, from inspection of the idea itself, that there is and can be no such being.

We can distinguish in Findlay's argument a philosophical premise to the effect that no existential proposition can be an analytic truth, and a theological premise to the effect that an adequate object of religious worship must be such that it is logically necessary that it exists. Of these two premises, I suggest that the former should be accepted but the latter rejected. We must deny, that is to say, the theological doctrine that God must be conceived, if at all, in such a way that 'God exists' is a logically necessary truth. We must deny this for precisely the same reason as Findlay, namely, that the demand that 'God exists' should be a necessary truth is, like the demand that a circle should be square, not a proper demand at all but a misuse of language. Only, whereas Findlay concludes that the notion of an adequate object of religious attitudes is an absurdity, we should conclude that that of which the idea is an absurdity cannot be an adequate object of religious attitudes; it would on the contrary be a totally inadequate object of worship!

Ontological Necessity

Let us then ask the question, which seems appropriate at this point, as to how religious persons actually think of the Being whom they regard as the adequate object of their worship. What aspect of the Judaeo-Christian experience of God lies behind the idea of necessary being?

The concept of God held by many of the biblical writers was based upon their experience of God as awesome power and holy will confronting them and drawing them into the sphere of his ongoing purpose. God was known as a dynamic will interacting with their own wills; a sheer given reality, as inescapably to be reckoned with as destructive storm and life-giving sunshine, the fixed contours of the land, or the hatred of their enemies and the friendship of their neighbours. God was not for them an inferred entity but an experienced reality. Some of the biblical writers seem to have been as vividly conscious of being in God's presence as they were of living in a material environment. Their pages resound and vibrate with the sense of God's presence, as a building might resound and vibrate with the tread of some great being walking through it. They thought of this holy Presence as unique – as the maker and ruler of the universe, the sole rightful sovereign of humans and angels, as eternal and infinite, and as the ultimate reality and determining power, in relation to whom his creatures have no standing except as the objects of his grace. But nowhere in the biblical thought about God is use made of the idea of logical necessity. The notion is quite foreign to the characteristically Hebraic and concrete utterances found in the Bible, and it forms no part of the biblical concept or concepts of God.

But, it might be said, was it not to the biblical writers inconceivable that God should not exist, or that he should cease to exist, or should lose his divine powers and attributes? Was it not inconceivable to them that God might one day go out of existence, or cease to be good and become evil? And does not this attitude involve an implicit belief that God exists necessarily and possesses his divine characteristics in some necessary manner? The answer, I think, is that it was to the biblical writers psychologically inconceivable – as we say colloquially, unthinkable – that God might not exist, or that he might change from a loving to a hating God. They were so vividly conscious of God that they were unable to doubt his reality, and they relied so firmly upon his integrity and faithfulness that they could not contemplate his becoming other than they knew him to be. They would have allowed as a verbal concession only that there might possibly be no God, for they were convinced that they were at many times directly aware of his presence and of his dealings with them. But the question whether the non-existence of God is *logically* inconceivable, or *logically* impossible, is a philosophical puzzle which could not be answered by the prophets and apostles out of their own first-hand experience. This does not of course represent any special limitation of the biblical figures. The logical concept of necessary being cannot be given in any form of religious experience. It is a product – as Findlay rightly argues, a malformed product – of philosophical reflection. A religious person's reply to the question, 'Is God's existence logically necessary?' will be determined by their view of the nature of logical necessity; and this is not part of his religion but part of his system of logic. The biblical writers had no views on the nature of logical necessity, and would doubtless have regarded the topic as of no religious significance. It cannot reasonably be claimed, then, that logically necessary existence was part of their conception of the adequate object of human worship.

Nevertheless, the biblical tradition, in its subsequent theological development, does contain an increasingly explicit understanding of God as necessary being. In this concept it is not logical but ontological or factual necessity that is attributed to the object of human worship. More than one type of non-logical necessity have been distinguished in philosophical literature. Kant, for example, speaks in the *Critique of Pure Reason* of 'material necessity in existence (*die materiale Notwendigheit im Dasein*) and not merely formal and logical necessity in the connection of concepts',[3] this material necessity being equivalent to what is sometimes termed causal necessity, that is, participation in the universal causal system of nature. Kant also speaks of another kind of factual necessity when he treats of the three modal categories of possibility, existence and necessity. He derives the latter from the necessary or analytic proposition in formal logic; but its schema in time is the existence of an object throughout all time (p. 184). This notion of necessary existence as existence throughout all time suggests the idea of a temporally unlimited Being, and this is an important part, although not the whole, of the concept of divine existence as ontologically necessary. The concept first appears in Anselm, in *Proslogion* III and especially in his *Reply to Gaunilo*. In *Proslogion* III we read that 'it is possible to conceive of a being which cannot be conceived not to exist'. As most naturally understood by the twenty-first-century philosopher, 'a being who cannot be conceived not to exist' would be presumed to mean 'a being whose non-existence is logically inconceivable, that is, logically impossible, or self-contradictory'. However, when we turn to Anselm's *Reply to Gaunilo*, we find that he states explicitly what he means by the notion of beings which can and which cannot be conceived not to exist. 'All those objects, and those alone,' he says:

> can be conceived not to exist, which have a beginning or end or composition of parts: also . . . whatever at any place or at any time does not exist as a whole. That being alone, on the other hand, cannot be conceived not to exist, in which any conception discovers neither beginning nor end nor composition of parts (*nec initium nec finem nec partium conjunctionem*), and which any conception finds always and everywhere as a whole.[4]

Here we have something quite different from the distinctively modern thought of 'God exists' as a logically necessary truth. We have instead the essence of the contrasting notion of God as sheer, ultimate, unconditioned reality, without origin or end.

Thomas Aquinas also uses the term 'necessary being' and uses it, I believe, in the sense of ontological or factual necessity. The conclusion of the Third Way argument is that 'there must exist something the existence of which is necessary (*oportet aliquid esse necessarium in rebus*)'.[5] In the preceding argument the mark of contingency is transiency or temporal finitude; and, by contrast, the mark of non-contingency, or of the necessary being of God, is existence without beginning or end – in other words, eternal being.

Another, and indeed more fundamental, aspect of the distinctively theological form of ontological or factual necessity is contributed by Anselm in the *Monologion*, where he draws the distinction between existence *a se* and existence *ab alio*. He says of God:

> The supreme Substance, then, does not exist through any efficient agent, and does not derive existence from any matter, and was not aided in being brought into existence by any external causes. Nevertheless, it by no means exists through nothing, or derives existence from nothing; since, through itself and from itself, it is whatever it is (*per seipsam et ex seipsa est quidquid est*).[6]

Thus, aseity (*a se esse*) is central to the notion of the necessary being of God.

From God's aseity, or ontic independence, his eternity, indestructibility and incorruptibility can be seen to follow. A self-existent being must be eternal, that is, without temporal limitation. For if he had begun to exist, or should cease to exist, he must have been caused to exist, or to cease to exist, by some power other than himself; and this would be inconsistent with his aseity. By the same token, he must be indestructible, for to say that he exists in total ontic independence is to say that there is and could be no reality able to constitute or to destroy him; and likewise he must be incorruptible, for otherwise his aseity would be qualified as regards its duration.

Again, to refer back to Findlay's discussion, it is meaningless to say of the self-existent being that he might not have existed or that he merely happens to exist. For what could it mean to say of the eternal, uncreated Creator of everything other than himself that he merely happens to exist? When we assert of a dependent and temporarily finite being, such as myself, that I only happen to exist, we mean that if such-and-such an event had occurred in the past, or if such-and-such another event had failed to occur, I should not now exist. But no such meaning can be given to the statement, 'A self-existent being only happens to exist', or 'might not have existed'. There is no conceivable event such that if it had occurred, or failed to occur, a self-existent being would not have existed; for the concept of aseity is precisely the exclusion of such dependence. There is and could be nothing that would have prevented a self-existent being from coming to exist, for it is meaningless even to speak of a self-existent being as *coming* to exist.

What may properly be meant, then, by the statement that God is, or has, necessary rather than contingent being is that God is, without beginning or end, and without origin, cause or ground of any kind whatsoever. He *is*, as the ultimate, unconditioned, absolute, unlimited reality.

Hartshorne's Argument

We have now distinguished the following two concepts: 1 the logically necessary truth of a proposition, arising from the meaning of the terms employed in it; and 2 the factual necessity of a Being who exists eternally and *a se*. These two concepts are quite distinct; logical necessity is not a case of ontological necessity, nor vice versa. The necessary existence of an object, *x*, is defined as the existence of *x* without beginning or end and without dependence upon anything other than itself. The logically necessary truth of a proposition, *p*, on the other hand, consists in the fact that *p* is so formed as to be true by definition. It is, it seems to me, essential to keep this distinction clear. From the concept of God as ontologically necessary we can derive the analytic truth that if God exists, he exists eternally and *a se*, but we cannot deduce that it is a logically necessary truth that God exists, that is, that the concept of an eternal Being who exists *a se* is instantiated in extra-mental reality. And yet this is precisely what Norman Malcolm and Charles Hartshorne try to do.[7] They observe (rightly) that while 'existence' is not a real predicate (that is, it cannot figure as an element in the concept of a kind of being), 'necessary existence' in the ontological sense *is* a real predicate and can be a constituent element in the concept of deity. However, having established that ontological necessity (eternal existence *a se*) is a real predicate, they proceed as though what they had established is the quite different conclusion that logically necessary existence is a real predicate. From this point they have no difficulty in proceeding by due process to the conclusion that since God has logically necessary existence, he must and therefore does exist. The argument is, however, fatally disrupted by the illicit shift of meaning between logical and ontological necessity.

Basically, the same criticism applies to both Malcolm's and Hartshorne's versions of the ontological proof; but since the latter has so conveniently formalized his argument, I will expound the criticism first and more fully in relation to Hartshorne's formulation, which is as follows:[8]

1. $q \to Nq$ 'Anselm's Principle': perfection could not exist contingently [hence the assertion that it exists could not be contingently but only necessarily true].[†]

2. $Nq \lor {\sim}Nq$ Excluded Middle.

3. ${\sim}Nq \to N{\sim}Nq$ Form of Decker's Postulate: modal status is always necessary.

4. $Nq \lor N{\sim}Nq$ Inference from (2, 3).

5. $N{\sim}Nq \to N{\sim}q$ Inference from (1): the necessary falsity of the consequent implies that of the antecedent (modal form of modus tollens).

6. $Nq \lor N{\sim}q$ Inference from (4, 5).

7. ${\sim}N{\sim}q$ Intuitive postulate (or conclusion from other theistic arguments): perfection is not impossible.

8. Nq Inference from (6, 7).

9. $Nq \to q$ Modal axiom.

10. q Inference from (8, 9).

Key
'q' for '(Ex) Px. There is a perfect being, or perfection exists.'
'N' for 'it is necessary (logically true) that'
'~' for 'it is not true that'
'v' for 'or'
'p → q' for 'p strictly implies q' or $N{\sim}(p \,\&\, {\sim}q)$
[†] The clause in square brackets does not appear in *The Logic of Perfection*, but was added at Hartshorne's request.

   The key proposition in this argument is the first, $q \to Nq$, because at this point it is essential to decide whether N is to be understood as signifying logical or ontological necessity. Hartshorne himself is quite explicit that he is using exclusively the former. N, he says, 'means analytic or L-true, true by necessity of the terms employed. This is the sense intended in the present essay' (p. 337). Concerning Hartshorne's argument, thus interpreted by himself, I wish to maintain:

1   that when N is interpreted as signifying logical necessity, prop. 1 has no kind of self-evidence, and indeed does not conform to any

prepositional form recognized in standard logical theory;

2 that in order to represent, as Hartshorne claims, Anselm's basic principle, N in prop. 1 must be interpreted as signifying ontological, rather than logical, necessity;

3 that when N is so interpreted, prop. 1 constitutes an acceptable premise, and leads by valid steps to prop. 6;

4 that in order to reach its conclusion in prop. 10, the argument, having established prop. 6 in terms of ontological necessity, must thenceforth proceed on the (false) assumption that prop. 6 has been established in terms of logical necessity; and that the proof is rendered invalid by this change of meaning of a key term in mid-course.

In support of these four theses I offer the following considerations:

1 Prop. 1, interpreted in terms of logical necessity, asserts that a certain proposition, q, strictly implies another proposition which is a proposition about q, to the effect that q is a logically necessary truth. That a proposition should strictly imply another proposition, which is a proposition about the first proposition, involves unformulated principles which form no part of accepted logical theory, and which require justifying considerations which Hartshorne has not supplied.

Further, to propose a logical transition from q to Nq, q being an existential proposition, is to reject one of the foundations of modern logic. Within the universe of discourse within which Hartshorne professes to be operating, and according to the canons to which he appeals at other points in his argument, one cannot treat an existential proposition as a logically necessary truth. When Hartshorne insists that in the unique case of God the existential assertion is an exception to this rule, he has in mind, I believe, the *ontological* necessity (that is, eternal aseity) which is part of the concept of God.

2 In his explanatory gloss, Hartshorne describes his prop. 1 as 'Anselm's Principle: perfection could not exist contingently [hence the assertion that it exists could not be contingently but only necessarily true]'. Now it is, I think, as certain as a historical judgement can be that Anselm did not use the concept of logical necessity which Hartshorne is himself professedly using, in which N 'means analytic or L-true, true by necessity of the terms employed'. For this is a distinctively modern understanding of necessity. Further, Anselm states explicitly what he means by 'a being which cannot be conceived not to exist', and the kind of necessity which he there describes is not logical but ontological. I have already cited some of the key passages in

Anselm's discussion, concluding with the sentence, 'That being alone, on the other hand, cannot be conceived not to exist, in which any conception discovers neither beginning nor end nor composition of parts, and which any conception finds always and everywhere as a whole.' Thus, in order for Hartshorne's prop. 1 to represent Anselm's principle, it must be interpreted in terms of ontological necessity: If Perfection exists, it exists eternally and *a se*.

3 From the premise that 'If Perfection exists, it exists eternally and *a se*' we can reach the further position, stated in Hartshorne's prop. 6, that the existence of Perfection is either (ontologically) necessary or (ontologically) impossible. For if an eternal and independent being exists, he cannot cease to exist, and his existence is thus ontologically necessary; while if such a being does not exist, he cannot come into existence, and his existence is thus ontologically impossible.

4 However, from this disjunction, according to which the divine existence is (ontologically) either necessary or impossible, we cannot derive the conclusion that Perfection or God exists. What we can deduce is that if there is a God, he has ontologically necessary (that is, eternal and self-existent) being. For the coming to exist and the ceasing to exist of an eternal Being are alike precluded; God exists either eternally or not at all. This is the maximum that can validly be derived from the concept of God as existing eternally and *a se*.

In order to proceed beyond this point to Hartshorne's conclusion that God exists (prop. 10), we have to make an illicit switch in the interpretation of N from ontological to logical necessity. Having established prop. 6 in terms of ontological necessity, we must now take it to have been established in terms of logical necessity: God's existence is either *logically* necessary or *logically* impossible. We can then argue, as Hartshorne does, that it has not been shown that the existence of God is logically impossible, and hence that it must be regarded as logically necessary. However, the argument is rendered invalid by the fact that prop. 6 has to be interpreted in terms of ontological necessity in relation to its supporting propositions, but in terms of logical necessity in relation to the propositions which are derived from it.

It should be emphasized at this point that I am not accusing Hartshorne of the fallacy of equivocation in his argument as he has himself presented it. He states explicitly that the proof is to be understood consistently in terms of logical necessity. What I am claiming is that, so interpreted, the argument does not even have an acceptable premise from which to begin. I note, however, that if the initial premise is interpreted in terms of ontological necessity, the first half of the argument becomes valid; and I suggest that it is this fact, aided by a dormant attention at this point to the distinction between the two concepts of necessity, that has led to the argument being regarded as cogent.

It must, however, be acknowledged that, while Hartshorne explicitly rests his proof upon the logical concept of necessity, he is well aware of the differing theological concept, and addresses himself to what he describes as 'the technical problem of reconciling the logical meaning of "necessary" with the ontological in the unique divine case'.[9] The phrase added in square brackets assumes that this has been accomplished. Hartshorne's suggestion is that this might be done by adapting Carnap's notion of meaning postulates (in *Meaning and Necessity*), these being promulgated within an artificially constructed language system thereby creating logical necessities within that language.

Hartshorne's suggestion is, apparently, that a meaning postulate might be formulated which would import the factual or ontological necessity which is part of the concept of God into an artificial theological language, with the result that in that language it will be L-true that God exists. The suggestion is, however, not further spelled out in Hartshorne's chapter. In particular, he does not formulate the meaning postulate on which he wishes to rely. It is, therefore, not easy to appraise his suggestion. But there are two features of Carnap's notion which seem to disqualify it for the use which Hartshorne proposes:

1 The Carnapian meaning postulates contain no existential quantifier. They do not assert existence, but only meaning equivalences. But the meaning postulate required for an ontological argument would presumably have to assert existence, and would thus diverge radically from the original Carnapian notion.

2 Meaning postulates perform a function within an artificial language; but Hartshorne's object is to make the ontological argument work within our natural language. No doubt it is possible to construct an artificial language for the purpose of proving the existence of God within it, or even such that the existence of God is axiomatic within it and does not need to be proved. But this would not affect the ontological argument propounded by Anselm in Latin and by Hartshorne in English. If we cannot prove God's existence in English it is not clear how we should be advantaged by being able to construct an artificial language in which we can prove it; for it would then only be proved to those who elect to use this special language.

Malcolm's Argument

The other important modern treatment of the second form of the Argument is that of Norman Malcolm in his much-discussed article, 'Anselm's Ontological Arguments'.[10] This defends the ontological proof on grounds which are essentially the same as those offered by Hartshorne and which are (as it seems to me) open to essentially the same criticism. Having already presented this criticism in relation to Hartshorne's version of the argument, the same point can now be applied more briefly to Malcolm's no less significant and thought-provoking discussion.

Malcolm summarizes the proof as follows:

> If God, a being greater than which cannot be conceived, does not exist, then he cannot *come* into existence. For if he did, he would either have been *caused* to come into existence or have *happened* to come into existence, and in either case he would be a limited being, which by our conception of him he is not. Since he cannot come into existence, if he does not exist, his existence is impossible. If he does exist, he cannot have come into existence (for the reasons given), nor can he cease to exist, for nothing could cause him to cease to exist nor could it just happen that he ceased to exist. So if God exists, his existence is necessary.[11]

Thus far we have an admirable account of the ontological concept of necessary being. If an eternal and independent being does not exist, he cannot come into existence (for he would not then be eternal); and if such a being does exist, he cannot cease to exist (for, again, he would then not be eternal). His existence is thus either necessary or impossible. But, we must immediately ask, is this necessity, and is this impossibility, logical or ontological? The correct answer is I think complex, at least to the extent that it must contain the following propositions, in which 'eternal being' is intended as short for 'eternal being who exists *a se*':

1 If there is an eternal being, his existence is ontologically necessary; but
2 it is not logically necessary that there should be an ontologically necessary being.
3 If there is no eternal being, it is not logically impossible that there should have been one; but
4 it is logically impossible that there should now come to be one.

The bearing of these four propositions upon Malcolm's ontological proof is as follows. Whether there is an ontologically necessary being (i.e. a being who exists eternally and *a se*) is a question of fact, although of uniquely ultimate fact. Given this concept of an ontologically necessary being, it is a matter of logic that if there is such a being, his existence is necessary in the sense that he cannot cease to exist, and that if there is no such being, none can come to exist. This logical necessity and this logical impossibility are, however, dependent upon the hypotheses, respectively, that there is and that there is not an ontologically necessary being; apart from the hypotheses from which they follow they do not entail that there is or that there is not an eternal self-existent being.

Hence, there is no substance to the dilemma: The existence of God is either logically necessary or logically impossible. And yet this is the dilemma upon which Malcolm's argument rests. The passage quoted above continues:

> Thus, God's existence is either impossible or necessary. It can be the former only if the concept of such a being is self-contradictory or in some way logically absurd. Assuming that it is not so, it follows that he necessarily exists.[12]

Here Malcolm is equating proposition (1), that the existence of an eternal being is either ontologically necessary or ontologically impossible, with proposition (2), that the existence of an ontologically necessary being is either logically necessary or logically impossible. The former (1) is validly derived from the concept of God as self-existent and eternal. The latter (2) receives its plausibility from its not being distinguished from (1). Once attention is focused upon the distinction between them, the plausibility of (2) disappears and the argument which depends upon it likewise loses its force.

Anselm's Argument

To complete this critique we must return to the source of the second argument in Anselm himself. Perhaps his most subtle piece of reasoning in the passages expounding his second form of ontological proof occurs in *Reply* I, and is formulated twice, in two successive paragraphs, the first of which is as follows:

> If that being (than which no greater can be conceived) can even be

conceived to be, it must exist in reality. For that than which a greater is inconceivable cannot be conceived except as without a beginning. But whatever can be conceived to exist, and does not exist, can be conceived to exist through a beginning. Hence, what can be conceived to exist, but does not exist, is not the being than which a greater cannot be conceived. Therefore, if such a being can be conceived to exist, necessarily it does exist.[13]

This argument from not-having-a-beginning can be set out as follows:

1 to be unsurpassably perfect is to be incapable-of-having-a-beginning;
2 to be nonexistent-but-capable-of-existing is not to be incapable-of-having-a-beginning; and
3 therefore to be unsurpassably perfect is not to be nonexistent-but-capable-of-existing.

What this argument proves is that God is not nonexistent-but-capable-of-existing, that is, that he is not contingently nonexistent. It does not however prove that he exists.

We can present the difficulty, again, in terms of the statement that 'whatever can be conceived to exist, and does not exist, can be conceived to exist through a beginning' (and is therefore not the greatest conceivable being, which is by definition eternal). This is in general a sound rule; but there is an exception to it, and the exception is precisely the case in question. On the one hand, an eternal being can be conceived to exist; and on the other hand, we can conceive that there is no such being. But it does not follow that we can conceive an eternal being to have a beginning. On the contrary, the notion of such a being precludes the thought that it should come or have come to be (at a certain point in time). We can, nevertheless, conceive that the notion of an eternal being is unexemplified – providing we understand that if it is ever unexemplified, it must be eternally unexemplified.

In his next paragraph Anselm restates his argument:

Furthermore: if it can be conceived at all, it [a being than which no greater can be conceived] must exist. For no one who denies or doubts the existence of a being than which a greater is inconceivable, denies or doubts that if it does exist, its nonexistence, either in reality or in the understanding, would be impossible. For otherwise it would not be a being than which a greater cannot be conceived. But as to whatever can be conceived, and does not exist – if there were such a being, its nonexistence, either in reality or in the understanding, would be possible. Therefore, if a being than which a greater is inconceivable can even be conceived, it cannot be nonexistent.[14]

This is essentially the same argument, and it must be challenged at the same point. Anselm says, 'But as to whatever can be conceived, but does not exist: If there were such a being, its nonexistence, either in reality or in the understanding, would be possible.' But, once again, the notion of an eternal being constitutes an exception to this rule. Let us suppose that there is no eternal being. It does not now follow that if there *were* an eternal being, its nonexistence would be possible. For it is by definition impossible for an eternal being to cease to exist. If there were an eternal being, its nonexistence would in that case be impossible. Nevertheless, it does not follow from this circumstance that there *is* an eternal being.

Let me put the criticism again in another way. We may paraphrase Anselm's argument as follows: Whatever does not exist but can be thought of as existing would, if it were to exist, be able to be thought of as not existing. But anything that can be thought of as not existing is not unsurpassably perfect. Therefore the unsurpassably perfect cannot not exist (that is, cannot be such that if it were to exist it would be able to be thought of as not existing).

Or again, more briefly: Whatever does not exist, but might exist, would if it were to exist be a contingent thing. But a most-perfect-conceivable cannot be contingent. Therefore a most-perfect-conceivable cannot not-exist.

The argument can be set out as follows:

1 every nonexistent-which-might-exist is a contingent;
2 no unsurpassably-perfect is a contingent;
3 therefore no unsurpassably-perfect is a nonexistent-which-might-exist; and
4 therefore every unsurpassably-perfect is other than a nonexistent-which-might-exist (that is, other than contingent).

Once again what is thus proved is that God is not a contingent being, or more precisely that he does not contingently not-exist. In being other than a nonexistent-which-might-exist, he *either* exists *or* is a nonexistent which could not exist (that is, whose existence is impossible). But what is not proved is that he exists. The second form of the argument is therefore invalid.

Notes

1 J. N. Findlay, 'Can God's Existence Be Disproved?', *Mind*, vol. 57, no. 226 (April 1958), p. 177. Reprinted in Antony Flew and Alasdair Macintyre (eds), *New Essays in Philosophical Theology*, London: SCM Press, 1955, p. 40.

2 Findlay, 'God's Existence', p. 55.

3 Immanuel Kant, *Critique of Pure Reason*, 2nd edn, 1787, p. 279.

4 Anselm, *Reply to Gaunilo*.

5 Thomas Aquinas, *Summa Theologica*, I, Q. 2, art. 3.

6 Anselm, *Monologion*, ch. 6.

7 Norman Malcolm, 'Anselm's Ontological Arguments', *Philosophical Review*, vol. 69 (January 1960), pp. 41–62; Charles Hartshorne, *The Logic of Perfection*, La Salle: Open Court, 1962.

8 Hartshorne, *Perfection*, ch. 2.

9 Hartshorne, *Perfection*, ch. 2.

10 Malcolm, 'Anselm's Ontological Arguments'.

11 Malcolm, 'Anselm's Ontological Arguments', reprinted in *The Many-Faced Argument*, ed. John Hick and Arthur McGill, London: Macmillan, 1968, p. 309.

12 Malcolm, 'Anselm's Ontological Arguments', reprinted in *The Many-Faced Argument*, p. 309.

13 Anselm, *Reply* I.

14 Anselm, *Reply* I.

Index

Ahmajinidad, Mahmoud xi
Al-Arabi xiii, 9
Akrami, Amir xi
Ambler, Rex 168
Analogy 8
Anselm xiv, 97–8, 99, 101–2,
    183–4, 191–3
Apartheid 122, 130–48
Apostles' Creed 68
Aquinas, Thomas ix, 4, 8, 183
Atonement 71, 72, 96–117
Augustine 5, 63, 99, 105
Axial age 24–5, 154

Baha'i faith 7
Bave, Vinoba xiv
Bergson, Henri 24
Bhagavad Gita 112
Biko, Steve 139
Brahman 9, 24
Brown, David 80
Brown, Judith 163–4
Brown, J. E. ix
Buddhism 4, 6, 7, 10, 11, 25,
    39–43, 56, 60–1, 71, 74
Bunyan, John 60, 62

Calvary 72
Calvin 103
Carnap, R. 189
Chalcedon 79, 85

Chatterjee, Margaret 164
Churchill, Winston 161–2
Clifford, W. K. 101
Cognitive freedom 23–4
Confucianism 4, 25
Conze, Edward 41
Cosmic optimism 35–45
Council of Trent 99–100
Crossan, John Dominic 95

Damasio, Antonio 57
Dawkins, Richard ix, 65, 152–4
Dunn, James 83, 87, 129
Dutch Reformed Church 140,
    151

Eckhart, Meister 8–9, 21, 41
Eliot, T. S. 30

Fall of humanity 100
Feminism 175
Findlay, J. N. 180–1, 182, 184
Fischer, Louis 161
Flew, Antony 3
Forgiveness 110
Fundamentalism 124

Gandhi, Mahatma ix, xiv, 62,
    115, 160, 161–78
Gauld, Alan 95
Global ethic 149–60

God
  answering prayers 1
  anthropomorphic 1
  as Trinity 11, 71, 72
  ineffable (transcategorial) 5
  omni-attributes 11
  personal 1, 4
  presence 27
Golden Rule 149–50
Gregory of Nyssa 99
Grensted, L. W. 116

Harnack, Adolf von 126
Hartshorne, Charles xiv, 17
  185–9
Hawkins, Stephen 61
Heidegger, Martin xii
Heiler, Friedrich 40
Heintz, John ix
Hell 38, 44, 58
Hinduism 11, 21, 25, 45, 60,
  167, 169
Hitchins, Christopher ix
Houlden, Leslie 66
Hume, David 54

Incarnation 69, 72, 75–87, 125
Interpretation 17–19, 33
Iran x
Irenaeus 63
Islam 2, 11, 44–5, 74, 118–29
Iyer, Rhaghavan 177

Jaspers, Karl 24
Jeremias, Joachim 108–9
Jesus xii, 25, 29, 43, 67, 69–70,
  80, 83, 121 127
  Resurrection 88–95
  Son of God 84, 12
  Teaching 69–70, 72, 110–11,
    120, 121–2

Virgin birth 77–8, 127
Joseph of Aramathea 88, 89
Josephus 92
Judaism 2, 9, 10, 44, 84, 111,
  120
Julian of Norwich 38, 62

Kant, Immanuel xii, 11, 20, 26,
  42, 183
Kaufman, Gordon 21
Khatami, Mohammed x
King, Martin Luther xiv, 115,
  165
Kundera, Milan 58–9, 62
Küng, Hans xiv, 74, 149

Lewis, C. S. 98
Libet, Benjamin 57
Ling, Trevor 30
Luther, Martin 29

Malcolm, Norman xiv, 179,
  190–1
Mandela, Nelson xiv, 69, 148,
  159, 165
Meaning 31–2, 33–5
Melanchthon 102
Mencius 150
Metaphor 75–6, 84
Meyendorff 117
Mill, John Stuart 34
Miracles 2
Mission 72–3
Morris, Thomas 80, 81, 83
Moses 25
Moule, Charles 86, 129
Muhammad 10, 25, 29
Mysticism ix, 14–30
Myth 7, 75–7
Myth of God Incarnate 66

Necessity
  logical 179–81
  ontological 181–5
Nehru, Jahwarhalal 172
New Testament 67–8, 88–91
Nicene creed 69
Nietzsche, Friedrich 1, 53–4
Nineham, Dennis 66
Nirvana 40–2

O'Collins, Gerald 80
Old Testament 71
Origen 98
Orthodox theology 113–14
Otto, Rudolf 21

Paul, St 29, 70, 71, 89, 92–4, 114
Penelhum, Terence ix
Penrose, Roger 57
Plato 25
Prayer 12
Pseudo-Dionysius 4, 6, 41
Purgatory 56
Pythagoras 25

Qur'an xii, 112, 118, 119, 121, 123–4
Quakers 169

Ramachandran, V. S. 56–7
Ramsey, Michael 86–7, 129
Rees, Martin 61
Reincarnation x, 53–6, 66
Religious experience 7, 9–10, 14–15, 19–20, 28–9
  institutions 7–8
Roll, William 95
Rose, Steven 57
Rumi xiii

Sabatier, August 112

Sanders, E. P. 82, 108, 109, 111
Sartre, Jean-Paul 55–6
Sawiki, Marianne 95
Schliermacher, Friedrich 114
Scillebeeckx, Edward 87
Schumacher, E. F. 174
Shakespeare, William 50
Shankara 21
Shaw, Bernard 50
Sikhism 74
Singer, Wolf 57
Smart, Ninian ix
Smith, Wilfred Cantwell 36
Smith, Robertson 24
Socrates 25
Sturch, Richard 80
Swidler, Leonard 155
Swinburne, Richard 77, 80–2, 83, 104–10

Tacitus 92
Taoism (Daoism) 4, 10, 11
Tertullian 72
Thich Nhat Hahn 165
Tillich, Paul 21
Transcendent 15–16, 17, 22, 26–37
Turner, Denys 6–7
Tutu, Desmond xiv, 141, 151, 159, 165

Vatican xiii

Webb, Mark 62
Westminster Confession 100
Whitehead, A. N. 21
Wiles, Maurice 66
Wisdom, John 32
Wittgenstein 32

Zoroaster 25, 71